Social Studies

All Day, Every Day in the
Early Childhood Classroom

Dedication
To my parents for your
constant support, and
to Dolores McClatchey, in
the year of your retirement

Join us on the web at
EarlyChildEd.delmar.com

Social Studies

All Day, Every Day in the Early Childhood Classroom

Melanie Wallace, Ed.D.

DELMAR
CENGAGE Learning™

Australia • Brazil • Japan • Korea • Mexico • Singapore • Spain • United Kingdom • United States

DELMAR
CENGAGE Learning

Social Studies: All Day Every Day in the Early Childhood Classroom
Melanie Wallace

Vice President, Career Education SBU:
Dawn Gerrain

Director of Editorial: Sherry Gomoll

Acquisitions Editor: Erin O'Connor

Developmental Editor: Patricia Osborn

Editorial Assistant: Stephanie Kelly

Director of Production: Wendy A. Troeger

Production Manager: J. P. Henkel

Production Editor: Joy Kocsis

Production Assistant: Angela Iula

Technology Project Manager:
Sandy Charette

Director of Marketing: Wendy E. Mapstone

Channel Manager: Kristin McNary

Marketing Coordinator: David White

Cover Design: Joseph Villanova

Composition: Cadmus Professional
Communications

For product information and technology assistance, contact us at
Cengage Learning Customer & Sales Support, 1-800-354-9706.
For permission to use material from this text or product,
submit all requests online at **www.cengage.com/permissions.**
Further permissions questions can be emailed to
permissionrequest@cengage.com.

Library of Congress Control Number: 2005000020

ISBN-13: 978-1-4018-8197-9

ISBN-10: 1-4018-8197-1

Delmar
10 Davis Drive
Belmont, CA 94002-3098
USA

Cengage Learning is a leading provider of customized learning solutions with office locations around the globe, including Singapore, the United Kingdom, Australia, Mexico, Brazil, and Japan. Locate your local office at:
www.cengage.com/global.

Cengage Learning products are represented in Canada by Nelson Education, Ltd.

To learn more about Delmar, visit **www.cengage.com/delmar.**

Purchase any of our products at your local college store or at our preferred online store **www.ichapters.com.**

Printed in Canada
2 3 4 5 6 7 8 9 10 12 11 10 09

Contents

Chapter 9   **Economics, Anthropology, and Archaeology / 255**

Chapter 10   **Bringing It to Life: Drama, Art, Music, Movement, Field Trips, Cooking, and Storytelling / 271**

Chapter 11   **Assessment / 305**

Preface

Building a solid background in social studies in the early years of life can provide an effective foundation for students as they move into the more complex development of civic responsibility, and character development in later years. This book is based on the assumption that *all children* can learn, given an appropriate and caring classroom environment. It is designed as a resource for early childhood pre-service teachers and also for those currently in service. It is intended to help teachers of young children (ages 3–8) provide an appropriate, well-designed, and well-integrated social studies curriculum.

DEVELOPMENTAL APPROPRIATE PRACTICES

This book is soundly based on the tenets of developmentally appropriate practice (DAP). It is theoretical and research based, supporting the belief that as teachers of young children we must embrace and recognize the differences in children's development, their individual growth, and their cultural backgrounds. References to the *National Standards from the National Council of the Social Studies* (NCSS) are included, representing teachers of young children and individual social studies disciplines. Structured around these important standards are ideas intended to address the ultimate goal of social studies in the schools—that of informing citizens to carry on the democracy.

INTEGRATED APPROACH

This book has an integrated approach based on the belief that young children do not learn best in isolated pockets of instruction. It is based from the perspective that a well-designed social studies program should span the entire curriculum for optimal learning. It adheres to the National Council of Social Studies standards and requirements and inclusion of these standards.

ORGANIZATION

There are 11 chapters in total, each beginning with an opening quote emphasizing different philosophical perspectives to encourage student critical thinking and reflection.

The intent of this text is to present a user-friendly guide for incorporating social studies topics into the every day, all day school lives of young children. To that end, I have incorporated several features in hopes of making the transition from student teacher to classroom teacher easier for the student.

SPECIAL FEATURES

- *Thematic Strands and Focus Questions* are at the back of each chapter, allowing the reader to make a connection between the material presented and the National Council for the Social Studies Standards. The Ten Themes are presented early in Chapter 1.

- *Connection to Children's Literature* boxes present ideas for incorporating children's literature selections into the different areas of the social studies

- *Read-Aloud Suggestions* provide helpful recommendations to students and teachers, focusing the reader on the content to be addressed in each chapter.

- *Group Activities* are provided to increase understanding of presented material and to engage the students in discussion about the content of the chapter.

- *Connecting to Administration* boxes provide helpful suggestions to encourage the student to involve campus administration in the early childhood classroom social studies activities. This feature allows the reader to consider the importance of the administrator when providing a developmentally appropriate social studies program in the early years.

- *Global Perspective* boxes allow the reader to have a different perspective on various issues. This feature offers suggestions for looking at issues presented in the text from different cultural points of view.

- *Connecting to Diverse Populations* boxes offer suggestions of ways to celebrate the diversity of the children in each classroom, as well as the diversity of the society in which children live.

Additional features include specific strategies, activities, and materials appropriate for use with special populations are included to guide in helping children in the general education population understand differences and similarities among children with special needs and themselves.

SUPPLEMENTS

An Instructors Manual to accompany *Social Studies All Day, Every Day* is available to instructors and provides instrumental resources, activities, essay, and discussion questions.

 An Online Companion™ is available for students to access a wealth of information designed to enhance this book including the following:

- Case studies
- Discussion/follow-up questions
- Suggested activities for university classrooms
- Suggestions for further reading: books, articles, Web sites
- Transparency masters for instructors to download
- A PowerPoint presentation is available online for instructors as an additional resource for class lectures, class discussions, and activities.

To access the Online Companion™ for *Social Studies, All Day, Every Day* go to http://www.EarlyChildEd.delmar.com

ABOUT THE AUTHOR

Melanie Wallace has served the education community in a variety of positions during the past 25 years. As a classroom teacher, she worked with early childhood special education third-, fourth-, and fifth-grade students. She served for 10 years as a primary school principal, where she also developed and directed one of the first employee child care facilities in the nation. She later served as a classroom teacher and literacy coach in Los Angeles, and as a professor and early childhood program director at the University of Texas at Arlington. A member of ACEI, NAEYC, and IRA, Dr. Wallace presents regularly at national and international conferences and works with individual school districts in mentor training and new teacher induction programs. Dr. Wallace received her Ed.D. from Texas Woman's University.

CHAPTER 1
Social Studies in the Early Childhood Classroom

OBJECTIVES

After reading this chapter, you should be able to:

➤ Describe the attributes of an excellent social studies teacher.

➤ Identify the disciplines that make up the social studies.

➤ Compare the "ideal" social studies classroom with less than ideal models.

➤ Discuss the implications of the No Child Left Behind legislation as it pertains to social studies instruction in the early childhood classroom.

➤ Interpret the National Association for the Education of Young Children's (NAEYC's) Code of Ethical Conduct (1989) in the context of how teachers can balance the responsibilities for teaching standards with developmentally appropriate practices.

In a completely rational society, the best of us would be teachers and the rest of us would have to settle for something else.

Lee Iacocca

Balancing curriculum requirements with an understanding of the unique needs of young children is essential for ethical teaching.

INTRODUCTION

What does an excellent social studies teacher look like? How does she plan effective lessons; how does she engage the students? Which concepts and skills does he choose to keep; which ones does he leave for the following school year? How in the world does she fit it all in?

After the parents, teachers are the most significant people in a young child's life. The **Association for Childhood Education International (ACEI)** and The **National Association for the Education of Young Children (NAEYC)** recognize the importance of exposure to good teaching in the early childhood years. Teachers of young children should be specifically trained in the multiple aspects inherent in working with young children. ACEI states that "to teach successfully at the elementary level, pre-service teachers need to study and have knowledge of the general **curriculum** taught at this level, as well as a strong foundation in educational psychology and child development" (ACEI, 1998). In the area of social studies, many teachers' own limited childhood memories of how they were taught involve "reading the chapter and answering the questions at the back of the book," and the rich possibilities of social studies instruction elude them. Today, after focusing on reading and math instruction, many

This teacher is presenting material in a meaningful fashion.

teachers might "get around to" a lesson or two from the social studies book. More often than not, they opt to give students bonus time to do independent reading or to complete other work. "We don't have time for social studies. We have to get ready for the reading and math tests," many teachers lament. Particularly in light of the recent **No Child Left Behind** legislation, which raises the bar for **high-stakes testing,** many teachers of young children are spending less time on social studies in favor of additional reading and math instruction. Not only is this inappropriate and unfair to the students, but it is also unnecessary. In this text, we explore ways to present, in depth, a wide range of the social studies lessons, while devoting the necessary time and intellectual energy to developing reading and mathematical skills. By engaging children in the social studies, we allow them to become critical thinkers and problem solvers. At the same time, through effective engagement in social studies, young students will become even better readers, writers, and mathematicians.

WHAT ARE THE SOCIAL STUDIES?

"Social Studies is the integrated study of the social studies and humanities to promote civic competence" (NCSS, 1994). Anthropology, archaeology, economics, geography, history, law, philosophy, political science, psychology, religion, and sociology, as well as content from the humanities, mathematics, and natural sciences are all a part of the social studies in the early years of school. An effective social studies curriculum is multidisciplinary and interdisciplinary. The primary purpose of social studies is to help young people develop the ability to make informed and reasoned decisions for the public good as citizens of a culturally diverse, democratic society in an interdependent world (NCSS, 1994).

At the primary level, children should learn social studies through integrated studies in the form of units constructed around themes (NCSS, 1994). Social studies is not a subject to be "done" at 2:15 on Friday afternoon—if we get around to it. Social studies can and should be integrated throughout the entire school year, day after day. It should be fun, exciting, and engaging.

Even in the interests of holding children's attention, however, the social studies curriculum should not be an endless succession of circus-like, disconnected activities. Rather, it should provide meaningful, integrated activities and assignments, which address the important concepts necessary to prepare young students to participate effectively in a democracy. Educational experiences should help children to develop their innate curiosity and to construct meaning. This is, possibly, our most important task as teachers.

"One of the most significant challenges faced by social studies teachers is knowing how to help children acquire the knowledge, skills, and values that prepare them for constructive participation in a democratic society, while organizing and conducting lessons that offer a blend of pleasure, intrigue, variety, active involvement, and excitement" (Maxim, 2003, p. 4). What a challenge! With enthusiasm, good planning, and a great deal of energy, early childhood teachers can arm the next generation of Americans with the tools needed to make the world a better place.

PUBLIC EDUCATION IN A DEMOCRACY

Social studies are the integrated study of social sciences and humanities to promote civic competence. Public schools were built on the vision, perfectly stated by Thomas Jefferson, that "light and liberty go together." His belief, shared by many of the other founding fathers, was that only an educated citizenry could meet the challenge of self-government.

The development of the public school system in the United States of America demonstrated our collective belief that quality education is the key to our society's future. As stated earlier, the primary purpose of social studies is to help young people develop the ability to make informed and reasoned decisions for the public good—a goal that under-girds the discussion in the remainder of this text.

In this time of high-stakes testing, the back-to-basics movement, and budget cuts, it seems difficult (or impossible) to add yet another thing to your school day. In this text, we explore ways to teach reading, math, social skills, physical education, and music through the social studies. Young children learn best in integrated settings (Bredekamp & Copple, 1997). It is inappropriate and ineffective to teach discrete facts and skills to young children in isolation from the broader perspective.

Fortunately, social studies concepts lend themselves to the good teaching inherent in an active, integrated, multisensory approach. The techniques and suggestions that we will explore together will not only make you a more effective teacher of young children, but they will also help engage your own creative energy and keep you interested in effective teaching for a long time.

INFLUENCES ON EARLY CHILDHOOD SOCIAL STUDIES INSTRUCTION

No Child Left Behind

The No Child Left Behind Act of 2001 (NCLB) was designed to improve student achievement and "change the culture of America's schools" (U. S. Department of Education, 2002). Built on President George W. Bush's belief that, "Too many of our neediest children are being left behind," the January, 2002 passage of NCLB reauthorized the Elementary and Secondary Education Act, which was the principal federal law affecting education from kindergarten through high school. This amendment represents a sweeping overhaul of federal efforts to support elementary and secondary education in the United States. NCLB is built on four pillars: accountability for results, an emphasis on doing what works based on scientific research, expanded parental options, and expanded local control and flexibility (U. S. Department of Education, 2002).

According to the U. S. Department of Education, an accountable education system involves: (1) states creating their own standards, (2) testing of every student's progress toward achieving those standards, (3) evidence of moving toward adequate yearly progress, and (4) public reporting of school and district performance. This narrow definition of academic success has become a political and economic issue. Many school districts, principals, and teachers are responding to the pressure of accountability in ways that are inappropriate for working with young children. While the standards must be addressed with all students, it is imperative that we, as teachers of young children, address the needs of the child first, taking into account each one's special strengths and needs.

Effects of NCLB on Social Studies Instruction

NCLB has indirectly affected social studies instruction in the primary grades because of its increased emphasis on assessment and accountability in the areas of reading and mathematics. As a result, many teachers have deemphasized the importance of social studies instruction in favor of spending more time preparing the students for mandated testing in reading and mathematics. In a well-meaning, but misguided, attempt to help students increase standardized test scores, many school districts, principals, and classroom teachers have chosen to spend extra time on basic skills in reading and math, at the expense of instruction in social studies—the very discipline that brought us public schooling in the first place. Again, the choice does not have to be made between the two. Basic skills in reading and mathematics can be taught very effectively through the important concepts and reading and analytical skills inherent in mastering the social studies. Particularly in light of this new legislation, it is essential for teachers of young children to understand the importance of social studies instruction and to develop creative ways to address the federal, state, and local mandates they face, while ensuring an appropriate education for their young students.

National Council for the Social Studies

The **National Council for the Social Studies (NCSS)** is the largest association in the country devoted to social studies education.

GROUP ACTIVITY — NO CHILD LEFT BEHIND

Obtain copies of No Child Left Behind: A Parent's Guide by writing to EDPubs, Education Publications Center, U. S. Department of Education, PO Box 1398, Jessup, MD 20794-1398, or e-mail your request to: edpubs@inet.ed.gov or call 1-877-433-7827. This free publication can be used to explore the law in detail.

1. Divide the class into small groups of three or four.
2. Pass out copies of No Child Left Behind: A Parent's Guide.
3. Have students read and discuss pages 1–5 in the Guide.
4. Introduce the use of the graphic organizer, the T-chart (see appendix for an example of the T-chart).
5. Have students examine the introduction and overview of NCLB by completing a T-chart, listing the pros and cons of the individual aspects of the law.
6. Come back together as a whole class group.
7. Have student groups identify a spokesperson to share their T-chart with the group.
8. Develop a class chart, compiling responses from each group.
9. Discuss the overall impact of NCLB.
10. Discuss the implications of NCLB on the instruction of social studies in early childhood classrooms.

Founded in 1921, NCSS supports educators in advocating for the social studies. Its mission is to provide leadership, service, and support for all social studies educators (NCSS, 1994). The National Council for the Social Studies serves as an umbrella organization for elementary, secondary, and college teachers of history, geography, economics, political science, sociology, psychology, anthropology, and law-related education. The Curriculum Standards for Social Studies were developed by a Task Force of the National Council for the Social Studies and approved by the NCSS Board of Directors in April 1994.

National Curriculum Standards in Social Studies

The National Curriculum Standards in the social studies were designed to inform teachers, policymakers, and parents concerning what students should be taught, how they will be taught, and how their performance in the social studies arena will be evaluated. In a rapidly changing world and in a time of information explosion, it is clear that teachers cannot teach everything and students cannot learn everything. The social studies standards provide criteria for making decisions about what to include in the curriculum. Among the most important elements of the social studies curriculum are the strategies and skills that teach students how to learn, how to make decisions, and how to work effectively with others.

The standards are divided into 10 thematic curriculum strands, which can be used by classroom teachers to provide goals for units of study, evaluate current practices, and develop ideas for instruction and assessment in the social studies. These 10 thematic strands form the basis of the social studies standards.

TEN THEMATIC STRANDS

- Culture
- Time, Continuity, and Change
- People, Places and Environments
- Individual Development and Identity
- Individuals, Groups and Institutions
- Power, Authority, and Governance
- Production, Distribution and Consumption
- Science, Technology, and Society
- Global Connections
- Civic Ideals and Practices

Source: NCSS, 1994, pp. x–xii.

The thematic strands "point to a core of fundamental knowledge drawn from many academic disciplines" (Krey, 1995). The strands draw from the social science disciplines of anthropology, archaeology, economics, geography, history, law, philosophy, political science, psychology, religion, and sociology, as well as appropriate content from the humanities, mathematics, and natural science (NCSS, 1994, p. 3). The strands serve as a framework for social studies curricula and guide the development of meaningful learning experiences in the early childhood classroom.

These standards give educators a way to examine the scope of the social studies curriculum as it corresponds to national goals.

What is this teacher trying to accomplish?

They provide early childhood teachers with a direction and framework for curriculum development. The standards are designed to serve three purposes:

1. To provide a framework for social studies programs K–12

2. To guide curriculum decisions by providing student performance expectations

3. To provide examples of classroom activities, which will guide teachers' instruction (NCSS, 1994, p. ix)

Excellence in social studies is achieved by programs and instruction in which students gain the knowledge, skills, and attitudes necessary to understand the world around them. Knowledge is constructed by children when they work to fit new information, experiences, feelings, and relationships into their existing schema. As teachers of young children, we must draw from various disciplines to develop this contextual understanding. It is important, however, to constantly be aware of the developmental needs of each child as an individual. Social studies content is appropriate only when presented in a meaningful fashion for each child in the classroom.

Developmentally Appropriate Practice

How can social studies be addressed in a developmentally appropriate program? The National Association for the Education of Young Children (NAEYC), the nation's largest professional organization of early childhood educators, first published a set of position statements in 1986 concerning developmentally appropriate practice. At the time, early childhood professionals were concerned with the escalation of the curriculum for young children. These concerns continue to grow in today's educational climate, particularly with the advent of the NCLB legislation, which ups the ante on high-stakes testing for young children.

In many cases, classroom teachers feel pressure to "teach to the test" or at the very least, to ignore the "fluff" and concentrate on the tested areas of the curriculum—reading and mathematics. In many classrooms, this means that social studies instruction is left out entirely or reduced to a fraction of the total early childhood curriculum.

CONNECTION TO CHILDREN'S LITERATURE

Leo the Late Bloomer

Leo the Late Bloomer, by Robert Kraus, is a wonderful, beautifully illustrated children's book. Leo is a little tiger who can't read or write or even eat neatly. Throughout the course of the story, Leo's father is concerned about Leo's developmental level. Leo's mother continues to reassure his father that "a watched bloomer never blooms." As the story continues, Leo eventually blooms! By the end of the story, he can read and write, and even eat neatly.

Discuss with your neighbor how this story of Leo relates to your classroom teaching, taking into account the following: (1) How can you use this story to reassure parents of their child's development? (2) How can you use this story to guide your curriculum planning? (3) What about the child who does not bloom? (4) What questions did this story bring to your mind?

Developmentally appropriate practices (DAP) result from the process of professionals making decisions about the well-being and education of children based on at least three important kinds of information or knowledge:

1. What is known about child development and learning

2. What is known about the strengths, interests, and needs of each child in the group

3. What is known about the social and cultural contexts in which children live (Bredekamp & Copple, 1997)

NAEYC's Position Statement on Developmentally Appropriate Practice (available at http://www.naeyc.org) states that children fail to progress as they should in school because many schools address a very narrow curriculum or use inappropriate and ineffective instructional approaches. Rote learning and a focus on narrowly defined academic skills are incompatible with the learning styles of young children. The social studies offer broad, complex concepts, perfect for helping students learn to apply skills and knowledge by developing problem-solving strategies and thinking skills.

Early childhood teachers must have a deep understanding of developmentally appropriate practice in order to meet the needs of young students, while also addressing the important standards expected from districts, state education departments, and national legislation. The excellent teacher does not view his or her responsibilities in terms of "either/or." It is both possible and necessary for the early childhood professional to address local, state, and national curricular requirements, while meeting the developmental needs of the individual student in the classroom.

The Controversy Surrounding Developmentally Appropriate Practice

The effectiveness of DAP has been debated since its inception in the 1980s. Some see the implementation of developmentally appropriate practices as a way of watering down the curriculum. By allowing children to construct their own knowledge, opponents of DAP believe that children are not being allowed to reach their full potential in the academic realm.

In the context of this book, *developmentally appropriate practices* are considered to be those practices based on what is known about (1) child development, (2) the individual child, and (3) the child in a cultural context, that truly meet the educational needs of each child in the classroom. By definition, this denies the notion that children would be offered a watered-down curriculum, as this would be inappropriate and would not meet the educational needs of that child in the long term. So, while the debate about DAP undoubtedly will continue, this text presents information based on the supposition that a rigorous curriculum can and should be presented to young children in a developmentally appropriate fashion.

A GLOBAL PERSPECTIVE: CONNECTING TO STUDENTS WITH SPECIAL NEEDS

We are *all* special education teachers. Within each classroom of 22 students are at least 22 different learning styles, thousands of combinations of interests, strengths and weaknesses, and combinations of cultural, experiential, and family backgrounds. Only by looking at each child, no matter the ability level, as an individual, can the early childhood teacher meet the particular needs represented. Groups that are truly heterogeneous, in which children of all cultural backgrounds and all levels of ability and disability work and learn together, are the richest environments for learning.

Working With Administration to Provide Developmentally Appropriate Instruction

Many elementary school principals have had little or no formal training or experience in working with young children (Egley & Egley, 2000). It is the responsibility of the early childhood teacher to keep the administrators informed of not only *what* is happening in the early childhood classroom but also *why*. An administrator charged with the responsibility of making sure that each student on the campus is prepared to pass the required standardized tests may pressure the staff to participate in developmentally inappropriate activities in order to ensure success. It is the responsibility of the early childhood teacher to educate the principal concerning the activities being used to achieve those standards with young children.

CONNECTING TO ADMINISTRATION

DEVELOPMENTALLY APPROPRIATE PRACTICE

Some ways to communicate with the administrator follow:

1. Post appropriate state or national standards and objectives in each of your learning centers. This helps the observer to make a connection between the active learning of the young child and the ultimate objective for that particular learning center.

2. Invite your principal to participate in some of the activities in the classroom. (Cooking activities are usually popular with busy administrators!) Before the visit, drop a note into the principal's box explaining which standards will be addressed during the visit. Make an opportunity to talk informally with the principal after the visit. Talk with him or her about the lesson and make sure to underscore the standards that were covered in the lesson.

3. Be sure to give the principal a copy of your weekly newsletter or lesson plan outline (discussed in Chapter 2). Even if he or she does not read it in detail each week, chances are, it will be scanned. At the very least, the principal will know that you are proactively making contact with parents and paying close attention to the standards that your students will be expected to meet.

4. Share brief and interesting articles about developmentally appropriate practice with your principal. Make an extra copy, highlighting any particular statements or examples that you would like him or her to make note of. Remember that the principal is a very busy person. Make it easy for him or her to access the information you are sharing.

5. Explain the specific materials and supplies that are needed for work with young students. Most principals will do whatever they can to provide for the needs of the teachers and students in their schools.

High-Stakes Testing

High-stakes testing is defined as testing programs intended to gather data about student achievement in order to hold students and schools accountable. Tests are considered "high stakes" if they carry serious consequences for students or educators. Some of those consequences include retention in a grade, exclusion from special courses of study, or withholding a diploma from a student. For the school, poor performance on high-stakes tests can lead to public embarrassment, sanctions, and reassignment of personnel (AERA).

High-stakes testing is here to stay. Teachers are now and will continue to be held accountable for the academic progress of their students. Standardized testing will be a fact of life for those entering the classroom as new teachers in the coming years. For the benefit of their young students, early childhood educators must learn to balance their students' individual developmental needs with the requirements of the educational hierarchy.

THE CODE OF ETHICAL CONDUCT

It is most important to understand and appreciate the core values represented in NAEYC's Code of Ethical Conduct. The Code of Ethical Conduct is available on the Web site of the National Association for the Education of Young Children (NAEYC) at http://www.naeyc.org.

When working with young children, in whatever content area, it is important to acknowledge and incorporate the Core Values represented in the Code of Ethical Conduct. Standards of ethical behavior in early childhood care and education are based on commitment to the core values that are deeply rooted in the history of our field. We have committed ourselves to:

- "Appreciating childhood as a unique and valuable stage of the human life cycle.
- Basing our work with children on knowledge of child development.
- Appreciating and supporting the close ties between the child and family.
- Recognizing that children are best understood and supported in the context of family, culture, community, and society.
- Respecting the dignity, worth, and uniqueness of each individual (child, family member, and colleague).
- Helping children and adults achieve their full potential in the context of relationships that are based on trust, respect, and positive regard."

(NAEYC Code of Ethical Conduct, 1989)

All instruction, regardless of the subject represented, must be approached within the important framework of ethical responsibilities to the children we teach. When sifting through the wide array of topics, standards, and concepts to be presented, it is most important to keep the developmental abilities of the students at the center of lesson planning.

Again, this does not mean that students should be presented watered-down lessons. Children deserve the challenge of a rigorous curriculum. The abilities of young children are frequently underestimated, and by doing so we do them a disservice. Young children are capable of understanding complex concepts when presented in an appropriate and interesting way. Because of the rigor of the curriculum suggested in this text, it is all the more important to look at each child's ability and to tailor the instruction to each child's **Zone of Proximal Development (ZPD).**

The ZPD, described through the work of Lev Vygotsky, is the child's ability, bounded at the lower end by what a child can accomplish independently, and at the upper end by what the child can accomplish with assistance. These boundaries are constantly changing as the child reaches new levels of accomplishment. For optimal instruction, teachers should provide activities just beyond the independent level but within the ZPD (Vygotsky, 1930/1978).

When balancing the needs of the individual child with the demands of the educational hierarchy and the student's parents, the early childhood professional faces many challenges. By basing all decisions made in the classroom on the early childhood professional's Code of Ethical Conduct, teachers are better able to make effective and appropriate decisions on each child's education.

THE HOW AND WHAT OF EARLY CHILDHOOD SOCIAL STUDIES INSTRUCTION

Many factors influence the effective instruction of young children. In addition to having specific knowledge of child development theory, effective teachers must have a broad knowledge base in the liberal arts. Decisions on *what* to teach are based on state and district standards and the classroom teacher's understanding of the developmental levels and interests of the children in the classroom.

What is this teacher's approach to teaching?

How to Teach Young Children

The **Association of Teacher Educators (ATE)** and the National Association for the Education of Young Children (NAEYC) jointly prepared a position statement in 1991 that addressed Early Childhood Teacher Certification. The position statement recognizes the importance of the need for qualified teachers through a child's early education. The position statement outlined five characteristics for an early teacher preparation program, which give an overview of "how" we need to approach the teaching of young children. They include:

1. Teachers must be educated in the liberal arts and knowledgeable about a variety of disciplines in order to recognize the learning embedded in children's activity.

GROUP ACTIVITY — ON THE HORNS OF A DILEMMA

1. Divide into small groups of three.
2. One group member will take on the perspective of the parent, one that of school principal, and one that of the classroom teacher.
3. Discuss the following scenario:

Javier is a typically developing 7-year-old, currently enrolled in a suburban elementary school, in the second grade. His teacher, Ms. Jones, a 27-year veteran of elementary teaching, has called in the parent and the school administrator to discuss the lack of progress that Javier is making. It is mid-October and school has been in session since early August. As a seasoned veteran, Ms. Jones knows that she will need documentation of Javier's lack of progress, so she has kept several of his written papers from social studies class, instead of sending them home as she has done with the other children.

Ms. Jones' social studies instruction is very structured and she schedules in two 30-minute social studies lessons each week, which she always completes. The classroom has only 13 social studies textbooks, but she has students share the books as they read and answer the questions. She augments the text information with worksheets that she has collected over the course of her 27-year career.

When the principal, Mr. Till, and Javier's mom, Mrs. Martinez, arrive for the conference, the teacher asks them to have a seat at the reading table, and takes out the folder of poorly completed written work and worksheets that she has collected from Javier over the last few weeks.

Your task is to develop a Reader's Theater script from the perspective of these three participants in Javier's conference. Be prepared to discuss reasons behind the participants' actions in the script, based on the Code of Ethical Conduct, the National Council for Social Studies, and the No Child Left Behind legislation.

This speaks to the importance of well-educated, well-grounded individuals assigned to the early grades. Early childhood teachers must know a bit about everything, and be interested and willing to learn more about topics they will be exploring.

2. Early childhood teachers must be well informed about developmental theories and their implications for practice.

Early childhood teachers must have a firm foundation in theory. Teachers of young children teach the whole child—the cognitive growth of a child cannot be separated from his or her growth in other areas.

   3. Early childhood teachers must understand the significance of play to children's educational development and develop skills in facilitating enriching play in early childhood classrooms.

Not only must teachers understand the importance of play, but they also need to be advocates for play in the young child's school day. Informing parents, administrators, and community members about the importance of play is imperative if teachers are to ensure the sanctity of this important aspect of childhood.

   4. Early childhood teachers must understand families as the primary context for children's learning and development, respect diversity in family structure and values, and develop skills in interacting with parents in ways that enhance children's educational success.

We do not teach in a vacuum. The family is the single most important influence on our students; every opportunity should be embraced to involve the family in our classroom. Newsletters, parent–teacher conferences, parent volunteers, and guest readers are just a few of the many ways we can involve *all* family members.

   5. Early childhood teachers need to acquire the ability to supervise and coordinate their teaching with other adults.

The old paradigm of teaching involves a vision of the classroom teacher as a solitary figure, planning and grading alone, interacting only with the children. To be truly effective, it is important for teachers of young children to work cooperatively with other teachers (NAEYC, 1997).

What to Teach Young Children

Knowledge of children is not enough for teachers to address the important question of what is to be taught in the social studies. Teachers of young children must be generalists, with a broad understanding of all areas of the curriculum, and be prepared to implement a variety of instructional strategies in each discipline. They

must have a solid understanding of the subject matter and methodologies necessary for effective social studies instruction.

Curriculum includes all of the concepts and information that
children are expected to learn. For guidance in social studies, the
National Council for Social Studies (NCSS) offers suggestions for
what to teach at different grade levels in the publication, *Expectations
of Excellence: Curriculum Standards for Social Studies.* This guide,
along with state standards and standards published within the organizations from the individual disciplines, will serve as excellent guidelines when planning the social studies curriculum and the year-long
plan for teaching.

The question of what should be learned takes on new meaning as states begin to establish standards for student performance at
every level and as the effects of NCLB manifest themselves into the
education of young students. Teachers of young children must ask
themselves, "What kinds of learning best serves students in the long
term?" Young children are capable of learning and understanding
complex concepts, but only if presented in appropriate, interesting,
and active ways.

Lilian Katz (1999) suggests four categories of learning:

1. Knowledge: Facts, concepts, ideas, vocabulary, stories, and
   many other aspects of children's culture

2. Skills: Small units of action. Physical, social, verbal, and counting
   skills are a few of the endless skills learned in early childhood.
   Skills can be learned from direct instruction and are improved
   with guidance, practice, repetition, drill, and application.

3. Dispositions: Habits or tendencies to respond to certain situations in certain ways. Examples of dispositions are curiosity,
   friendliness, meanness, creativity, bossiness. Katz reminds us
   that it is important to keep in mind the difference between
   having writing skills and having the disposition to be a writer,
   or having reading skills and having the disposition to be a
   reader (Katz, 1995).

4. Feelings: Subjective emotional states. Some examples of
   learned feelings are competence, confidence, and security.
   "Feelings about school, teachers, learning and other children
   are also learned in the early years" (Katz, 1999, p. 2).

Content in early childhood classrooms comes from several sources:
the child, society, and the content itself. The content in the social studies is vast and offers great opportunity for meaningful instruction

with young children. The challenge to teachers is to know the students and the cultural context from which they come and choose the most appropriate and meaningful content to present. Teachers must be prepared to take full advantage of each child's natural abilities and interests when planning and developing effective lessons.

Skills inherent in an excellent social studies program include acquiring information, manipulating data, constructing new knowledge, and participating in group work. These are not discrete skills, but rather an interconnected framework. Facts should not be taught in isolation, but must be embedded in a connected fashion within the knowledge, skills, and concepts that are ultimately sought. When an appropriate social studies curriculum is implemented, students achieve a deep understanding of the required skills as they participate in interesting and relevant activities.

Values can be developed by through systematic social studies experiences. These include such fundamental rights as "the right to life, liberty, individual dignity, equality of opportunity, justice, privacy, security, and ownership of private property. They include as well the basic freedoms of worship, thought, conscience, expression, inquiry, assembly, and participation in the political process" (NCSS, 1994). Through effective instructional strategies, teachers can guide their young students to explore these important values.

Integrated Curriculum

Interdisciplinary learning capitalizes on natural connections that cut across content areas. Integrated lessons are organized around themes and projects rather than along traditional subject-matter boundaries. This kind of learning encourages children to become active learners rather than passive listeners of the facts. There is a consensus among early childhood educators that young children learn by doing (Charlesworth & Miller, 1985; Dunn & Kontos, 1997; Katz, 1999; Newberger, 1997). They want to learn, and do learn from everything around them.

Interdisciplinary, cross-curricular teaching can increase students' motivation for learning by increasing their level of engagement. When students see the value of what they are learning, they become more actively engaged and tend to participate more fully in interdisciplinary experiences. When children learn concepts in context instead of in isolation, they tend to be more involved and derive deeper meaning from their instruction. The following chapters deal more specifically with ways to prepare the environment for learning and with ways to make lessons come alive for your students.

The important thing to remember about interdisciplinary learning is that life itself is interdisciplinary! Experience is not compartmentalized into tiny, discrete aspects. Everything that we do in real life is integrated, and likewise is the way that young children learn best. When planning social studies instruction, consider the lessons as an integral part of the entire school day. How can the skills and concepts be embedded into the other subject areas of the curriculum? In real life, we don't stop and say, "Now I'm going to work on interpersonal interactions" or "Now I will memorize the names of the states and capitals." We learn all of these things within a meaningful context, and in a multidisciplinary fashion. Let's offer that same benefit to our young students.

CHARACTERISTICS OF AN EXCELLENT SOCIAL STUDIES CURRICULUM

The stated purpose of public schools, to prepare citizens for life in our democracy, is well served through the social studies curriculum. The development of the four goal areas in the social studies—(1) knowledge, (2) skills, (3) values, and (4) citizenship—are critical for an effective social studies program for young children. Ultimately, social studies curricula should strive to help develop citizens who embrace the democratic ideals of our nation and who have developed critical thinking and problem-solving skills necessary to help solve global problems.

An excellent social studies program is characterized by the implementation of a variety of teaching strategies and resources. Although the social studies curriculum varies between different states, districts, and even classrooms, what should be consistent is the emphasis on problem-solving, critical thinking, and the development of research skills.

There continues to be some debate concerning the importance of student knowledge of basic facts. For young children, memorization of facts and dates is simply not appropriate. The debate, as it relates to older children and young adults, can belong to another author. I believe, however, that understanding broad meanings and *learning to learn* are the important goals of a social studies curriculum for young children.

Decision-Making

Social studies should form the basis of a curriculum that helps students develop the skills needed to solve the problems of our world. By learning to analyze a problem effectively, clarify their feelings about that problem, and reflect on good decisions, students will go into the world prepared to make a difference. Children are not born with the ability to make effective and reflective decisions. Classroom teachers must give students the background knowledge necessary to make good decisions. They must be provided with strategies to apply what they know and opportunities to practice in a supportive, nonjudgmental environment.

THEORETICAL BACKGROUND FOR EFFECTIVE SOCIAL STUDIES INSTRUCTION

This text does not delve deeply into early childhood theory, as those foundations have been covered in other courses. It is important to remember, however, that teachers of young children should be firmly grounded in excellent research and have a firm theoretical base from which to practice. As effective practitioners, it is important to reflect continuously on the theories and ongoing research that form the basis of the profession. While most teachers will adopt different aspects of theory, based on individual experiences, interests, beliefs, and most importantly, individual student profiles, it is very important to have a broad knowledge of theory. Take some time to review theoretical foundations materials at intervals throughout your teaching career. Many times, you will gain a deepened understanding of a particular theory based on classroom experiences and the children in individual classrooms.

The most popular theories among early childhood teachers are those of Jean Piaget and Lev Vygotsky These theorists' work forms the foundation of the constructivist approach that is the basis of DAP. **Constructivism** is a philosophy of learning that "refers to the idea that learners construct knowledge for themselves—each learner individually (and socially) constructs meaning —as he or she learns" (Hein, 1991, p. 1).

Jean Piaget

Jean Piaget (1896–1980) was one of the most influential researchers in the area of developmental psychology. He believed that the factor that distinguishes humans from other living beings is our ability to do "abstract symbolic reasoning." He believed that biological maturation establishes the preconditions for cognitive development. Piaget's view of early cognitive and concept development is one of the most popular and well known among early childhood educators. Those particularly interested in social studies instruction find Piaget's work very valuable.

Charlesworth and Miller (1985) have shown that all basic concepts in social studies can be constructed through appropriate classroom activities. Leading constructivists interpret Piaget's work in different ways, but all agree that children should work with concrete materials and maintain active involvement.

BASIC PRINCIPLES FOR IMPLEMENTATION OF PIAGET'S WORK

1. Learning should be child-centered.
2. Learning should be self-initiated.
3. Learning should involve real objects.

4. Learning should be individualized.
5. Learning should involve social interaction.

Source: Piaget & Inhelder, 1969.

Lev Vygotsky

Lev Vygotsky (1896–1934) was a Russian developmental psychologist who was discovered by the Western world many years after his untimely death, at the age of 37. Vygotsky's work became known in the United States during the 1980s and was influential because it allowed reconciliation between the competing views of children as (1) unfolding butterflies—left to their own devices and (2) la tabula rasa—a blank slate, just waiting for the chalk.

Vygotsky's work involved the importance of social interaction as children learn. Scaffolding, the use of social interaction as a support for learning, is a basic tenet of Vygotsky's theory. One of his most important contributions was the concept of the *zone of proximal development*, the term he coined to describe the gap between a child's current individual level of development and his emerging level of development—the things that the child can do with the help of a more competent peer.

Vygotsky believed that learning could occur through play, formal instruction, or the interaction between the learner and a more experienced peer. He believed that every function of a child's development appears twice: first on the social level and then on the individual level (Vygotsky, 1930/1978, p. 57). This offers an excellent basis for planning social studies instruction for our young children.

Sociocultural Factors

In addition to the theories of Piaget and Vygotsky, sociocultural factors must be taken into consideration. It is important to remember that, although theory and research inform our teaching, they are only a portion of what should influence that teaching. Piaget's approach suggested that the child constructs knowledge, intelligence, personality, and social and moral values. To provide meaningful instruction, teachers must engage the children in activities by which they construct their own knowledge.

"Every classroom has a socio-moral atmosphere that either hinders or promotes children's development" (Devries & Zan, 1995, p. 4). **Sociomoral atmosphere** refers to the entire environment in the classroom—the relationships among the children, between the teacher and the children, between the parents and teachers, and so forth. Constructivist classrooms are characterized by mutual respect between the teacher and the children.

Social Development

Erikson, Sears, Piaget, Maslow, and Rogers have all focused on the social development of the young child (Charlesworth, 2004, p. 467). As children enter school, they become less dependent on their families as their major social task becomes developing relationships with other children. A well-developed classroom environment (discussed in detail in Chapter 4) encourages independence and interdependence. The early childhood teacher sets the tone for a risk-free environment, where young children can interact with others, growing in social competence.

With a firm theoretical background and an understanding of current research, the excellent social studies teacher uses personal experiences and knowledge and a growing understanding of each child and family represented in the classroom to plan and carry out instruction. Theories, although important to know, are helpful only to the extent they provide a basis for understanding what teachers observe with individual students.

PREPARING TO TEACH THE CHILD FROM A DIFFERENT CULTURE

In creating a culturally responsive environment for young children, one of the most important steps that the teacher must take is to engage in self-analysis, to examine his or her own attitudes toward different ethnic, racial, gender, and social class groups (Banks & Banks, 1995). By writing life stories and reflecting on one's own experiences with diverse cultural groups, a teacher can gain self-awareness about his or her own beliefs and biases. Only through understanding one's own beliefs about racism and bias can the early childhood teacher provide a culturally relevant environment for his or her young students. Spend some time writing the story of your own life, as it relates to bias and beliefs about diverse cultural groups. Have you had any experiences with discrimination; if so, can you describe them? How did you overcome bias in your own experience, and what strategies might you employ to help students in your classroom? Share your thoughts with a partner, looking for similarities and differences in your experiences.

SUMMARY

Teaching young children is an exciting and meaningful profession. Few others provide such an opportunity to make a real difference in the future of our world. Even though public schools were established specifically for the purpose of developing an informed citizenry, many teachers find it difficult to provide adequate time for social studies instruction. Particularly in light of the No Child Left Behind legislation, which ups the ante for high-stakes testing, many teachers are opting out of teaching social studies all together in favor of spending more time on reading and math instruction, which is assessed on the state-mandated standardized tests.

Based on the work of the National Council for Social Studies (NCSS) and the National Association for the Education of Young Children (NAEYC), guidelines have been established for teachers of young children that encourage the use of developmentally appropriate practices to teach the important skills and concepts inherent in the social studies. The work of Jean Piaget and Lev Vygotsky forms the theoretical base for the constructivist approach to teaching in the social studies.

Teaching young children is a complex task. This chapter outlined some of the important organizations, theories, and ethical considerations to ponder when planning an effective social studies curriculum for young children. Building an early childhood/elementary classroom curriculum around the social studies is not only possible, but it is also fun and effective. The chapters that follow will delve more deeply into the specific ways this can be done.

▶ THEMATIC STRANDS AND FOCUS QUESTIONS

Individual Development and Identity

1. How can developmentally appropriate practices in the early childhood social studies classroom enhance young children's individual development and identity?

2. Which theoretical underpinnings guide the individual development of children in early childhood programs?

Individuals, Groups, and Institutions

1. What influences do schools and government agencies have on the practice of the early childhood social studies teacher?

2. How have the groups representing young children and their teachers responded to the changing educational needs of children?

Power, Authority, and Governance

1. How do national, state, and local mandates affect early childhood social studies instruction?

2. How does the early childhood professional balance the implementation of developmentally appropriate practices and mandates from national, state, and district authorities?

Civic Ideals and Practice

1. How does the development of the public school system relate to civic ideals?

2. How can early childhood teachers prepare young children for active participation in our democracy?

KEY TERMS

Association for Childhood Education International (ACEI)

Association of Teacher Educators (ATE)

Code of Ethical Conduct

constructivism

curriculum

developmentally appropriate practices (DAP)

graphic organizer

high-stakes testing

interdisciplinary learning

National Association for the Education of Young Children (NAEYC)

National Council for the Social Studies (NCSS)

No Child Left Behind (NCLB)

scaffolding

sociomoral atmosphere

Zone of Proximal Development (ZPD)

REFERENCES

AERA (American Educational Research Association). (2000). *AERA position statement concerning high-stakes testing in preK-12 education.* Washington, DC: Author.

ACEI (Association for Childhood Education International) (1998). ACEI position paper: Preparation of elementary teachers. http://www.acei.org/prepel.htm (Accessed August 26, 2004).

Banks, C., & Banks, J. (1995). Equity pedagogy: An essential component of multicultural education. *Theory Into Practice*, 34(3), 152–158.

Bredekamp, S., & Copple C. (1997). *Developmentally appropriate practice in early childhood programs.* Washington, DC: National Association for the Education of Young Children.

Charlesworth, R. (2004). *Understanding child development* (6th ed.). Clifton Park, NY: Thomson Delmar Learning

Charlesworth, R., & Miller, N. (1985). Social studies and basic skills in the kindergarten. *The Social Studies*, 76, 34–37.

Devries, R., & Zan, B. (1995). *Creating a constructivist classroom atmosphere. Young Children*, 5(1), 4–14.

Dunn, L., & Kontos, S. (1997). Developmentally appropriate practice: What does research tell us? (Eric Document Reproduction Service No. ED413106)

Egley, E., & Egley, R. (2000). Teaching principals, parents, and colleagues about developmentally appropriate practice. *Young Children*, 55(5), 48–51.

Hein, G. (1991, October). *Constructivist learning theory: The museum and the needs of people*. Paper presented at the CECA Conference in Jerusalem, Israel, October 15-21, 1991.

Katz, L. (1999). Another look at what young children should be learning. *ERIC Digest* ED430735, 1.

Krey, D. (1995). Operationalizing the thematic strands of social studies for young learners. Silver Spring, MD: National Council for the Social Studies.

NAEYC (National Association for the Education of Young Children). (1989). Code of ethical conduct.http://www.naeyc.org/resources/position_statements/pseth98.htm (Accessed February 4, 2004).

NCSS (National Council for the Social Studies). (1994). *Expectations of excellence; Curriculum standards for social studies*, Bulletin 89. Washington, DC: Author.

NAEYC (National Association for the Education of Young Children). (1997). NAEYC position statement: Early childhood teacher certification. http://www.naeyc.org/resources/position_statements/pscert98.htm (Accessed August 26, 2004).

Newberger, J. (1997). New brain development research—a wonderful window of opportunity to build public support for early childhood education! *Young Children*, *52* (4), 4–9.

Piaget, J., & Inhelder, B. (1969). *The psychology of the child*. New York: Basic Books.

U. S. Department of Education. (2002). Introduction: No Child Left Behind. http://www.ed.gov/nclb/overview/intro/index.html (Accessed February 1, 2004).

U. S. Department of Education. (2003). *No Child Left Behind: A parent's guide*. Washington, DC: Author.

Vygotsky, L. (1978). *Mind and society* (A. Blunden & N. Schmolze, Trans.). London: Harvard University Press. (Original work published 1930)

▶ SUGGESTED READINGS

Elkind, D. (1988). *The hurried child: Growing up too fast too soon*. New York: Perseus Books.

Kraus, R. (1994). *Leo the late bloomer*. New York: HarperTrophy.

NAEYC (National Association for the Education of Young Children). Position statement on developmentally appropriate practice. http://www.naeyc.org.

NCSS (National Council for the Social Studies). (1994). *Expectations for excellence*. Silver Spring, MD: National Council for the Social Studies.

No Child Left Behind: A parent's guide. (2002) Washington, DC: U.S. Department of Education.

CHAPTER 2
Creating a Learning Environment

OBJECTIVES

After reading this chapter, you should be able to:

➤ Design a social studies learning environment appropriate for young children.

➤ Develop learning centers that meet the needs of young students, based on social studies goals and objectives.

➤ Discuss the importance of active involvement in the learning process.

➤ Evaluate your own cultural background as it relates to teaching in diverse settings.

➤ Identify the uses of technology to guide the intellectual development of young children.

My heart is singing for joy this morning. A miracle has happened! The light of understanding has shown upon my little pupil's mind, and behold, all things are changed.

Anne Sullivan

Classrooms should reflect the multiple ways that children interact and learn.

INTRODUCTION

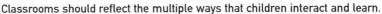

"Successful schools are unique places, not simply spaces" (NCSS, 2004). As teachers of young children, it is our responsibility to create engaging places of learning. In the minds of many teachers, the question becomes, "How can I make social studies fun and still maintain control of the classroom and focus on the standards for which I am responsible?"

Teachers of young children face a huge challenge in balancing the responsibility of making sure that students acquire the knowledge, skills, and values necessary to prepare them for citizenship with the desire to provide lessons that interest and involve the students in an active way. The social studies offer an excellent, meaningful basis for building thematic instruction that both interests children and develops higher-level thinking skills.

John Dewey (1938) offered some advice on this delicate balance between fun and work. When discussing social studies instruction, he said, "Play degenerates into fooling, and work into drudgery" (p. 286). As professionals, we must develop strategies that blend the interests of the students with the teaching of necessary standards. Children come to school curious about the world around them. It is up to the classroom teacher to tap into that curiosity and teach children how to question, find the answers to their questions, and solve problems through critical thinking.

Young children are eager learners. Social studies are the perfect avenue to help students maintain their zest for learning and their natural curiosity. When learning is fun and meaningful, students become interested and view social studies as an important part of their lives. Therefore, when preschool and primary classrooms are stimulating and support that natural sense of curiosity and wonder, students are able to cultivate their innate drive to learn and explore.

Environments that encourage play and offer an interesting variety of activities are most beneficial to a child's learning. While many believe that the younger the child, the more informal the learning should be, informal instruction is beneficial for learners of all ages. The curriculum should include a variety of opportunities for children to interact with materials, the environment, other children, and adults in an ongoing and meaningful way.

When developing an appropriate learning environment for young children, the early childhood educator must take many factors into consideration. One of the most important aspects of any classroom is the underlying foundation of respect.

By practicing respect for all students, teachers, and parents represented in the school community, the early childhood teacher models the most important element of any early childhood environment. For children to feel secure and ready to learn, the teacher must provide an accepting atmosphere for all children represented in the classroom (Salmon & Akaran, 2001).

PROVIDING AN ACCEPTING ATMOSPHERE FOR ALL CHILDREN

The U. S. Bureau of Census reports that the population of the United States is growing more culturally diverse every year (U. S. Bureau of the Census, 2000). The Children's Defense Fund (2004) indicates that this is particularly evident among families with young children.

Children become aware of differences in color, language, gender, and physical ability at a very young age. With the growing diversity in public school classrooms, it is becoming more and more important for teachers to develop an understanding of the specific needs of the diverse cultures represented in the early childhood classroom. Teaching practices need to be developed with careful attention to the cultural context in which the students live.

A GLOBAL PERSPECTIVE

CONNECTING TO PEOPLE OF ALL CULTURES

R-E-S-P-E-C-T

1. Have each person in the class pair up with someone he or she does not know.
2. Pairs introduce themselves to each other.
3. Each pair spends 5 minutes talking about respect.
   a. What does it mean to you?
   b. How is it manifested in the way you treat other people?
   c. What do you expect from others in terms of respect?
4. After 10 minutes, come together as a whole group.
5. Chart the ideas, as they are expressed by the pairs.
6. Remember that respect is crucial to any situation, but particularly important when dealing with issues of diversity.
7. The following are some important aspects to remember about respect:
   a. It's not about agreeing with each other.
   b. It's about understanding about the other person.
   c. Know each other's names and the correct pronunciations.
   d. What is said in the classroom, stays in the classroom.
8. Talk about the way that this kind of activity could or should be used in the early childhood classroom.

Obtain a copy of the soundtrack to *South Pacific*. Play the "You've Got to Be Taught" track. This song begins by telling us, You have to be carefully taught to hate and to be afraid of the people who are different. People who have different colored skin or eyes of a different shape—taught to hate the people that our relatives hate. Listen to the song and take some time to talk about the lyrics. Are they true? At what point do young children begin to see differences in people? At what point would they begin to hate? How can the early childhood teacher guide young children to be accepting of others?

Cultural Awareness

Culture is a fundamental building block in the development of a child's personal identity. It encompasses the values, beliefs, attitudes, laws, and ways of doing things characteristic of a particular community and is made up of all the influences in a child's environment. To understand the concept of culture, teachers and students must analyze

TABLE 2-1
Working With Culturally Diverse Students: Teacher Behaviors and Student Outcomes

TEACHER BEHAVIOR	STUDENT OUTCOME
Appreciate student differences and similarities.	Students learn to appreciate differences and similarities of other students.
Model respect for cross-cultural understanding.	Students replicate teacher behaviors and develop positive relationships with students from different cultural backgrounds.
Incorporate objectives for affective development.	Positive self-esteem is developed.
Consider children's cultures and language skills when developing lessons.	Continuous learning occurs at appropriate levels.

Based on the research of Burnette (1999); Derman-Sparks, L. and the ABC Task Force (1989); Salmon & Akaran (2001).

language, family, religion, government, and education of different groups of people.

A belief in the value of human diversity is a prerequisite for effective early childhood teaching. When developing the **classroom environment,** it is important to consider the way that environment supports each teacher's philosophy and curriculum. Understanding the cultural differences represented in each classroom is a first step in developing a culturally responsive curriculum.

Respect for all children is integral to every aspect of daily life in the classroom. Early childhood teachers play an important role in helping children to develop positive attitudes and respect for the differences represented in the classroom. "Teachers must have time for emotionalizing feelings about others, examining their prejudices, and working toward informed actions" (Hunt, 1999, p. 40). Sharing life experiences on race and diversity helps teachers to reach a common understanding about the importance of learning about and celebrating similarities and differences among people.

Certain teacher behaviors and instructional strategies enable teachers to build stronger relationships with their culturally diverse students (Burnette, 1999). Many of the strategies are standard practices of good teaching, but some are specific to working with students from diverse cultures. See Table 2–1 for teacher behaviors and student outcomes.

Many early childhood teachers have not had extensive interactions with people from diverse cultures. When beginning to develop the learning environment for young children, it is often effective for the early childhood teacher to explore his or her

GROUP ACTIVITY

THINKING ABOUT CULTURE

1. Spend some time getting to know about your own culture.
2. Talk to members of your extended family. How did your family traditions come about?
3 Where did your family originate? Can the traditions, dispositions, and interests that are common among your family members be traced back to those roots?

4 Have you had any experiences with discrimination; if so, can you describe them?
5 Talk with your neighbor about what you know about your cultural heritage and how that background affects your teaching and interaction from children with a different background.
6 Discuss these questions with other students and compare feedback.

understanding of culture from a personal perspective (Neugebauer, 1994). Spending time reflecting on one's own cultural heritage is an important step in preparing to teach students of diverse backgrounds.

Every classroom is diverse to a degree, whether the differences arise from gender, ethnicity, race, socioeconomic status, religion, capability, disability, interests, or other factors. Establishing a classroom climate of caring and respect is an important part of teaching young children. To do this, the entire curriculum must incorporate an appreciation of diversity. The teacher must be the model for setting a standard of commitment to **multicultural education** in the classroom (Hunt, 1999).

There are many valid reasons for early childhood teachers to embrace multicultural approaches to the education of our young students. We want our students to feel welcome and important. By validating their cultural background, we can encourage them to feel like a part of the classroom culture (Bredekamp & Rosegrant, 1992). In addition, understanding of other cultures allows children to accept the differences of others. The American boxer Muhammad Ali said, "Prejudice comes from being in the dark;

sunlight disinfects it." Let us, the educators of the new generation, be that sunlight.

Goals for Encouraging an Accepting Classroom Environment

Louise Derman-Sparks and the ABC Task Force (1989) suggest four goals for encouraging an accepting classroom environment:

1. Foster each child's construction of a knowledgeable, confident self-identity.
2. Foster each child's comfortable, empathetic interaction with diversity among people.
3. Foster each child's critical thinking about bias.
4. Foster each child's ability to stand up for her- or himself and for others in the face of bias.

Teaching about diversity is not a part of the curriculum that occurs occasionally, listed specifically in the lesson plan book or on the weekly schedule. Teaching children about diversity is an ongoing, integral part of an effective classroom environment. This important aspect of the curriculum teaches the importance of respecting others, valuing their differences and similarities, and becoming more caring members of the greater society.

Approaches to Teaching About Culture

In general, there are four main approaches to teaching young children about culture: multicultural education, **anti-bias curriculum**, global education, and international education. While the desired goals for all four approaches are similar, there are subtle differences in the way the four approaches are designed.

Anti-Bias Curriculum

In 1989, Louise Derman-Sparks and the ABC Task Force wrote the anti-bias curriculum handbook as a guide for teachers of young children, with the basic goal of helping children develop a positive-self concept without an attitude of superiority. The book encourages teachers to integrate anti-bias curriculum throughout the school day, not as a stand-alone curriculum.

Multicultural Education

Multicultural education has as its goal exposing children to a variety of cultures. The teacher makes it a point to examine the different cultures represented in the classroom. If the classroom population has little diversity, the teacher would present as many cultural experiences as possible through the curriculum. Such practices as examining family traditions around the world expose children to differences among cultures at an early age.

Global Education

Global education is usually explored with older children—those in middle and high school. The goal of global education is to help students recognize the interconnectedness of the world. It involves developing a student's ability to look at problems and events from different perspectives. Global education is inherently abstract, so is less appropriate for very young children. Working with young children to develop their abilities to view the world from different perspectives would be an appropriate objective, however, which would lead to success in dealing with a global education curriculum in later years.

International Education

International education is structured to expose children to a single culture for an entire school year. Over the course of that year, students might study the clothing, food, music, dances, shelter, economy, family structure, and celebrations of a particular culture. Through this type of study, children are able to move beyond superficial knowledge to a deeper, more meaningful understanding of that culture.

Family and Cultural Competence

The concept and reality of the family has changed drastically in recent decades. In this text *family* is considered as any unit that defines itself as a family. Family characteristics will continue to become more and more diverse and complex. Early childhood teachers need to understand and acknowledge these changes to effectively serve the children and families represented in each classroom.

Collaboration with parents is essential to the development of families' awareness of the importance of their role in supporting their child's development and learning. In NAEYC's position statement on developmentally appropriate practice, the fifth guideline for decisions about developmentally appropriate practice—Establishing reciprocal relationships with families—stresses that teachers need to share their knowledge of the child and understanding of children's learning as a part of day-to-day communication with families. Involving parents in daily classroom activities can be useful in a variety of ways. In addition to allowing the teacher to understand more fully the cultural background of each child in the classroom, through regular parental involvement, the teacher can model techniques and strategies for learning and behavior management.

Regular interaction with parents also increases trust and cooperation between the teacher and the parents. Parents are a rich resource of topics for the early childhood social studies curriculum. Become aware of their special gifts and talents, as well as their diverse cultural and experiential backgrounds, and tap into those resources when planning for social studies instruction. Inviting parents to share their travel experiences, special cooking or craft skills, or demonstration of cultural dance is a powerful way to involve parents in the classroom and to enrich the education of the students.

Special Populations

Every child is special and unique. The classroom teacher is challenged with children at all levels of development, children with a wide range of experiential backgrounds and intellectual abilities. While every child is special and has particular instructional needs, two broad groups of learners are discussed in this chapter. We first discuss the special needs of children coming from a different language background. These students bring particular needs to the early childhood classroom, which are addressed through appropriate instruction. The second group consists of students who have been identified with special needs based on any one of a number of factors and who present special challenges to the classroom teacher. Inclusive classrooms, those embracing children with disabilities in a number of areas, are growing in number and are an effective way to meet the needs of young children with special needs.

English Language Learners

More immigrants arrived in the United States during the 1990s than in any other single decade. This means that the number of public school students in need of language instruction has increased dramatically (Bureau of U. S. Citizenship and Immigration Services,

2001). A survey of state education agencies found that in 2000–2001, more than 4 million students with limited English proficiency were enrolled in the nation's public schools. This is more than 10 percent of the total pre-K–12th grade public enrollment, making linguistically and culturally diverse classrooms the rule rather than the exception.

Meeting the needs of such a **heterogeneous group** of students is challenging in the social studies classroom. Aside from the obvious benefits of understanding the English language, social studies concepts frequently involve an underlying knowledge of American culture as a basis for further conceptual development.

For a child whose native culture is very different from the American culture, learning social studies can be quite difficult (Lee & Fradd, 1998). U. S.-born students have a preexisting schema into which they can fit in the new information being presented. Children from different cultures do not have this framework. In addition, children from different language backgrounds may have difficulty understanding the teacher's accent and will probably not comprehend the meaning of colloquialisms or some analogies. It is particularly important for the classroom teacher to be aware of these limitations as complex social studies concepts are explored.

For young children, adjusting to a new language and culture is a challenging and difficult process that may take several years. An active, integrated curriculum is essential if these students are to achieve their full potential. It is important for the classroom teacher to remember that English language learners can understand and reason at a much deeper level than they have vocabulary to express. Recognizing and appreciating cultural differences in the classroom makes a huge difference. Valuing the students' cultures and learning about those differences are important starts in working with a child from a different language and cultural background.

When working with children from different language backgrounds the early childhood teacher has a responsibility to create an appropriate environment to encourage learning. While many of the strategies for working with children from non-English-speaking backgrounds are the same as those for all children, some special considerations need to be taken into account.

All students deserve equal access to the social studies curriculum. The early childhood teacher must adopt instructional approaches that help make the material comprehensible to all children. Some suggestions for helping make this happen are: (1) use hands-on materials, such as maps, globes, and realia; (2) provide students with biographies of famous people from a wide variety of cultural groups; (3) supplement textbooks with children's literature—both fiction and

CONSIDERATIONS FOR WORKING WITH CHILDREN LEARNING ENGLISH

* From what country has the child immigrated?
* What language(s) is spoken in the home?
* What does the teacher need to know about that culture that could impact instruction (gestures, eye contact, classroom etiquette, etc.)?
* What was the child's schooling experience in his native country?
* What level of schooling did the parents achieve?
* How can the teacher communicate effectively with families who do not speak English?

* What strategies can the teacher use to engage, one-on-one, with the child learning English?
* How can the teacher include words from the child's home language into classroom print materials?
* How can the teacher include books reflecting the cultures and languages of the children enrolled in the early childhood classroom?

nonfiction; (4) be alert to language, concepts, and values that may be unclear because of cultural differences (Thonis, 1981).

Children With Special Needs

Many young children have special needs, making their learning a greater challenge. While all children must be considered *children* first, some conditions require specific help and specialized instruction. It is sometimes difficult to determine whether a child at an early age has a specific disability or if he or she is simply developing in a particular area at a slower rate. Appropriate instruction, based on the individual development of each child in the classroom, allows every child to progress in a steady manner.

Some identifiable special needs include children with intellectual disabilities, visual or hearing impairment, orthopedic or other physical disabilities, emotional disturbance, and speech and language disorders, to name a few. Students with all levels of ability and disability will be a part of the early childhood classroom. While there are specialists who tend to the specific needs of children with disabilities, the general education classroom teacher is an integral part of the team.

The Individuals With Disabilities Act (IDEA)

In 1975, the U. S. Department of Education passed **P.L. 94–142**, which was the first law to ensure that each child with a disability be given a **free appropriate public education (FAPE).** Prior to P.L. 94–142, approximately one million children with disabilities were shut out of schools and hundreds of thousands more were denied appropriate services (Office of Special Education Programs, U. S. Department of Education, June 1997). This law formed the basis for **IDEA**, or the **Individuals with Disabilities Education Act** of 1997. This Act strengthened academic expectations and accountability for the nation's 5.8 million children with disabilities. In addition, the Act bridges the gap between the curriculum for typically developing children and those children with disabilities.

One of the most interesting and promising byproducts of IDEA has been the implementation of inclusive classrooms in public schools. In these classrooms, children with disabilities are "included" in regular education classrooms to varying degrees (Odom & Diamond, 1998; Odom, Teferra, & Kaul, 2004). Early childhood teachers are particularly successful in establishing inclusive classrooms, because of their natural tendency and training in meeting individual needs. Young children are especially accepting of others, and when led by a caring and skilled teacher, they view all students as equal members of the classroom.

When establishing the environment for the classroom, keep in mind the special needs of the students you will be serving. It takes some forethought, as center space is planned, materials are made accessible to all, and maneuvering space is provided, to accommodate all of the children who make up the class population.

The American writer James Baldwin said, "Children have never been very good at listening to their elders, but they have never failed to imitate them." This quote rings particularly true as we think about developing an atmosphere of acceptance in our early childhood classrooms. Young children have an uncanny way of seeing our real selves. While we may be able to fool our adult colleagues concerning our true feelings about working with diverse populations, we will never fool our students. As we plan our classrooms to create an accepting, nurturing environment for our young students, every book, activity, instructional material, and interaction must be viewed through a filter of anti-bias. Learning about diversity is not a lesson that we present twice a week—it is a lifestyle and an attitude that permeates every activity.

Inclusion

In an increasing number of early childhood and elementary classrooms, teachers and parents are finding the benefits of educating young children with special needs together with their same-age peers. In most public schools, children with disabilities are included in the regular education classroom, either for a portion of the day or for the entire day (Odom & Diamond, 1998).

Those who favor **inclusion** believe that children with special needs can be effectively included in the regular education classrooms for a portion of the day, with the remainder of the school day being spent with specialists focusing on the specific needs of the individual child. **Full inclusionists** believe that children with special needs must be placed full-time in the general education classroom, making them full-fledged members of the class. The child with special needs would not come and go from the classroom. In either case, the general education teacher, who is planning and implementing social studies instruction in the classroom, is responsible for meeting the needs of all of the children in the classroom.

The key to making inclusion successful is to educate oneself about the best ways to help each child, whatever his ability or disability, reach his full potential. A common thread throughout this text is the idea that all of us are special education teachers—whether we are specifically trained as such or not. Each child in each classroom has a particular set of strengths and needs, and it is the responsibility of the classroom teacher to meet each of those needs. A wide range of active, appropriate lessons will serve to meet the needs of the children with disabilities in each classroom, as well as those of the typically developing children in the class.

Early childhood teachers are particularly well suited to working with children with disabilities, as the basis of early childhood education is knowing and meeting the needs of the individual child (Shade, 1996). Establishment of an environment in which the social, physical, emotional, and intellectual development of all children is acknowledged and encouraged creates a rich backdrop for the learning of all children.

Even if the general education teacher is not specifically trained to work with children with disabilities, these students will be a part of the classroom community. A wide variety of disabilities is represented in inclusive early childhood classrooms. To meet the needs of each child, it is important to gain an understanding of the disabilities represented and to find effective ways to work with the students with special needs. See Table 2–2 for some types of disabilities.

TABLe 2-2
Types of Disabilities Represented in an Inclusive Early Childhood Classroom

CONDITION	DESCRIPTION	SUGGESTIONS FOR ADAPTING CURRICULA IN THE EARLY CHILDHOOD CLASSROOM
Visual impairments	A range from lack of vision to corrected vision.	• Be aware of lighting conditions. • Orient the child to classroom layout. • Provide tactile, manipulative, and auditory experiences. • Tell students what will be happening.
Hearing impairments	A range from total hearing loss to correctable hearing.	• Seat the child in front for good visibility. • Speak at a normal volume and speed. • Avoid speaking with your back to the child. • Use visual/tactile aids.
Health impairments	Chronic problems, including but not limited to: asthma, diabetes, epilepsy, heart defects, sickle cell disease, cancer.	• Consult with the child's parents, physician and school nurse while planning child's program. • Encourage the child to be as independent as possible. • Develop a plan for keeping children current with lessons when they are absent for long periods of time.
Physical/orthopedic impairments	Missing or nonfunctional limbs, muscles, or joints. Conditions such as arthritis, muscular dystrophy, cerebral palsy, spina bifida.	• Consult with physical/occupational therapists during planning. • Arrange the environment to accommodate child's movement and equipment. • Work toward independence for the child.
Learning disabilities/difficulties	Average or above average intelligence, but has difficulty learning.	• Consistent behavior management. • Multisensory approach. • Work in cooperation with parents.
Autism	"Severely incapacitating lifelong developmental disability characterized by certain types of behaviors and patterns of interaction and communication." (Hunt & Marshall, 2001)	• Maintain a well-organized, predictable classroom environment. • Reduce noise level. • Be consistent with consequences. • Use verbal and visual cues for communication with the child.
Intellectual/cognitive disability	Intellectual challenge based on multiple criteria.	• Present material in short segments using multisensory approach. • Break tasks into many small steps. • Concentrate on strengths, not weaknesses.

Adapted from Charlesworth, R. (2004).

THE TEACHER

In any classroom, the single most important element necessary for success is the teacher. His or her understanding of child development, knowledge of the subject matter to be presented, and understanding of the appropriate teaching strategies needed to deliver that instruction are integral to the success of the students enrolled in the early childhood classroom. Although social studies instruction requires specific skills and materials, an effective early childhood teacher is well prepared to be an effective social studies teacher.

There is consensus among early childhood educators that young children learn by doing; they learn by ongoing interaction with all kinds of people, material, and equipment (Piaget & Inhelder, 1969; Tharp & Fritz, 2003), Young children want to learn! Almost every child enters school with a zest for learning and a passion for engagement in the curriculum, but sadly, by third or fourth grade, many students have lost that love for school, and a majority of middle school students would rather be anywhere else. As teachers of young children, we can help our students to affirm the love of learning; indeed, it is our job to do exactly that.

What are the characteristics of an excellent teacher? What makes a single teacher memorable long after we leave that classroom?

GROUP ACTIVITY: THE PERFECT SOCIAL STUDIES TEACHER

1. With university students interested in teaching at the same grade level, form small groups of three or four.
2. Have a variety of art materials available: large paper, markers, yarn, glue, scissors, and so forth.
3. Have groups design the "perfect social studies teacher." Anything goes! Use all of your talents—poetry, song, dramatics, games, and so forth.
4. Share the representations of the exemplary social studies teacher, making a composite as different groups share.
5. Discuss ways that you can achieve "exemplary" status as a social studies teacher in your early childhood classroom.

How can new teachers become that life-changing influence for young children (Tertell, Klein, & Jewett, 1998)?

The Social Studies Teacher

If you were to draw a picture of the exemplary social studies teacher, what would you include? What kinds of instructional strategies would the exemplary teacher use? How would the environment be prepared for maximum learning? What kinds of materials and books would be available to the students in the classroom? How would the children be engaged in the learning? Although, on the surface, an exemplary social studies teacher appears to carry out her duties in an effortless manner, in reality, she is (much like the duck in the old story) paddling like crazy under water!

The characteristics of an excellent social studies teacher can be categorized into three different areas: (1) understanding of children—as individuals, as groups, and from a cultural perspective, (2) understanding of the planning process, and (3) understanding of the instructional process (Bredekamp, 1992; Bredekamp & Copple, 1997). We will explore the three areas and the ways in which they interact to form a basis of effective instruction for young children.

Understanding Children

To present an effective social studies curriculum, teachers must first understand the children they teach. Early childhood teachers must have a firm understanding of child development—what do typically developing children at this age look like? What concepts are they able to grasp? How do they learn most effectively? In addition, the early childhood teacher must know and understand each individual child in the classroom (Tomlinson & Kalbfleisch, 1998). If there are 20 children in a first-grade classroom, there will be 20 different profiles of learning at any given time. No two children are the same, and even the same child changes often.

What is that individual child capable of; what is he interested in? What prior experiences and understandings does she bring to this particular concept? Finally, what cultural differences do the children bring to this lesson? How will one child view the lesson in light of his home experiences as it compares to the understanding of another child, from a different cultural background? All of these elements are underpinnings of the planning and implementation of effective social studies lessons.

Understanding the Planning Process

Knowing the National Council for Social Studies (NCSS) Standards is an essential start for understanding the planning process for social studies instruction. With a thorough knowledge of these standards and those set forth by the individual district and state education department, the early childhood teacher will more readily be able to formulate the goals and objectives for effective social studies instruction. It is important to become familiar with these standards for the grade level being taught, as well as those for the grade level before and after yours. It is helpful to keep several copies of the standards available for planning.

A broad-based knowledge of the disciplines related to social studies is another important element of the planning process. To teach something to another person, we must first have a firm grasp of the information ourselves. Those hours of history, geography, anthropology, and economics in your university training will prove to be very important when beginning to plan for teaching the social studies. When planning thematic units for young students, the teacher will probably find it necessary to review and augment what has been learned in the content areas. We always learn more by teaching content to others.

After examining the NCSS standards and the state and district curriculum standards, choose a focus that will interest and challenge the students. Choose to present a few important concepts in depth, rather than making a superficial coverage of many. This requires important and difficult choices to the classroom teacher. The exemplary social studies teacher must make difficult decisions and creative choices to give students the benefit of deep knowledge and an understanding of a few important concepts from which to build in future school years.

Presentation of important social studies concepts must have meaning in the lives of young children. Choosing a common concept, such as "family," to tie the activities together will lend meaning to the instruction for the students. When planning, look at the different learning profiles of the students in the class. Plan a balance of activities that will meet the needs and interests of each child. Look for a balance of instructional strategies and activities that will allow children to work in active groups, in partnership with other children, as well as individually.

Review the instructional resources available. Planning is a dynamic and ongoing process in the life of an exemplary social studies teacher. To provide children with a variety of meaningful materials and resources, the teacher must be constantly searching for appropriate, new, and interesting materials to use in the classroom. The planning process is explored in detail later in the text, but it is important to note here that one of the critical elements of exemplary social studies instruction is that of ongoing, effective planning.

Understanding the Instructional Process

Excellent teaching is excellent teaching, no matter what subject is taught! The social studies, however, offer an outstanding array of important and meaningful concepts from which to "do" excellent teaching. Engaging students in analyses of important social issues, ethical concerns, and values offers good teachers vast opportunities to practice their art. Social studies offer opportunities to help students develop higher-order thinking skills and skills in problem-solving (Goffin & Tull, 1985). The possibilities for excellent teaching in the social studies are exciting. In reality, the teacher's imagination is the only limitation in providing varied and meaningful lessons for students.

With young children, many believe that teachers must first emphasize the relationships among people, places, events, ideas, and values offered in the social studies curriculum. Students must be provided with the opportunity for working in large groups, in small groups, and in pairs to develop ideas and understandings. Young children need an appropriate environment, materials, and adequate time to explore that environment in order to cultivate these ideas and to express them in meaningful ways. The early childhood teacher must also find ways to assess what the students have learned in appropriate and authentic ways.

THEORY INTO PRACTICE

In Chapter 1, we briefly discussed the importance of Jean Piaget and Lev Vygotsky's work, as it relates to teaching social studies to young children. When Piaget's ideas are applied to classroom instruction for young children, the recommended teaching strategies tend to focus on ways to help children to construct growing conceptual frameworks. This kind of instruction focuses on process rather than product (Kamii, 1981). Vygotsky's work also encourages constructivist approaches, and emphasizes the importance of interaction among peers in the learning process.

By increasing opportunities for young students to participate actively in problem-solving activities, language development is facilitated, thinking skills are enhanced and the child's ability to consider other points of view grows (Bergen, 2000b; Epstein, 2003). Teachers can expand everyday activities into problem-solving opportunities by encouraging children to make decisions, plan, predict, and evaluate the outcomes of their activities. Using open-ended materials such as blocks, sand, water tables, and art materials, in easy reach of students, encourages problem-solving.

Play Theory and Social Development

Play is an essential component of a quality program for young children. As they play, children develop problem-solving skills, use language to carry out their activities, and learn about other people by talking and listening to them. Play nurtures children's development in all areas: intellectual, social/emotional, and physical. In Chapter 10, we discuss the importance of play in more detail. In this chapter on developing an appropriate environment for young children's learning, we explore the importance of developing an environment where play is valued as a way of learning.

The Association for Childhood Education International (ACEI) believes that play is "a dynamic, active, and constructive behavior—is an essential and integral part of all children's healthy growth, development, and learning across all ages, domains, and cultures" (Isenberg & Quisenberry, 2002). Their advocacy for maintaining play as a regular part of the school day has led the way in opening the conversation about the value of play in a public school setting.

According to Fromberg (1990), play is the "ultimate integrator of human experience" (p. 223). Play reflects the social and cultural contexts in which children live and is a key facilitator for learning and development across domains. Piaget (1962) defined play as assimilation, or the child's efforts to make environmental stimuli match his or her own concepts. According to Piaget, play reflects what the child has already learned. In contrast to this view, Vygotsky stated that play actually facilitates cognitive development by allowing children to practice what they already know and by actually learning new things.

Both Vygotsky (1978) and Piaget (Piaget & Inhelder, 1969) believed that sociodramatic play leads to symbolic thought.

Theorists across the spectrum concur that play occupies a central role in children's lives and that the absence of play is an obstacle to healthy development. Learning requires an interactive balance of gaining facts and skills and making the information one's own (Fromberg, 1990). A major way that children take ownership of new information is by playing with it. Some in leadership roles in the public schools consider play to be a waste of time. On the contrary, "play is not wasted time but rather time spent building new knowledge from previous experience" (Bruner, 1972, cited in Harris, 1986, p. 263).

"The early childhood teacher is the facilitator of play in the classroom" (Fox, 2004, p. 3). By providing materials related to thematic instruction, links can be made between the child's play and the social studies curriculum. Props for creative dramatics can be placed in centers to encourage review and extension of concepts being studied in the social studies curriculum. Art materials should be made available to children to encourage integration of social studies concepts. Accessories for the block center can be added to reflect the theme of the social studies lessons.

Beginning school does not signal the end of children's need for play in learning. Traditionally, play in the elementary school setting has been viewed as meeting nonacademic, social, or physical education goals. However, many forms of play can make an important contribution to a young child's language, literacy, and social studies learning. Play continues to be important for supporting cognitive and social development throughout the school years. Structured playtime that occurs in a well-designed learning environment can provide rich opportunities for young children to construct knowledge related to social studies. Concrete experiences are the basis for deep understanding and development of complex concepts in the social studies.

Teachers must be knowledgeable about the ways that play enhances learning and development in order to make convincing arguments to administration about providing opportunities and time for children to play. Early childhood professionals must help administration, parents, community members, and other teachers to understand that a curriculum incorporating play strengthens and supports a child's intellectual and social development.

It is important that, as teachers of young children, we maintain the joy inherent in learning and growing. This joy is beautifully illustrated in the Jack Prelutsky/Lane Smith/Dr. Seuss book, *Hooray for Diffendoofer Day!*

Hooray for Diffendoofer Day!

Read Dr. Seuss' book, *Hooray for Diffendoofer Day!* This engagingly illustrated book, written in that unmistakable Dr. Seuss style, chronicles the Diffendoofer School's unique teaching and learning strategies. Unfortunately, one day, the principal, Mr. Lowe, announces that the students will be tested, and if they do not do well, they will all be transferred to dreary Flobbertown. Miss Bonkers makes the distraught children feel better as she reminds them of all the things they have learned; most importantly, she reminds the students that they have been taught how to *think*. After reading the book, talk about its implications in relation to your design for your classroom environment. What does this story remind us about teaching, learning, and instructional strategies? Discuss how you will deal with high-stakes testing in your own classroom.

As illustrated in *Hooray for Diffendoofer Day!* School principals are busy, responsible people. While the overwhelming majority of principals have the best intentions and hopes for the students and teachers in their schools, they are bombarded with conflicting information, mandates, and pressures. It is the responsibility of the early childhood teacher to keep the principal informed of the latest research as it relates to young children, and to communicate with him or her concerning important aspects of the early childhood curriculum.

Talk with your principal in the spring, as he or she is developing the schedule for the next school year. Discuss your concerns and preferences for extended periods of time, and be sure to tell your principal *why* you are requesting a particular schedule. Understand that the principal is dealing with a balancing act—trying to work the schedule to accommodate many children and teachers, as well as state-enforced time and scheduling mandates.

Make your preferences known, but understand that you may not get your first choice! Any schedule is ultimately workable. Have regular conversations with your principal about your classroom schedule, as well as other needs. My principal always said, "the princi*pal* is your *pal*." And, it is really true.

SCHEDULING

School principals are charged with making the school run smoothly. One duty of the elementary principal is to prepare the schedule for every classroom in the school. Making sure that lunch, recess, music, art, physical education, library, special education, speech therapy, and English as a second language (ESL) schedules mesh for a large number of children is no small feat! When planning for the early childhood classroom, it is important to have large blocks of uninterrupted time available for project learning and for children's extended play and interaction.

THE PHYSICAL ENVIRONMENT

Early childhood teachers must introduce students to important concepts at their own level of awareness, through active exploration of the environment. Research suggests that early childhood curricula should provide opportunities for children to interact with peers, teachers, and aspects of their environment, and to engage in active rather than passive activities (Katz, 1987). Setting up the environment for active engagement, allowing for a wide range of abilities and interest levels, and offering multiple opportunities for children to master complex understandings are integral to the effective social studies curriculum (Diffily, 2002; Shade, 1996). Preparing the physical environment for active learning is one of the most important tasks of the effective early childhood teacher.

The Social Studies Classroom

Our responsibility as educators is to imagine and create places of learning. Social studies educators should be leaders in this effort (NCSS, 2004). Young children are active learners. They touch, feel, create, and experiment with their surroundings. Teachers must structure the classroom environments, schedules, and curricula to include and encourage this active involvement.

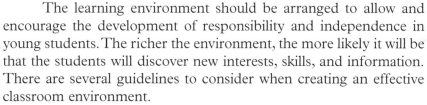

An environment for active engagement.

The learning environment should be arranged to allow and encourage the development of responsibility and independence in young students. The richer the environment, the more likely it will be that the students will discover new interests, skills, and information. There are several guidelines to consider when creating an effective classroom environment.

Safety must be the foundation upon which classroom environments are built. When setting up the classroom, it is most important that the teacher is able to easily observe all areas of the classroom at all times. Particularly important is the viewpoint from the reading table, since you will be working there with small groups while others work in centers. Be particularly aware of this when designing areas for learning centers.

Children need easy access to age-appropriate materials, supplies, books, and toys. The classroom should be set up in such a way as to encourage children to do things for themselves. If materials and supplies are at their level, well organized, and labeled, children are able to work much more effectively and independently. Appropriate guidelines, procedures, and rules must be developed and enforced in order to allow children to use an appropriate environment in a growing and independent way.

Easy access to books on social studies topics can help make your instruction come alive for students!

To encourage engagement in social studies lessons, the classroom should be set up with your teaching style and your students' learning styles in mind. Desks or tables should be arranged in configurations that allow students to interact with each other, encouraging social competence. There should also be a large area for students to assemble, either on a rug or by bringing their chairs, in a circle for read-alouds and interactive writing activities.

The physical environment is very important in a young child's learning. Educators of young children are greatly influenced by Jean Piaget's theory of child development, in which he stated that children learn through active, multisensory exploration of the environment (Piaget, 1969). In an early childhood setting, a child assimilates new information through sensory experiences with the environment.

The classroom environment reflects the teacher's philosophy and goals. In most cases, the physical characteristics of the classroom to which the teacher is assigned do not reflect his or her own choices. Perhaps the room is too small. Maybe desks have been installed in the classroom instead of the small tables requested. Perhaps there is no sink in the classroom and the only restroom is down the hall!

While these are all challenges, to be sure, with a firm understanding of developmentally appropriate practice and a roadmap for

IMPORTANT CONSIDERATIONS WHEN SETTING UP THE PHYSICAL ENVIRONMENT

- You should be able to see all areas of the classroom.
- Have materials organized for easy access to young learners.
- Arrange classroom with your teaching style and students' learning styles in mind.
- Don't be afraid to change the configuration of the classroom as students' needs change.
- Arrange areas for social interaction and for individual work.
- Arrange centers to facilitate independence.
- Arrange quiet areas (library center) away from louder areas (block center).

the curriculum to be used during the school year, the early childhood teacher will be able to work effectively within these constraints. It is important to remember, however, that the most important ingredient of a developmentally appropriate classroom is *the teacher*.

Room arrangement is an important way that the teacher communicates expectations for behavior and achievement to students, parents, and administration. Furniture (or the lack of it) gives immediate information about how students are to behave in a given setting. Consider the message given when children walk into a classroom with desks lined up in rows, all facing the front chalkboard. Does this signal a classroom where social interaction is valued? In contrast, consider the child's perception upon walking into a classroom with those very same desks grouped in four's, facing each other, with that same chalkboard covered in bright paper, hosting an interactive bulletin board. What are the messages given, before ever meeting the teacher?

In providing an appropriate environment, where all children feel important and valued, teachers must evaluate the cultural appropriateness of the physical classroom. Are the similarities and differences of the students in the classroom celebrated? Does the classroom reflect the different cultures represented by the students, within the walls of the school, and the greater community? Are there books about

What message does this environment send to children?

black, Hispanic, Jewish, and Asian families, as well as families with a single mom or dad, a grandparent acting as parent, families representing all of the different configurations that are represented in our diverse society? Are there dolls, cooking utensils, photographs, musical instruments, clothing, and music from a wide variety of cultures in the home living center? Do the bulletin boards represent the variety of cultures represented in the classroom and in society?

Particularly for teachers who have grown up in a somewhat homogeneous environment, having never developed relationships with people of other cultures, omission of these culturally diverse materials can be made, with no intention of bias or ill-will. Using materials rich in cultural diversity can underscore the importance of children being exposed to the reality of living in a diverse world.

Learning Centers

Learning centers are an important part of an early childhood classroom environment. Learning centers are areas set up in the classroom that are designed to encourage independent understanding of the concepts presented. While most preschool and kindergarten teachers incorporate learning centers in their classrooms, the use of centers

CREATING AN ACCEPTING PHYSICAL CLASSROOM ENVIRONMENT

Provide bulletin boards, materials, and books that:

1. Reflect the backgrounds of the children, workers, and families represented in the classroom, the school, and the greater community.
2. Reflect people's daily lives accurately—people working, playing, eating, and relating to one another.
3. Reflect a balance of gender roles.
4. Reflect accurate images of elderly people.
5. Reflect a diversity of family configurations.
6. Reflect the lives of important people through history in a balanced way.
7. Reflect realistic images of people with disabilities.

Providing visuals that reflect diversity is important in helping young children develop a positive self-image.

diminishes as the students move up the grade levels. Centers can be effectively used in the upper elementary grades, allowing children to extend their social studies instruction with small group activities, independent study, and application of previously learned material.

Moving from a total-class, teacher-directed model of teaching to individualized center activities is one way to create more student involvement. Learning centers are one way of organizing materials and addressing multiple learning styles within a manageable structure. They also provide a way of truly integrating the curriculum, by placing books having to do with the social studies theme in the reading center; having firefighter, police officer, and chef hats in the dramatic play area; or by having copies of a reader's theater script developed by the class after reading a favorite book about George Washington, available in the Theater Center.

Adding books to the library center that address multicultural issues of ethnicity, family structure, and religious celebrations is one effective and simple way to prepare the environment to address the multicultural needs of the students in the classroom. Adding props to the housekeeping area that reflect the diversity of the students in the classroom is another way to involve students in authentic multicultural study.

The classroom environment should nurture the total development of our students and provide opportunities for children to participate individually, in teams, and in small groups. Current research confirms that young children learn most effectively when they are engaged in interactive participation rather than in passive activities (Bruner, 1999).

If classroom environments are designed to nurture the overall development of young children, then learning centers should be at the core of the environmental design (Isbell, 1995). Learning centers allow children to participate in self-directed activities, at their own levels of learning and understanding. Learning centers are especially useful for maintaining student engagement. "Centers in primary classrooms produce wonderful and exciting results. Children not only discover, practice, and master the knowledge and skills expected of them, but they do so with real understanding" (Sloane, 1999, p. 82).

Centers are integrated learning at its best. At whatever grade level, when students are engaged in center work, they talk (oral language), use small motor skills (physical coordination), work together on projects (social skills), and develop a sense of responsibility and problem-solving skills. The use of learning centers facilitates these different configurations. While the teacher is working with a small group of students in directed lessons, other groups of students can be engaged in meaningful activities, in small groups or individually, in those centers.

When designed appropriately, learning centers offer endless possibilities for extension of concept development for students at

Interactive participation is important to a child's development.

every level of development and understanding. Learning centers offer rich possibilities for extensions and re-teaching of important social studies concepts. Through the use of centers, students develop a strong sense of themselves as learners and develop a sense of responsibility for their own learning. "Center-based classrooms are ideal environments for implementing developmentally appropriate practice with primary students. They provide the setting for teachers to act as true facilitators of learning. Children are treated as individuals and learn at their own pace through activities that tap their interests" (Sloane, 1999, p. 82).

Types of Learning Centers

One of the most difficult tasks for a teacher is designing effective curricula for the wide variety of ability levels represented in the early childhood classroom. Learning centers, by the very nature of their design, allow children to work at their own levels of ability and interest. As with all preparation for learning, planning a learning center needs to begin with knowledge of the developmental and knowledge levels of the students in the classroom, along with the goals and objectives for learning. With those two things in mind, it

An art center can be a great learning environment.

is exciting and fun to plan learning centers that will engage and interest the students.

The implementation of learning centers demands extra work (at least initially) for the teacher. While learning centers are generally developed to encourage exploration and interaction with diverse materials, clear objectives must be established for each center. One approach to tying standards to the centers is to post the objectives or standards in each center. Not only does this reinforce students' focus on the task at hand and the teacher's focus on specific standards while planning and updating the centers for use in each thematic unit, but posting standards also gives a clear message to the administrators and parents that students are not "just playing" as they circulate through the centers. At a glance, anyone visiting the classroom can see that these students are focused on learning. Posted standards also offer students a reminder that their work in centers is standards based and important.

Learning centers offer a multitude of advantages for effective teaching. They afford an opportunity for social development and for the development of independence in young children. When working in learning centers, students must work cooperatively. They must negotiate the use of materials and supplies and work together to problem-solve and plan. During center time, students develop independence through self-selection of centers and self-initiated completion of the center tasks.

When centers are designed appropriately, each child can work at his or her own level of development. Attention in choosing materials and lessons that are open ended and flexible make learning centers work well for every child in the classroom.

By engaging different learning styles in the centers, the needs of each child can be addressed. Learning centers allow the classroom teacher to meet the needs of each child by providing different levels of instructions, geared to individual abilities.

Use of well-developed learning centers allows the teacher to work with small groups of students or individual students while the other students are purposefully engaged in meaningful learning. Seatwork is rarely an effective way to "keep students busy" while working with small groups or individuals. Learning centers offer an exciting and effective alternative to worksheets.

The physical environment is an important aspect of the overall early childhood classroom experience. There are a multitude of elements to consider when developing the physical learning space for young children. Much like preparing the canvas before painting a masterpiece, the development of the classroom environment is a critical part of the early childhood teacher's responsibility.

THEMATIC LEARNING

One effective way of addressing the social standards is through the use of themes in instructional units. Themes focus on a single topic of interest to students. A theme provides a core for classroom activities by building on the natural interests of learners. Themes draw concepts together under a single umbrella, allowing students to recognize the relevance of the learning that is occurring.

There are many definitions for **theme.** For our purposes, we will consider that a theme explores the human dimensions of any important topic. An effective themed unit creates connected relationships and meanings that foster higher levels of thinking, feeling, and understanding. Beyond the specific facts to which students will be exposed in the thematic studies, the *meanings* will be remembered and internalized.

Connections within a themed unit are developed through **generalizations,** which are broad statements that relate to and provide a focus for a theme. Generalizations clarify the central concepts of the theme, forming "valid statements about relationships between or among concepts. The statements summarize information and are removed from specific situations" (McGuire, 1991, p. 44). Generalizations give a foundation for instruction and can come from several sources.

SOME TIPS FOR DEVELOPING LEARNING CENTERS TO FOSTER LEARNING

1. Have a clearly stated purpose for the center. Post objectives in each center.
2. Introduce new centers to students slowly—preferably no more than one new center introduction per day.
3. Practice the activity presented in the center with the entire group before students work independently in the center.
4. Develop a management process for center work.
5. Develop a range of options at each center, designed to meet the developmental levels and learning styles of each child in the classroom.
6. Make sure each learning center has a way to keep track of the work done by the students in the center.
7. Establish standards of behavior for use in the learning centers.
8. Don't use centers as a reward for completion of "real" work. The center work merits participation in its own right.

A comfortable learning center for social studies.

1. Divide into small groups of three or four students interested in teaching the same grade level.
2. Give each group a large sheet of graph paper, pencil, and ruler.
3. Student groups will design a "dream classroom."
4. Small groups will present their dream classrooms to the whole group, providing theoretical and practical background for their choices.

When choosing a theme, start with a list of topics that are of interest to a particular grade level and from a synthesis of the standards required for your grade level. Thematic units consist of a series of learning experiences that are focused on a particular topic, idea, or generalization. Each unit consists of specific learning outcomes for students. When working to build a unit, the classroom teacher often starts with a traditional classroom topic such as *explorers, ecology,* or *democracy.* This topic is then developed into a theme by focusing on the human dimensions of the topic, related standards, essential questions, along with the core concepts and generalizations that make up this topic.

Teachers are constantly faced with the dilemma of having too many things to teach and not enough time to teach them. Thematic organization makes it possible to use classroom time more efficiently by focusing on a variety of curricular areas across the theme. By having a strong thematic organization, teachers are better able to provide students with learning experiences that make more efficient use of their time and match the way students actually learn.

COOPERATIVE LEARNING

What children can do together today, they can do alone tomorrow (Vygotsky, 1962). The ways that students perceive each other and interact with one another has traditionally been a neglected aspect of instruction. Johnson and Johnson (1994) report that there are three basic ways students can interact with each other as they learn. They can (1) compete to see who is "best," (2) work individually toward a goal without paying attention to other students, or (3) work cooperatively with a vested interest in each other's learning as well as their own.

Throughout their academic and professional careers, students will face situations in which each of the three patterns is in play. Students will need to work effectively in each. Social studies instruction lends itself to developing the cooperative spirit in students. Having students work cooperatively is a powerful way for them to learn. This strategy has positive effects on the classroom climate and student learning, by teaching students to work as a team.

TECHNOLOGY IN THE EARLY CHILDHOOD CLASSROOM

Technology plays a significant role in the lives of all Americans. From computers to video cameras and calculators, to technologies we've yet to imagine, today's young children will interact with technology throughout their lives. Early childhood teachers have the responsibility of helping children use technology appropriately, to integrate technology into the classroom curriculum, and to choose technology applications to guide the intellectual development of all children in the classroom.

Computers

Electronic technology is widely used at home, at school, and in the workplace and is a valuable educational resource in the early childhood classroom. Many school systems have incorporated opportunities for children to become familiar users of technology as a learning tool into the curriculum. "To become productive adults in an increasingly computer-oriented society, children should have the opportunity to become comfortable with computers early in their lives" (Haugland, 2000a, p. 12).

"Research has also moved beyond the simple question of whether computers can help young children learn. They can. What we need to understand is how to best aid learning, what types of learning we should facilitate, and how to serve the needs of diverse populations" (Clements, 1999, p. 93). "For technology to fulfill its promise as a powerful contributor to learning, it must be used to deepen children's engagement in a meaningful and intellectually

A computer center can work as a "discovery center."

authentic curriculum" (Murphy, DePasquale, & McNamara, 2003, p. 2).

In some cases, however, computers are used in ways that are developmentally inappropriate. The research (Clements, 1994) indicates that in early childhood classrooms, computers supplement and do not replace activities and materials such as blocks, sand and water tables, books, and dramatic play props, but when technology is used, it is frequently for drill. To apply technology in an effective way, teachers of young children must employ their knowledge of child development and curriculum when making decisions concerning its use in their classrooms.

According to the National Association for the Education of Young Children's (NAEYC's) position statement on Technology and Young Children, "Used appropriately, technology can enhance children's cognitive and social abilities" (NAEYC, 1996, p. 2). Computers are exciting to children and well-designed software can provide an excellent extension of the social studies curriculum. Unfortunately, one study, done by the U. S. Congress in 1995, found that "... most teachers use these technologies in traditional ways, including drills in basic skills and instructional games" (p. 103). Benefits of computer use in early childhood settings depend on the kind of experiences provided to the children. The potential benefits of regular, appropriate interaction with computers is huge, including "improved motor skills, enhanced mathematical thinking, increased creativity, higher scores on tests of critical thinking and problem solving..." (Haugland, 2000b).

The use of technology in the curriculum must be based on the individual needs of the children in the classroom and the curriculum to be addressed. The National Educational Technology Standards developed by the International Society for Technology in Education (ISTE) outlined the knowledge and skills appropriate for children in the early years (ISTE, 1998). These can be used as a guide for computer application in the early childhood classroom. These standards can be accessed through the homepage of the International Society for Technology in Education at http://www.iste.org.

The National Technology Standards suggest that, in the preschool years, children should have opportunities to explore openended, developmentally appropriate software programs in a playful environment. As they enter the primary grades, students can extend these experiences to use of technology tools as a part of the academic program. As children become more able to read and write independently, they can be given more opportunities to work with technology in the classroom. The teacher's responsibility is to prepare the environment, matching the curriculum goals with the child's level of ability and interests, and the technology available.

Young children learn by doing. Experiential learning enhances understanding in a diverse classroom, by providing all of the students with similar experiences. Instead of using technology for "drill and kill" activities, the effective early childhood teacher will use the technology available to support active learning. Technology should be integrated into classroom activities and must be available to the students and be a part of the regular classroom environment. Students should be allowed to use the technology on a regular basis, not as a reward for finishing work early or for good behavior. Their tasks should be authentic.

Technology allows for effective use of cooperative learning strategies, as well. Encouraging students to work in pairs or small groups, employing the technology available in the classroom or school, is effective in team building and peer tutoring in the early childhood classroom.

Numerous software packages are available for use in early childhood classrooms. The challenge is for the classroom teacher to identify software that meets the developmental needs of the students and matches the curricular needs of the social studies lesson plan. The National Association for the Education of Young Children

Encourage students to work together collaboratively.

(NAEYC) offers guidelines for choosing effective software for young children. This information can be accessed through the NAEYC homepage at http://www.naeyc.org.

The internet has revolutionized the way we do research, communicate, and learn. For young children, it provides a variety of learning opportunities that "enhance problem solving, critical thinking skills, decision-making, creativity, language skills, knowledge, research skills, the ability to integrate information, social skills, and self-esteem" (Haugland, 2000b, p. 13).

Caution must be taken when using the Internet in the classroom. Children must understand that they cannot share personal information over the Internet, and the teacher must monitor their Internet sessions carefully. Placement of computers in the classroom in positions easily visible to the teacher is essential.

Use of computers in the classroom offers wonderful possibilities. As with any material or tool, the *way* that they are used is most important. Integrating computer use into the overall social studies curriculum, through the use of appropriate software and Web sites, and teaching and encouraging students to use the Internet for research are effective ways to enrich the social studies curriculum using the computer.

Creating a classroom Web site is an effective way to communicate with parents about the learning that is taking place in the classroom, as well as providing an activity that supports research and writing on the part of the students. A Web site encourages students to learn to use digital cameras and word processing programs by offering an authentic use for their work.

PowerPoint, Tape Recorders, Cameras, Video, and DVD

The use of technology goes beyond the use of computers in the classroom. Tape recorders, cameras, video, and DVDs are all effective tools, when used appropriately in the social studies curriculum. These technologies allow young children to explore, discover, and display their learning in diverse and meaningful ways.

Use of Digital Cameras, Video, DVD, Tape Recorders, and PowerPoint Presentations

Other technologies can enrich the social studies curriculum for young children. Use of videos and DVDs, on a limited basis, can help illustrate and bring to life different aspects of the social studies curriculum. Movie clips can be used effectively to introduce a topic, to summarize a unit of study, or to extend student information on a particular aspect within the unit of study.

Students enjoy using digital cameras and video cameras in their performances. This mode of chronicling their work serves as a motivating factor and a way for students to share their work with other students and with their parents. Digital imagery has been used effectively to document children's learning and to communicate that learning to parents. As the technology has become easier to use and less expensive, it has shown promise for use by young children. To incorporate the use of digital cameras in the classroom, the teacher needs to begin by teaching students to use and care for the equipment appropriately. Specific guidelines for use of the cameras need to be in place before allowing students work with them independently.

Use of student-made PowerPoint presentations helps enhance the understanding of concepts presented in the social studies lessons. As students work collaboratively to create PowerPoint presentations, they scaffold one another's learning and deepen their own understanding of the content. Student presentations also offer an excellent forum to showcase their learning for assessment purposes.

Listening centers, CD players, and even old filmstrip projectors can be used effectively in learning centers, with small groups of students. Technology can enrich and extend the social studies curriculum and is limited only by the imagination of the early childhood teacher.

Technology is here to stay in the early childhood classroom. It can have a positive impact on student learning, if used effectively in an early childhood curriculum that supports creativity and critical thinking (Bergen, 2000a). Teachers must be knowledgeable about the range of appropriate technology applications and it is the early childhood teacher's responsibility to expose children to developmentally appropriate and challenging uses of technology. Use of these tools to promote learning and social interaction will help young students to become confident and skilled users of technology, as well as more capable students of the social studies.

SUMMARY

The **methodologies** and strategies for bringing the social studies alive for young children are vast. Depending on the concept to be explored and the developmental levels of the students in the classroom, a wide variety of meaningful activities and strategies can be implemented. While planning the environment in which young students will be learning, the teacher must first examine his or her own beliefs about learning, about children, and about the cultural backgrounds represented in each classroom.

Well-designed, active learning centers allow for and encourage practice and extension of skills presented in the social studies. They are an important part of a well-designed classroom environment. Technology offers a variety of opportunities for independent learning, cooperative experiences, and research in the early childhood classroom. These kinds of learning make social studies instruction meaningful to young children and help to prepare them for a lifetime of effective citizenship.

Preparing the environment for learning, through study and interaction with diverse populations, is the first step in developing an open and appropriate environment for young children and is one of the most important aspects of effective childhood teaching. Understanding the different ways that children learn and taking time to think about the flow of traffic, material selection and storage, and seating options further guide the establishment of the effective early childhood classroom. When conceptualizing the classroom as a palette for "painting" a place for children to learn and grow, the possibilities are endless.

THEMATIC STRANDS AND FOCUS QUESTIONS

Culture

1. How does the early childhood teacher prepare an environment that embraces the cultural diversity represented in each classroom?

2. Which materials reflect the value of each individual in the classroom and the greater community?

Individual Development and Identity

1. How does the physical environment encourage the development of the child's individual identity?

2. How can the classroom teacher structure the physical environment to maximize individual autonomy and development in the classroom?

Power, Authority, and Governance

1. How did IDEA affect the early childhood classroom?

2. Why was federal intervention required to provide a "level playing field" for people with disabilities in the public schools?

Global Connections

1. What activities can the early childhood educator use to introduce the concept of the interconnectedness of the world's people?

2. Which materials can be used in the early childhood classroom to encourage the understanding of global connections?

▶ KEY TERMS

anti-bias curriculum
classroom environment
cooperative learning
free appropriate public education (FAPE)
full inclusionists
generalizations
heterogeneous group
Individuals with Disabilities Education Act (IDEA)
inclusion
informational texts

learning centers
methodology
multicultural education
P.L. 94–142
play
project
realia
standards
technology
thematic learning
theme

▶ REFERENCES

Bergen, D. (2000a). Linkng technology and teaching practice. *Childhood Education, 76* (4), 252–253.

Bergen, D. (2000b). *Brain research and childhood education.* Olney, MD: Association for Childhood Education International.

Bredekamp, S., & Rosegrant, T. (Eds.). (1992). *Reaching potentials: Appropriate curriculum and assessment for young children* (Vol. 1). Washington, DC: National Association for the Education of Young Children.

Bredekamp, S., & Copple, C. (Eds.). (1997). *Developmentally appropriate practice in early childhood programs.* Washington, DC: National Association for the Education of Young Children.

Bronfenbrenner, U. (1986). Ecology of the family as a context for human development. *Developmental Psychology, 22,* 723–742.

Bruner, J. (1999, April) Keynote Address in Global Perspective on Early Childhood Education (pp. 9–18). A workshop sponsored by the Committee on Early Childhood Pedagogy, National Academy of Sciences, and the National Research Council, Washington, DC: PS–027–463.

Burnette, J. (1999). Critical behaviors and strategies for teaching culturally diverse students. *ERIC Digest,* E584.

Bureau of U. S. Citizenship and Immigration Services. (2001). *Immigrants, Fiscal Year 2001.* Washington, DC: Author.

Children's Defense Fund. (2004). *The state of America's children.* Washington, DC: Author.

Charlesworth, R. (2004). *Understanding child development* (6th ed.). Clifton Park, NY: Thomson Delmar Learning.

Clements, D. H. (1994). The uniqueness of the computer as a learning tool: Insights from research and practice. In J. L. Wright & D. D. Shade (Eds.), *Young children: Active learners in a technological age* (pp. 31–49). Washington, DC: National Association for the Education of Young Children.

Clements, D. H. (1999). Young children and technology. In Nelson, G.D. (Ed.). *Dialogue on early childhood science, mathematics, and technology education* (pp. 92–105). Washington, DC: American Association for the Advancement of Science.

Derman-Sparks, L., & the ABC Task Force (1989). *Anti-bias curriculum: Tools for empowering young children*. Washington, DC: National Association for the Education of Young Children.

Dewey, J. (1938). *Experience and education*. New York: Collier Books.

Diffily, D. (2002). Classroom inquiry: Student-centered experiences. *Social Studies for the Young Learner*,*15*(2), 17–19.

Epstein, A. (2003). How planning and reflection develop young children's thinking skills. *Young Children, 58*(5), 28–36.

Fox, J. E. Back-to-Basics: Play in Early Childhood. http://www.earlychildhood .com/Articles/index (Accessed February 5, 2004).

Fromberg, D. P. (1990). Play issues in early childhood education. In C. Seefeldt (Ed.), *Continuing issues in early childhood education* (pp. 223–243). Columbus, OH: Merrill.

Goffin, S., & Tull, C. (1985). Problem solving: Encouraging active learning. *Young Children, 40*(3), 28–32.

Haugland, S. (2000a). Early childhood classrooms in the 21st century: Using computers to maximize learning: Part II. *Young Children, 55*(1), 12–17.

Haugland, S. (2000b). Computers and young children. *ERIC Digest*, EDO-PS-00-4.

Hunt, R. (1999). Making positive multicultural early childhood education happen. *Young Children, 54*(5), 39–42.

Hunt, N., & Marshall, K. (2001). Exceptional children and youth (3rd ed.). New York: Houghton Mifflin.

Isbell, R. (1995). *The complete learning center book*. Beltsville, MD: Gryphon House.

Isenberg, J., & Quisenberry, N. (2002). Play: Essential for All Children. A Position Paper of the Association for Childhood Education International. http://www.acei.org/playpaper.htm (Accessed April 16, 2005).

ISTE (International Society for Technology in Education). (1998). *National educational technology standards for children*. Eugene, OR: Author.

Johnson, D. W., Johnson, R. T., & Johnson, H. (1994). The nuts and bolts of cooperative learning. Edna, MN: Interaction Book Company.

Kamii, C. (1981). Application of Piaget's theory to education: The preoperational level. In I. E. Siegel. D. M. Brodinsky, & R. M. Golenkoff (Eds.), *New directions in Piagetian theory and practice*. Hillsdale, NJ: Lawrence Erlbaum.

Katz, L. G. (1987). Early childhood education: What should young children be doing? In S. L. Kagan & E. F. Zigler (Eds.), *Early schooling: The national debate*. (pp. 151–167). New Haven: Yale University Press.

Lee, O., & Fradd, S. (1998). Science for all: Including students from non-English language backgrounds. *Educational Researcher*, May.

McGuire, M. E. (1991). *Teaching and learning in the social studies: Master in teaching handbook*. Seattle, WA: Seattle University.

Murphy, K., DePasquale, R., & McNamara, E. (2003). Meaningful connections: Using technology in primary classrooms. *Beyond the Journal*, November.

NAEYC (National Association for the Education of Young Children). (1996). Technology and Young Children—Ages 3 through 8. Washington, DC: NAEYC.

NCSS (National Council for Social Studies). (2004). Curriculum Standards for Social Studies: Introduction. http://www.socialstudies.org/standards/introduction (Accessed April 20, 2004).

Neugebauer, B. (1994). *Alike and different: Exploring our humanity with young children*. Washington, DC: NAEYC.

Odom, S. L., & Diamond, K. E. (Eds.) (1998). Inclusion in early childhood settings [Special Issue]. *Early Childhood Research Quarterly*, 13(1).

Odom, S., Teferra, T., & Kaul, S. (2004). An overview of international approaches to early intervention for young children with special needs and their families. *Young Children*, 59(5), 38–43.

Piaget, J. (1962). *Play, dreams, and imitation in childhood*. New York: W.W. Norton.

Piaget, J., & Inhelder, B. (1969). *The psychology of the child*. New York: Basic Books.

Salmon, M., & Akaran, S. (2001). Enrich your kindergarten program with a cross-cultural connection. *Young Children*, 56(4), 30–32.

Seuss, D., Prelutsky, J., & Smith, L. (1998). *Horray for Diffendoofer Day!* New York: Alfred A. Knopf.

Shade, D. (1996). Are you ready to teach young children in the 21st century? *Early Childhood Education Journal*, 24(1), 43–44.

Sloane, M. (1999). Engaging primary students: Learning resource centers. *Childhood Education*, 75(2), 76–82.

Tertell, E. A., Klein, S. M., & Jewett, J. L., (1998). *When teachers reflect: Journeys toward effective, inclusive practice*. Washington, DC: National Association for the Education of Young Children.

Tharp, R., & Fritz, S. (2003). From high chair to high school: Research-based principles for teaching complex thinking. *Young Children*, 58(5), 38–44.

Thonis, E. (1981). Reading instruction for minority students. In *Schooling and language for minority students: A theoretical framework* (pp. 147–181). Sacramento, CA: California Department of Education.

Tomlinson, C., & Kalbfleisch, M. (1998). Teach me, teach my brain: A call for differentiated classrooms. *Educational Leadership*, 56(3), 52–55.

U. S. Bureau of the Census. (2000). *Population change and distribution*. Washington, DC: U.S. Bureau of Census.

U. S. Congress. Office of Technology Assessment. (1995). Teachers and technology: Making the connection. (OTA–HER–616). Washington, DC: GPO. ED 386 155.

U. S. Department of Education. IDEA. http://www.ideapractices.org (Accessed August 31, 2004).

U.S. Department of Education, Office of Special Education and Rehabilitative Services (OSERS). (2004). IDEA 2004 Resources. http://www.ed.gov/policy/speced (Accessed June 1, 2004).

Vygotsky, L. (1962). Thought and language. Cambridge, MA: MIT Press.

SUGGESTED READINGS

Clark, B. (2001). *Regendering the school story: Sassy sissies and tattling tomboys.* New York: Routledge.

Derman-Sparks, L. (1992). Anti-bias, multicultural curriculum: What is developmentally appropriate? In S. Bredekamp & T. Rosengrant (Eds.), *Reaching potentials: Appropriate curriculum and assessment for young children.* Washington, DC: NAEYC.

Egley, E., & Egley, R. (2000). Teaching principals, parents, and colleagues about developmentally appropriate practice. *Young Children,* 55(5), 48–51.

Gould, P., & Sullivan, J. (1999). *The inclusive early childhood classroom: Easy ways to adapt learning centers for all children.* St. Paul, MN: Redleaf Press.

Holler, J., & Klein, K. (1990). *What's the difference: A children's guide to cultural diversity.* New York: Oceana.

NAEYC (National Association for the Education of Young Children). (1993). *Understanding the ADA.* Washington, DC: Author.

Stuve-Bodeen, S., & Devito, P. (1998). *Let's Paint the octopus red.* New York: Woodbine House.

CHAPTER 3
Many Ways of Knowing
Multiple Intelligences Theory

OBJECTIVES

After reading this chapter, you should be able to:

➤ List the eight intelligences identified by Howard Gardner and describe each.

➤ Discuss the importance of the intrapersonal intelligence as it relates to social studies instruction.

➤ Compare the traditional view of IQ with that of Howard Gardner's Theory of Multiple Intelligences.

➤ Develop a thematic unit, addressing the Multiple Intelligences as described by Howard Gardner.

➤ Express what you have learned about Multiple Intelligence theory through the use of your own "intelligences."

It is of the utmost importance that we recognize and nurture all of the varied human intelligences, and all the combinations of intelligences. We are all so different because we all have different combinations of intelligences...If we can mobilize the spectrum of human abilities, not only will people feel better about themselves and more competent; it is even possible that they will also feel more engaged and more readily able to join with the rest of the world community in working for the broader good.

Howard Gardner (1987)

It is important to nurture our future leaders.

INTRODUCTION

Children's minds work in vastly different ways. Teachers of young children are constantly looking for effective ways to reach their students. What seasoned teachers and parents have always known intuitively, Harvard psychologist Howard Gardner articulated in his Theory of Multiple Intelligences

(1983), which suggests that there are "eight intelligences" or "ways of know-ing." At the suggestion of Multiple Intelligences enthusiasts, Gardner has explored a variety of other intelligences for inclusion in the theory, but has not formally added others to date. While formally identifying eight intel-ligences, however, Gardner (1995a) says, "there are probably 5,000 different intelligences."

While all people possess each of the intelligences to different degrees, each person is inherently stronger in some than in others. Particularly when dealing with difficult concepts such as those represented in the social studies, it is important to teach children through their strengths, continuing the scaffolding of their understanding in the other intelligences. With this in mind, it is imperative to vary the instruction in the classroom.

HOWARD GARDNER'S THEORY OF MULTIPLE INTELLIGENCES

Dr. Howard Gardner, professor and director of Harvard Univer-sity's Project Zero, is a pioneer in the understanding of multiple intelligences. Traditionally, schools have valued a student's abilities primarily in the areas of verbal/linguistics and mathematics. But, as we all know, people are "smart" in many different ways. History is replete with stories of heroes, inventors, and visionaries who did poorly in school but had great intellect. It is our mandate, as teach-ers of young children, to nurture those future leaders (as well as the followers!) as we teach. The social studies offer a particularly rich opportunity to use Howard Gardner's Theory of Multiple Intelligences.

There are many misconceptions about intelligence. One of these, which has been disproved by modern research, is that intelli-gence is fixed. Another misconception is that there is only one intel-ligence. In Gardner's view, intelligence is made up of many kinds of abilities. He proposes that every individual possesses several differ-ent and independent capacities for solving problems and creating products and ideas. The categories of multiple intelligences are the following: verbal/linguistic, logical/mathematical, musical, visual/spatial, interpersonal, intrapersonal, bodily/kinesthetic, and natural-ist. In addition to the notion that there are many different *ways* of being smart, Gardner proposes that, through appropriate interaction and teaching, children can *become* smarter. As a person in the busi-ness of working with young children, I find this a much more attrac-tive view of intelligence.

Accepting Gardner's Theory of Multiple Intelligences has many implications for teachers in terms of classroom planning and instruction. While verbal/linguistic and logical/mathematical intelligences are traditionally valued in public schools, to reach every student, each intelligence must be considered important when planning engaging and effective activities to meet social studies standards. Effective teaching requires that teachers structure the presentation of material in such a way as to engage most or all of the intelligences at some point in the instruction and assessment. To be effective, teachers must recognize and teach to a broader range of skills and talents.

For example, a second-grade history standard might read, "The student understands how historical figures and ordinary people helped to shape our community, state, and nation." When teaching toward this standard, a teacher might read a variety of children's books concerning the individuals to be studied, sing songs and teach simple dances from the era, prepare foods representative of the times, and allow students to develop and perform Reader's Theater scripts based on the lives of the historical figures studied. This kind of curriculum presentation not only engages the students in the learning, but also allows the teacher to reinforce the material in a variety of ways and to reach each child in his or her own area of strength. This allows the children to develop a deeper understanding of the subject matter. We reach more students when we show them many representations of every topic.

Howard Gardner (1997) said, "The greatest enemy of understanding is coverage. If we try to cover everything, by the end of the day people will have learned very little and will have understood nothing." As we plan for instruction in the social studies, it is important to remember Gardner's warnings. Choose a fewer number of important topics to study in depth, rather than trying to cover the entire curriculum superficially. Development of thematic units, as discussed in Chapter 2, is one effective way to integrate the curriculum, allowing for deeper study of a few important concepts.

When planning the early childhood curriculum for social studies, it is important to incorporate the arts, self-awareness, communication, and physical education, in order to meet the learning styles and interests of all children. Such instructional methods as role playing, cooperative learning, storytelling, and musical performances are effective ways to engage all students in the important conceptual learning being presented. It is not necessary, possible, or even preferable to incorporate every intelligence into every lesson. Make meaningful connections between the subject matter being studied and the variety of strategies and methods available to teach those subjects. Incorporate several

In-depth study into a few topics is preferable to "covering" many topics.

activities that address varied learning styles/modalities into every lesson, making sure to address *all* intelligences at some point during the unit.

Every classroom is made up of students with varying strengths. As stated earlier, Howard Gardner's Theory of Multiple Intelligences puts forth the notion that all people possess each of the intelligences in varying degrees. Gardner also states that people can develop their abilities in the different areas of intelligence. The group activity "Find Someone Who..." offers a tiny glimpse into the strengths of your classmates.

FIND SOMEONE WHO...

Provide each class member with a "Find Someone Who..." chart. Students will spend 10–15 minutes getting to know people in the classroom by finding different class members who have particular characteristics represented in the statements on the chart. Each class member should find a different class member to sign his or her chart in the appropriate square.

Find Someone Who...	Can draw a picture of his/her feelings about this activity.	Can identify his/her strongest "intelligence."
Loves to dance, run, or engage in other daily exercise.	Knows all of the words to a song popular in his or her senior year of high school (make them prove it!)	Meditates regularly.
Can balance his or her checkbook.	Has read a novel for fun in the past month.	Prefers working in pairs or cooperative learning groups to working on a project individually

USING MULTIPLE INTELLIGENCES THEORY IN EARLY CHILDHOOD CLASSROOMS

Multiple Intelligences Theory has been adapted and interpreted by many writers. These interpretations have offered a variety of perspectives on practical ways to apply Gardner's theory to classroom teaching. Gardner's Theory of Multiple Intelligences is particularly relevant when working with young children who are in the beginning stages of developing their talents. By providing opportunities for students to participate in a variety of meaningful activities that incorporate many aspects of intelligence, we allow them to explore and hone their skills in different areas.

In his 1994 book, *Creating Minds: An Anatomy of Creativity Seen Through the Lives of Freud, Einstein, Picasso, Stravinsky, Eliot,*

Graham, and Gandhi, Gardner explores the lives of these creative geniuses, making the point that, while each person possessed the inherent genius that would ultimately make him famous, each had to be exposed to an opportunity to develop that intelligence.

Gardner's theory offers teachers a guide for creating personalized instruction for the individual children in the classroom. It also offers assistance in helping students to become the learners they *can* be. Acknowledging and honoring each child's gifts in the academic setting enables each child to better meet his or her full learning potential.

Chapman (1993) outlined several applications of Gardner's theory, which are particularly relevant to those who work with young children. He extrapolated from Gardner's work that:

1. Intelligence can be taught.
2. Everyone has stronger areas of intelligence.
3. Everyone has weaker areas of intelligence.
4. Weaknesses can be strengthened.
5. One's brain is as unique as a fingerprint.

When working with the youngest learners, these points can and should be taken to heart. Each child should be approached with the idea that his or her intelligence is not fixed, and comprises a unique combination of strengths and weaknesses. Early childhood teachers hold the key to strengthening weak areas through appropriate and meaningful instruction. Howard Gardner's Theory of Multiple Intelligences offers a framework for beginning that important work.

Howard Gardner's theory reflects what we already know about children—that each one brings a different set of strengths and talents. Offering many ways for students to access important information is a hallmark of teaching to the multiple intelligences. These multiple intelligences are not measurable by a traditional IQ test. In any particular child, some of the intelligences are more prominent than others, but all are present in each child and all can be enhanced through instruction and practice. As we consider intelligence in a broader way, discovery of children's potential is opened up to us in a far more exciting way than we could have ever dreamed!

Gardner's work beseeches us to teach to the whole-child and whole-brain and supports the active experiences that underlie a developmentally appropriate program for young children. Active involvement, play, experiential education—all work in conjunction with Gardner's important concepts.

Gardner states that "It sometimes surprises readers to learn that, as the author of the theory of multiple intelligences, I have no special allegiance to the notion of seven intelligences, let alone the seven specified in *Frames of Mind* and *Seven Ways of Knowing*. I am confident that if there are seven intelligences, there must be more, and I am sure that each of these intelligences has subcomponents as well" (Gardner, 1991, p. vi).

Effective schooling for all children should combine the important benefits gained through multisensory, active learning, which will provide effective learning and more fully developed capabilities.

Individual Profiles

Individual children possess greater strengths in some intelligences and less in others. If every child possesses each intelligence, as Gardner suggests, then students must be presented with opportunities for exploration and growth of each of these. Presentation of the curriculum in a variety of ways is very important if we wish to develop the complex concepts necessary for young children's understanding of the world.

Children vary in size, shape, intellectual ability, developmental rate, and learning style. Research clearly tells us that we must attend to individual differences as we teach. "The brain constantly searches through existing neural networks to find a way to make sense of incoming data" (Wolfe, 1998, p. 63). We know that young children are the most eager of all students. The challenge for the classroom teacher is to maintain that excitement and wonder of learning that students possess when they enter school. This is particularly important in terms of the social studies. To maintain and support young children's natural sense of wonder, we must support each child, using his or her particular interests and learning styles to introduce and expand social studies knowledge and understandings.

MULTIPLE INTELLIGENCE THEORY AND BRAIN RESEARCH

Recent brain research has broadened our definition of intelligence and proven, scientifically, what teachers of young children have always known—children learn and develop in different ways. Research clearly tells us that attending to individual differences is imperative as we work to develop curriculum and instruction that are responsive to each child in our classrooms. Since the scientific community has now validated

A Fine, Fine School by Sharon Creech

Obtain a copy of Sharon Creech's *A Fine, Fine School* and share with the class. In this wonderful children's book, Mr. Keene is a principal who loves his school. He is so pleased with all of the learning that is going on in the school that he extends class time to weekends. "This is such a fine, fine school! I love this school! Let's have more school!" (p. 15). He then extends the school year to include summer days and holidays—leaving no time for students and teachers to pursue other interests such as climbing trees, learning to swing, and training the dog. While the principal basks in the glory of his "fine, fine school," students and teachers are experiencing a steady decline in their enthusiasm for school.

What does this book tell us about the importance of school? Is there such a thing as too much of a good thing? Does the message in *A Fine, Fine School* tell us anything about homework? Talk with your neighbor about providing a balance of academic and nonacademic direction for your young students.

our common knowledge about the way children learn, the appropriate education of young children has been enhanced.

Brain research has shown us that:

1. Intelligence can be enhanced and amplified.
2. "Intelligence" can be taught to others.
3. There are many forms of intelligence—many ways that we can "know."
4. Intelligence is a plural entity, but it works as one (Lazear, 1991, p. ix).

INTELLIGENCE

The notion of intelligence has been examined from a number of different perspectives. Through the ages, people have tried to define, measure, and study intelligence through a number of instruments, and have come up with a variety of theories about intelligence.

Schools have traditionally focused on the use of IQ scores to predict the probability of a child's success in school. IQ tests have been misused to label children, to delay entry into school, or to deny entry into specific programs. This is particularly harmful for young children who may not have had a rich experiential background, who may have developmental delays, or who may have test anxiety. Many believe that standardized testing reflects biases against minority students or those from families of low socioeconomic status (Kamii, 1990; McGowan & Johnson, 1984).

Howard Gardner's Theory of Multiple Intelligences offers a new look at intelligence, which is particularly useful in the early childhood classroom. The major points of this important theory are outlined below.

Intelligence Can Be Enhanced and Amplified

For most of our history in education, it has been believed that intelligence is fixed at birth. Traditionally, children have been pigeon holed from their entrance into school as "bluebirds" or "buzzards." Many times, children who were placed in the "low group" remained there throughout their school careers, never being given a chance to move forward. Children were taught and socialized according to those early calculations of their intelligence—usually based on a single dimension of intelligence, the verbal/linguistic. If a child can speak, listen, read, and write well, then he or she is considered "intelligent." If not, he or she is out of luck.

Howard Gardner's work is based on the notion that intelligence can be enhanced. If teachers believe that every child brings specific gifts to the early childhood classroom, those gifts can be built upon and enhanced. Through appropriate instruction and interaction with the environment and other students, Gardner's theory gives hope that the intelligence of all students can be enhanced.

"Intelligence" Can Be Taught to Others

Recent research in brain development has shown us that at any age and almost any ability level, one's IQ can be improved. The research has shown us that we can all learn to be more intelligent—given the right teacher and teaching methods! Educational implications based on this research are endless. In the past, we have, all too easily, given up on the children who have more difficulty learning in the way that they have been taught. Gardner's research beseeches the early childhood teacher to *find* the appropriate and effective ways to reach each child. The stakes are too high to give up on a single student.

Many Forms of Intelligence

There are many ways that children "know" about the world. The IQ test, the SAT, or the state-mandated achievement tests are only one kind of measurement of intelligence. Teachers do students and society a disservice when they look only at those narrowly defined measures of intelligence. It is the teacher's responsibility to work diligently to find ways to reach every child and to measure the "intellectual worth" of that child in multiple ways. Standardized tests will continue to be used to assess student ability. It is doubtful that the use of the SAT will be discontinued as an element of the college application process any time soon. It is also important, therefore, to help children develop strategies to do well on these kinds of assessments, while taking a broader view of intelligence in general.

Intelligence Is a Plural Entity, but It Works as One

There are many ways that we use our multiple intelligences together to find appropriate solutions to complex problems. Usually, the stronger intelligence comes forward to take over the lead in the problem-solving activity; but by doing so, it works to enhance the weaker intelligences. When students are given problems to solve and are allowed freedom to choose the ways in which they solve those problems, all of their intelligences benefit. The stronger intelligences are enhanced, while the weaker ones gain practice and grow with every opportunity to be used.

AN OVERVIEW OF HOWARD GARDNER'S MULTIPLE INTELLIGENCES

In Gardner's theory, people do not exist as single "intelligences," but rather as a blend of eight intelligences, in varying degrees. Gardner describes the study of the individual intelligences much in the way that scientists study individual elements in the Periodic Table. This is helpful only in terms of study. Rarely do elements occur in isolation, just as "intelligences" do not occur in isolation.

Verbal/Linguistic Intelligence

Verbal/linguistic intelligence is related to language, both written and spoken. People with this ability possess a strong sensitivity to the meanings and nuances of words and are skilled in using them. Poets, authors, attorneys, and teachers typically exhibit verbal/linguistic intelligence.

Western society highly values verbal/linguistic intelligence. As mentioned earlier, we frequently label children as "intelligent" or "not intelligent" early in their education careers on the basis of their verbal/linguistic skills. Standardized testing relies heavily on verbal/linguistic intelligence. Since many teachers exhibit verbal/linguistic intelligence, we often use this strength in our teaching.

Logical/Mathematical Intelligence

Logical/mathematical intelligence is associated with deductive reasoning, inductive thought, and scientific thinking. This intelligence involves the capacity to recognize patterns, to work with abstract symbols (numbers), and to discern relationships and connections. Mathematicians, engineers, and computer programmers demonstrate a high degree of logical/mathematical intelligence.

The logical/mathematical part of the brain represents a mix of left- and right-brain hemisphere processes. The majority of the work of Jean Piaget was based in the logical/mathematical intelligence. Piaget believed that we first meet the logical/mathematical intelligence through manipulation of objects as infants. From that point, the logical/mathematical intelligence moves to more and more abstractions as a child matures.

Schools, especially in the upper grades, also value the logical/mathematical intelligence. Standardized testing almost always incorporates this intelligence.

Visual/Spatial Intelligence

Visual/spatial intelligence involves the ability to visualize an object and to create mental images and pictures of objects. The human brain thinks in images, and these images are the "roadmaps" that help us make sense of our lives. Images are formed by every experience we have. Sailors, surgeons, sculptors, cartographers, and architects have a high degree of visual/spatial intelligence.

Which intelligences are these children demonstrating?

Puzzles help children develop their visual/spatial intelligence.

Bodily/Kinesthetic Intelligence

One of the most important and interesting findings of current brain research is the connection between body and mind. Through our bodies, we experience the external world and come to make sense of it. The external body is a huge, elaborate receptor that allows us to receive thousands of bits of information. **Bodily/kinesthetic intelligence** is related to physical movement and an understanding of the physical body. Dancers, actors, and athletes have a high degree of bodily/kinesthetic intelligence. While our society values those highly gifted in the bodily/kinesthetic area, such as professional athletes and actors, this intelligence is rarely recognized as important in typical elementary classrooms.

Musical/Rhythmic Intelligence

Every culture in the world has been highly influenced by music and rhythm. In terms of both evolution and individual human development, no intellectual capacity develops earlier. From birth, a child responds to the tones of his or her mother's voice. Singers, composers, conductors, and instrumentalists have a high degree of **musical/rhythmic intelligence.**

Use of music and rhythm activities can create more connections when one is learning a new piece of information than would normally happen during a learning episode. Music can be used effectively to increase memory and to improve perception.

Interpersonal Intelligence

Working with and getting along with other people is one of the most important things we can teach our students. Whatever profession or walk of life students will ultimately choose, the ability to get along with others in a productive and positive way is one of the most important aspects of a quality life. The ability to cooperate, communicate, and collaborate provides the foundation for effective citizenship. Religious and political leaders, teachers, therapists, and counselors have a high degree of **interpersonal intelligence.**

In *Frames of Mind,* Howard Gardner states that the interpersonal and intrapersonal intelligences tend to use all of the other forms of intelligence in their operation. By offering opportunities for students to participate in cooperative learning activities, in learning centers, and in projects, we allow them to develop this important intelligence.

Use of music and rhythm are ways to help children learn.

Intrapersonal Intelligence

Intrapersonal intelligence has to do with knowing ourselves. An important Howard Gardner quote on this topic comes from the video, *How Kids Are Smart*. When talking about the intrapersonal intelligence, Gardner says, "Intrapersonal intelligence is probably the most

Encouraging students to work in pairs or small groups helps to develop interpersonal intelligence.

important of the intelligences. Many times, by the time we figure out what we want to be, where we want to live, and who we want to live with, it's all over" (Gardner, 1995a).

Intrapersonal intelligence involves mindfulness: understanding of one's own thoughts, feelings, and actions in an objective way. It is the ability to step back and analyze a given situation.

Naturalist Intelligence

In 1994–1995, Gardner took a sabbatical and used the time to review evidence for the existence of new intelligences. He concluded that there was ample evidence for a **naturalist intelligence** (Gardner, 2003). The naturalist intelligence involves and ability to understand features in the natural environment. People with a high degree of intelligence in the naturalist realm are able to make sense of patterns in nature. Botanists, biologists, farmers, ranchers, and park rangers generally have a high degree of naturalist intelligence. This intelligence can be nurtured by giving students responsibilities to care for plants and animals in the classroom environment.

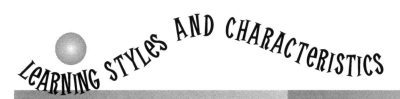

LEARNING STYLES AND CHARACTERISTICS

Learning Style	Characteristics
Verbal/linguistic	Ability to read, write, speak, and listen
Logical/mathematical	Ability to use numbers, logic, critical thinking, and to see patterns
Visual/spatial	Ability to think in terms of images and pictures
Bodily/kinesthetic	Ability to learn from movement, manipulation of objects
Musical/rhythmic	Ability to use rhythm and music to make connections to other learning
Interpersonal	Ability to work well with other people Ability to "read" other people's wishes and intentions
Intrapersonal	Ability to understand oneself
Naturalist	Ability to understand features in the natural environment

Adapted from the work of Howard Gardner.

According to Gardner, all people possess each of the intelligences in varying degrees. By closely observing children, we can begin to understand the strengths that they bring to the academic setting and plan ways to encourage growth in weaker areas.

Developing interpersonal skills is a vital part of the social studies curriculum.

GROUP ACTIVITY

KIDWATCHING AND MULTIPLE INTELLIGENCES THEORY

With a partner, observe young children in a classroom setting, during free-choice center time. Using the explanations for the eight multiple intelligences described by Howard Gardner, make note of the following:

- Choose five children to observe for one hour. If possible repeat the observation on another day.
- Which centers do the children choose? What do these choices tell you about their Multiple Intelligences profile?
- Which children seem to make friends easily?

- Which children seem to enjoy being alone?
- Which children seem to possess leadership abilities? What behaviors make you think so?
- Which children are particularly interested in reading/writing, math, art, physical activity?
- How could the classroom you observed be more responsive to children's different abilities? How will you prepare your own classroom to meet the needs of the individuals in the class?

After observing and making note of the intelligences represented by specific students in a classroom, the next step for bringing the Theory of Multiple Intelligences to life in your classroom is to begin to look at instruction in light of the eight intelligences.

GROUP ACTIVITY

PALETTE FOR DESIGNING LESSONS FOR MULTIPLE INTELLIGENCES

1. With a partner, identify a single standard, a skill, or a concept that you will be presenting to your students in the social studies lesson.
2. Take a piece of manila paper, crayons, and/or markers.
3. Draw a large artist's palette.
4. At the top of the paper, write the skill, standard, or concept that you will be addressing.
5. Within the palette diagram, identify at least one way that you will address each of the "intelligences" as you teach that skill, standard, or concept.
6. Share with the class.
7. Make note of the way that your pair chose to represent the topic to be addressed— did you draw, use words, make a song?
8. What does this activity tell you about your own learning style?

HOW MULTIPLE INTELLIGENCES THEORY WORKS

Each individual presents a specific profile of the intelligences, which are as unique as one's fingerprints. Gardner believed that an intelligence is sparked by certain kinds of stimuli inherent to the particular intelligence. He identified a traceable path toward proficiency in the development of each intelligence—moving from basic to complex to higher order. While he noted that all individuals pass through the various stages, only those with unusual talents may develop the highest level of proficiency.

A variety of factors can cause the intelligences to expand. A kindergartener who comes from a home where reading is valued and practiced on a regular basis will come to school with a more highly developed verbal/linguistic intelligence than the child from a family who does not read with him. While people are born with specific capacities for each development, they must also be exposed to opportunities to develop their special intelligences well beyond what they were born with. *Brain-compatible* classrooms are those that provide five elements: trust and a sense of belonging, meaningful content, enriched environment, intelligent choices, and adequate time (Chapman, 1993).

In a brain-compatible classroom, children have a feeling of belonging. In this kind of classroom, it is understood by the teacher that children will learn at varying rates. In addition, brain-compatible classrooms provide meaningful content for the students. The effective teacher can readily align national, state, and local standards with Multiple Intelligences approaches to teaching. Brain-compatible classrooms offer an environment that makes students feel comfortable and that offer constructive choices as to the *way* that students complete assignments. As long as the learning goal is met, students are able to choose the materials and format that their work will take. In addition, students must be given adequate time to complete assignments.

Teachers must make smart choices about *what* is important to teach and *how* that learning is most beneficially accomplished. It is

A GLOBAL PERSPECTIVE — CONNECTING TO CHILDREN FROM DIVERSE CULTURES

Culture shapes the way that a person sees his or her world, while determining his or her values and attitudes about learning. Generally, when we refer to "culture," we mean the values, customs, traditions, history, art, folklore, music, and other institutions shared by a group of people. While culture permeates all aspects of our lives, some of the traditional ways that we see cultural differences are:

- The role of religion
- Traditional foods; traditional dress
- Views on youth and old age
- Views on the structure of the family
- Views on the roles of women

- Views on the importance of the individual versus the family/community
- Views on the ways that wealth is measured
- Views on body language/the boundaries of personal space (eye contact, hugging, etc.)
- Views on the importance of education

Discuss, with a partner, children from diverse cultural backgrounds with whom you have worked in your student teaching or observations. How do their specific cultural differences impact their learning in the classroom? How can you use Multiple Intelligence Theory to help bridge the cultural gaps they may experience?

important to note, however, that children occasionally need to be led to participate in activities that would not necessarily be their first choice, in order to enhance less developed intelligences. For example, if a child chooses to work only in the block center, week after week, he will miss learning opportunities in other areas of the curriculum. The savvy teacher will know when to intervene, and will guide the child to learn from and enjoy varied aspects of the social studies curriculum.

Howard Gardner emphasizes the importance of taking into account the strengths of the individual children in the classroom. In a 1995 interview, he suggested that " the heart of MI perspective—theory and practice—inheres in taking human differences seriously" (Gardner, 1995b, p. 208). In that interview in Phi Delta Kappan, Howard Gardner summarized three ways in which Multiple Intelligence Theory can be used most effectively in schools. First, he commented that teachers using Multiple Intelligence Theory cultivate skills and capabilities that are valued outside of school. For instance, if our culture recognizes the benefits of musical intelligence, then this becomes a priority of the school. Second, teachers with a background in Multiple Intelligence Theory are more interested in developing key concepts and critical thinking than in "covering" the material in the textbook. Finally, Multiple Intelligence teachers value and teach to the individual student in the classroom. Focusing on instructional strategies that take into consideration the strengths of individual students, the teacher does not treat all children the same.

Social studies lends itself particularly well to the application of Multiple Intelligence Theory. The complex concepts presented in social studies are best explored through active, varied experiences for children. By giving students choices of activities, the children are able to tap into their own strengths and build on those strengths to develop their weaker areas. By varying the instruction in the classroom, students' understanding and motivation to learn will be increased.

It is important for the effective early childhood teacher to communicate regularly with parents, other staff members, and administration concerning all aspects of classroom instruction. Particularly when using nontraditional, active educational experiences, the early childhood teacher may be viewed as "playing" or not as serious as those teachers who use a drill-and-kill curriculum. Of course, just the opposite is true. Those educators who take into consideration the multiple intelligences profile of each student in the classroom, and plan instruction to augment those strengths, are the most serious and effective educators of all.

CONNECTING TO ADMINISTRATION

MULTIPLE INTELLIGENCES AND STANDARDS

Share the article, "Multiple Intelligences Meet Standards" by Jan Greenhawk, published in the September 1997 issue of *Educational Leadership*. This excellent article begins with a quote from parents, "Yes, this multiple intelligences stuff is great, but when do you stop doing the fun stuff and begin teaching my children the basics?" (Greenhawk, 1997, p. 62). While this article began by addressing the concerns of parents, I have found that administrators often have the very same concerns. All of this "fluff" is good, but principals want to know that the students are being taught the information that will eventually be tested on the state-mandated tests.

After giving the principal time to read the article, make an appointment to talk with him or her about how you are using the Theory of Multiple Intelligences in your classroom. Give specific examples of standards that you are targeting in your classroom, and connect them to the standards for which students will be held accountable.

Occasionally, send an e-mail to your principal, along with a digital photo of the children engaged in an activity. Add an explanation of how you are using Multiple Intelligence Theory to address the standards. This will be a great way for you to connect to your principal (without having to schedule several visits with the busy administrator), and to validate the importance of the active involvement in your classroom. It will make him or her feel confident in your focus on standards—especially when he or she walks by your classroom, with the students fully involved in a dance or song, or other activity.

SUMMARY

Harvard psychologist Howard Gardner has identified at least eight "intelligences," putting forth the notion that people are smart in many different ways. Traditionally, schools have identified intelligence primarily through the verbal/linguistic and logical/mathematical intelligences. Gardner's theory has great implications for early childhood classroom teachers. It puts teeth into what teachers of young children, have always known—that each child brings his or her own gifts to the classrooms. It is the responsibility of the early childhood teacher to meet the needs of the individual child, using his strengths and strengthening his weaknesses.

Teaching with multiple intelligences in mind helps to present information in interesting ways and lends itself to authentic assessments. As teachers work to vary strategies and meet the needs of individual students using Multiple Intelligence Theory, they expand their teaching repertoire and make instruction more meaningful for the students.

It is not necessary, or even desirable, to incorporate every intelligence into every lesson. It is simply important to be aware of the ways that different students learn and to be aware of the different intelligences represented in the class. Even if a particular student is not strong in the intelligence that you are primarily addressing in a lesson, you are working to strengthen that intelligence. By focusing on two or three of the intelligences in a single lesson, your chances of reaching every student are greatly enhanced.

THEMATIC STRANDS AND FOCUS QUESTIONS

Culture

1. How can the use of Multiple Intelligences Theory address the cultural differences represented in the early childhood classroom?

2. How can understanding the multiple intelligences described by Howard Gardner help the early childhood teacher to develop an understanding of cultural differences among all children?

Individual Development and Identity

1. How can the early childhood teacher's understanding of Multiple Intelligences Theory guide individual development of young children?

2. What is the importance of the Intrapersonal Intelligence and how does it relate to social studies instruction?

▶ KEY TERMS

bodily/kinesthetic
intelligence
interpersonal
intrapersonal
logical/mathematical
musical/rhythmic
naturalist
Theory of Multiple Intelligences
verbal/linguistic
visual/spatial

▶ REFERENCES

Chapman, C. (1993). *If the shoe fits...how to develop multiple intelligences in the classroom.* Palatine, IL: IRI/Skylight.

Gardner, H. (1983). *Frames of mind.* New York: Basic Books.

Gardner, H. (1987). Developing the spectrum of human intelligences. *Harvard Educational Review,* May, 76–82.

Gardner, H. (1991). *The unschooled mind.* New York: Basic Books.

Gardner, H. (1994). *Creating minds: An anatomy of creativity seen through the lives of Freud, Einstein, Picasso, Stravinsky, Eliot, Graham, and Gandhi.* New York: Basic Books.

Gardner, H. (1995a). *How are kids smart? Multiple intelligences in the classroom.* New York: National Professional Resources.

Gardner, H. (1995b). Reflections on multiple intelligences: myths and messages. *Phi Delta Kappan, 77*(3), 200–209.

Gardner, H. (1997, October). Keynote address to the Wisconsin Education Association Council, Milwaukee.

Gardner, H. (2003). Multiple intelligences after twenty years. Paper presented at the American Educational Research Association, Chicago, IL, April 21, 2003.

Greenhawk, J. (1997). Multiple intelligences meet standards. *Educational Leadership,* September, 62–64.

Kamii, C. (1990). Cognitive learning and development. In B. Spodek (Ed). *Today's kindergarten* (pp. 67–90). New York: Teachers College Press.

Lazear, D. (1991). *Seven ways of knowing.* Palastine, IL: IRI/Skylight.

McGowan, R. J., & Johnson, D. L. (1984). The mother–child relationship and other antecedents of childhood intelligence: A causal analysis. *Child Development, 55,* 810–820.

Wolfe, P. (1998). Revisiting effecting teaching. *Educational Leadership,* November, 61–64.

SUGGESTED READINGS

Cheech, S. (2001). A fine, fine school. New York: Harry Bliss.

Jensen, E. (2003). How Julie's brain learns. Cable in the classroom. http://www
.ciconline.org (Accessed May 26, 2004).

Gardner, H. (1995). *How are kids smart? Multiple intelligences in the classroom.* New
York: National Professional Resources.

Greenhawk, J. (1997). Multiple intelligences meet standards. *Educational Leadership,* 55(1), 62–64.

Koralek, D. (2003). Encouraging young children to develop and enhance their
thinking skills. *Young Children,* September, 10–11.

Tomlinson, C., & Kalbfleisch, M. (1998). Teach me, teach my brain: A call for
differentiated classrooms. *Educational Leadership,* 56(3), 52–55.

CHAPTER 4
Planning for Social Studies

OBJECTIVES

After reading this chapter, you should be able to:

➤ Discuss the elements of a direct instruction lesson.

➤ List focus and closure activities for specific social studies lessons.

➤ Define constructivism and discuss this concept as it relates to social studies instruction in an early childhood classroom.

➤ Develop a skeleton year-long plan, using social studies themes.

➤ Analyze social studies lessons based on Developmentally Appropriate Practices (DAP).

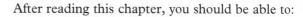

By failing to prepare, you are planning to fail.

Benjamin Franklin

Effective teachers frequently plan cooperatively.

INTRODUCTION

In an effective school, the halls are filled with teachers talking about their classes—lessons that worked, upcoming instruction, activities, and materials. In this chapter, we address planning on several different levels. Beginning with a strategy for year-long planning, and moving into unit planning, then weekly and daily planning, this chapter will help the reader match national, state, and local standards to daily plans and activities. We also address ways to include families and the school community in planning and implementing meaningful and effective lessons.

All successful classroom activities depend on good planning. This includes discovering meaningful ways to integrate the knowledge and prior experiences of your students into the curriculum. A wide variety of materials and strategies are available to the well-prepared teacher, many of which are discussed in this chapter. Other resources are available in the appendix. The better your plan, the better your lesson, and the more meaningful the instruction will be.

A DIRECT TEACHING MODEL: THE MODEL FOR EFFECTIVE TEACHING AND SUPERVISION

Constructivist learning is the basis of instruction for most early childhood teachers. While many early childhood teachers believe that children construct their own knowledge, directed lessons are required for some kinds of social studies instruction. Knowledge of a formal lesson cycle is an important tool in an effective teacher's repertoire. By knowing how to implement a **formal lesson cycle,** teachers are better prepared to implement other kinds of learning opportunities for their students. Understanding the facets of the formal learning cycle can help teachers identify areas to be addressed for each unit **topic.** This can also help the early childhood teacher in identifying areas to augment or repeat throughout a unit of study.

Although there are many models for implementing a formal lesson, the one presented here is that developed by Dr. Madeline Hunter. The early childhood teacher can refer to Madeline Hunter's easy-to-understand Model for Effective Teaching and Supervision (METS) to identify areas of the unit of study to be presented initially and those needing review or extension by the individual child.

As firm constructivists, some early childhood teachers struggle to justify the use of a rigid and structured learning cycle. While the early childhood teacher would not use the formal lesson cycle for every lesson, understanding and implementing a direct model of instruction can serve to structure the lesson, delivering needed information.

The Model for Effective Teaching and Supervision is based on seven basic elements (Hunter, 1982):

1. Objectives
2. Standards
3. Anticipatory set
4. Teaching
   Input
   Modeling
   Check for understanding
5. Guided practice/monitoring
6. Closure
7. Independent practice

Objectives

Before ever beginning a lesson, the teacher needs to have a clear idea about the **objectives** to be addressed. Objectives are most effectively chosen through study of the standards provided by each state or district, or from the national organizations for the discipline being taught (i.e., National History Standards, etc.). Each objective will be addressed many times throughout the school year. In addition, within each lesson, many objectives will be addressed. The teacher will choose two or three of the most important ones to list in the lesson plan. Bloom's Taxonomy is an excellent tool for guiding teachers in development of higher-order objectives, and is discussed in detail later in this chapter

Standards

From this overall plan, the teacher will choose specific objectives, based on the national, state, and local standards that are required for each subject area. The National Council for Social Studies (NCSS, 1994) provides a curriculum framework from which teachers of young children can build their curriculum. Most individual districts provide curriculum standards as well. National standards for social studies can be accessed online at http://www.ncss.org.

Anticipatory Set

The **anticipatory set** is the "hook" that grabs the attention of the student and focuses it on the learning that is about to be introduced. This could be a simple statement, "Today we are going to talk about...", or it could be a photograph, a song, a read-aloud, a costume, or a set of questions. Anything to capture the interest and attention of the students and draw that attention to the learning at hand is a very important part of your overall planning.

Children's literature provides an excellent source for the anticipatory set. Many titles are available for almost every topic explored with young children in the social studies. Book lists are included in the subject matter chapters of this text and in the on-line companion. Chapter 6 describes, in detail, ways to choose appropriate books for social studies instruction.

Teaching Presentation

This is the actual "meat" of the lesson. Teaching presentation involves three aspects: Input, Modeling, and Checking for Understanding.

Input

In the input phase, the teacher provides the information that the students need for the lesson. This can be in the form of a lecture, film, read-aloud, and so forth. At this point, the teacher is actually "putting in" information that will be used by the students at a later time. In nondirect instruction lessons, the "input" may be in the form of exploration or discovery.

Review of the information presented in Chapter 3 concerning Multiple Intelligence Theory is important in this phase of the lesson cycle. Many people mistake a formal lesson cycle as one consisting of only lecture or more traditional, straightforward presentations. This does not have to be true! The more creative and interesting the presentation, the more likely that the students will remember and focus on the learning at hand.

Modeling

Modeling involves showing the students examples of what is expected from them. For instance, a teacher may model the creation of a map legend for a lesson that is being taught on cartography. The teacher may model a comprehension strategy, by having students assemble at the front of the room for an interactive writing lesson, using chart paper to record student responses.

Checking for Understanding

Checking for understanding is a critical piece of the lesson cycle. In this phase of the lesson, the teacher makes sure that every child has a firm understanding of the information that has been presented up to that point. This may be done by questioning strategies, using whole-group responses (such as "thumbs up" to indicate a "yes" answer), or through the use of individual chalkboards or dry erase boards. The important aspect of this phase of instruction is to make sure that all children understand the information presented so far, before allowing them to practice. If a child practices incorrectly, it takes a great deal more time to undo that learning. If a student does not understand a particular concept, it is important to re-teach in a different way (not just louder and slower!) before allowing the child to practice and move on to the next concept.

Questioning and Questioning Strategies. When interacting with young children, it is important to ask open-ended questions that encourage children to observe, describe, or imagine the possibilities of different answers, and then to explain the reasons for their answers. This is particularly important and meaningful in social studies instruction, as the subject matter lends itself to interpretation and reflection. Open questions are *not* those with a single possible answer (Example: "Who signed the Declaration of Independence?) Such simple questions as, "What do you think about...?" are effective ways to encourage young children to really think about the implications of an event in history or a concept in geography.

Several important aspects of effective questioning need to be considered when working with young children:

1. Ask the question first, wait a few seconds in order to engage the minds of all of the students, and *then* call on a student to answer. (By calling on a student first, then asking the question, all other students tune out and breathe a sigh of relief that they will not have to answer the question!)

2. Provide **wait time**—wait approximately 3 seconds before moving on to another student to ask the question. This gives every student in the class time to reflect on the answer.

3. Be nonjudgmental in response to student answers on higher-level questions. Synthesis-level and evaluation-level questions often have several appropriate answers. Even though the teacher may have a specific answer in mind, it is important to be open to other interpretations.

4. Avoid answering your own questions.

5. Always tell students when they are incorrect, then tell them the correct answer. It is important to correct misinformation before students incorporate that misinformation into their knowledge base.

6. Let them down easy. If a student responds incorrectly, it is important to correct the misunderstanding, while maintaining the dignity of the learner.

7. You may choose to prompt the student. Asking leading questions, giving hints, or other examples can help stimulate student responses.

8. Reinforce correct responses.

9. Maintain a certain level of tension in the classroom during questioning. This will keep students attentive.

10. Vary question types and call on different students.

11. Don't use round-robin questioning. Students will disengage when their turns are over.

12. Call on all students, not just volunteers.

13. Avoid asking, "Are there any questions?" or "Does everyone understand?" (Very rarely will any child step up and say that he or she doesn't understand!). A better way to assess understanding is to use active participation devices to check for understanding.

There are numerous strategies for actively engaging students in classroom discussions. The key to "checking for understanding" is providing a way for the teacher to see, at a glance, if all students are engaged in the learning and understanding the material presented (Humboldt State University, 2002). Several suggestions of active participation strategies follow.

ACTIVE PARTICIPATION STRATEGIES

1. Thumbs up/thumbs down whole-class assessment. ("I'll read several statements about the lesson we just read. If the statements are true, give a "thumbs up" signal. If they are false, give a "thumbs down" signal.)

2. Independent brainstorming activity. (Have students jot down as many thoughts as they can on a scratch paper. Discuss after 3–5 minutes.)

3. Students write questions. ("Write one question about what we have just been studying. Try it out on your neighbor.")

4. Discuss with a partner. ("In your own words, explain to your partner how the concept of *movement* is described in the book we just read.")

5. Unison responses. ("We'll check the answers to this worksheet together. I'll say the number of the question, then you respond with the answer on your paper. If the answers are mixed, we'll stop to discuss. If not, we'll move on.")

Guided Practice

Guided Practice is exactly what it sounds like: practice, under the direct guidance of the teacher. By circulating through the classroom as students practice newly learned skills, a teacher is able to catch misconceptions and misunderstandings before a child practices the task incorrectly. This is a time for a teacher to be actively involved in monitoring student work and thought processes. If a teacher sees that the child is having difficulty, it is important to *immediately* work with the child to remediate the problem. It is imperative that the child not practice incorrectly.

Closure

Closure is an important part of the lesson which is frequently left out. An effective closure is not simply, "Close your books and get ready to go home." In addition, it is not, "Do you have any questions? Good."

An effective closure is as important as an effective opening. This is the point in the lesson in which students form a coherent picture of the learning that has taken place, a time to help them organize the information into their current schema. This is a time for the teacher to reinforce important points that have been discussed, and to emphasize the learning that has taken place.

One strategy is to ask students to either write or tell one important thing that they learned during the lesson. This can be effectively used as a **sponge activity**, when students are lining up for lunch or for dismissal. This procedure accomplishes several different things. First, it lets the teacher know if students are "on the right track." Have they gleaned the important points from the lesson? Second, it brings to the forefront of the students' minds the work that has been done. Another strategy for closure might be the "ABC to XYZ." In this strategy, each student chooses a letter from the "closure basket." Then the student thinks of a word beginning with that letter that summarizes what was learned in the unit. Write all the responses on a chart, and transfer them to a class book, having the children illustrate their letters and summarizing words. By creating a class book at the end of a unit, students have an opportunity to revisit the important points learned in each unit throughout the course of the school year.

Many parents complain that when their children are asked what they learned at school, they say "nothing." We know that they did not spend the day doing "nothing." It is important that the parents of our students fully understand the hard work that their children have been engaged in throughout the day. Through the kinds of closure activities discussed above, students have a ready answer. Remind them (or let them remind you) of what they have learned every day, as they leave the classroom.

Independent Practice

Independent practice is one of the most important parts of any teaching session. Once students have mastered a skill or developed a concept, they must practice it in order to truly *learn*. **Distributed practice** is a part of independent practice. It involves having students practice a skill or the application of a concept several times in the early days of learning that skill. Later, revisit the skill occasionally throughout the remainder of the school year.

Independent practice does not necessarily have to be done by a student on his or her own. Group work can also serve as independent practice. The important point of this component is that students practice what has been mastered. The teacher knows that the student has mastery because he or she has monitored students throughout the guided practice portion of the lesson. During independent practice, students solidify the knowledge that they have learned. I once worked with a great principal who used to say, "Tell them what you are going to tell them. Tell them. Tell them what you told them." This reinforcement is a very good idea.

A FINAL WORD ABOUT A DIRECT TEACHING LESSON

Much has been said about the inappropriate nature of a direct instruction lesson in an early childhood classroom. Long lectures, with the teacher droning on for hours and using endless overhead transparencies, are not appropriate for anybody, most especially not young children. It is imperative, however, that teachers of young children understand the components of a complete lesson cycle and build those components into the active learning environment that is provided for young students.

A lesson does not, cannot, and should not always be completed in a 45-minute period, with all seven components of the lesson cycle "covered." A lesson for young children may last for a week or a month, with the teacher working through several iterations of the lesson cycle before the concept is firmly embedded. Some themes or skills are best learned through constructivist activities, through independent research, a project, cooperative learning, or a myriad of other teaching strategies. Understanding the nature of the formal learning cycle, however, is an important base from which teachers of young children can make decisions concerning the best way to present information in the social studies.

TEACHING METHODS AND STRATEGIES

There are many effective ways of working with young children. The excellent early childhood teacher will choose from a well-stocked toolkit of methods and strategies tailored to fit the objectives of the lesson and the individual children in the classroom.

The Discovery Method

A teacher may choose to use a **discovery method** of lesson delivery, allowing the students to explore on their own, in a thoughtfully designed environment. Discovery learning can be facilitated by guided learning strategies, which focus on active, hands-on opportunities. Discovery learning is based on the notion that experience has the most important role in acquiring new knowledge. Through experiences with others and interaction with a prepared physical environment, students construct their own knowledge.

In terms of social studies curriculum, discovery learning would be accomplished by setting up the environment with appropriate materials, allowing adequate time to explore those materials, and the opportunity for students to study and interact with materials and information based on social studies objectives. In a discovery classroom, the teacher serves as a guide, facilitating the interaction with the materials and asking appropriate questions to allow students to discover the concepts on their own.

Inquiry Teaching

Inquiry teaching is the process of asking and answering key questions. In an inquiry lesson, the students develop questions, collect and organize data related to the questions, analyze the data, and draw conclusions from the data in order to answer those questions. This method, as applied to social studies, imitates the way that historians, economists, and other social scientists conduct research.

Inquiry teaching involves five steps: (1) identification of the question; (2) development of a hypothesis; (3) gathering and organizing evidence; (4) Evaluation, analysis, interpretation of data; and (5) conclusions, inferences, and generalizations. Because of the active, interactive nature of inquiry teaching, cooperative learning is an effective grouping strategy for students solving problems in this manner.

Cooperative Learning

Johnson, Johnson, and Smith (1991) define **cooperative learning** as "the instructional use of small groups so that students work together to maximize their own and each other's learning." There are five essential elements for effective small-group learning: (1) student interdependence, (2) face-to-face interaction, (3) individual accountability, (4) emphasis on interpersonal and small-group skills, and (5) process for group review.

There are many ways that these five elements can be structured to promote teamwork in the social studies classroom. When teaching students to work in cooperative groups, it is important to make the students themselves responsible for certain duties (record keeper, timekeeper, spokesperson, etc.). Another strategy for helping students develop a team spirit is to provide only a limited amount of materials; this facilitates sharing. Students need to be taught to self-evaluate. Johnson and Johnson are the pioneers in cooperative learning strategies. They have written many excellent books on the subject, which would be beneficial to the teacher interested in incorporating these strategies in the social studies classroom. Some of those titles include:

Cooperation and Competition: Theory and Research (1989)

The Nuts and Bolts of Cooperative Learning (1994)

Creative Controversy: Intellectual Challenge in the Classroom (1995)

Some Cooperative Learning Ideas

A mix of different abilities, learning styles, interests, and backgrounds works best when putting together a cooperative learning team. It is important for the teacher to know the individual children, with an awareness of their strengths and interests, before assigning them to cooperative groups. These groups should not be self selected.

The cornerstone skill for effective cooperative learning groups is the development of interpersonal skills. Students must be taught and encouraged to (1) make eye contact, (2) be encouraging to team members, (3) use quiet voices, and (4) disagree in acceptable ways. These are skills that must be taught, reinforced, and required by an actively involved and observant teacher.

Before beginning cooperative groups for the first time, it is important to develop some ground rules. This can be done most effectively with the children themselves. If they make the rules, they are more likely to keep them! Some examples might be (1) listen to others, (2) contribute—it is selfish to deny others the benefit or your thoughts, (3) try everything before asking the teacher, (4) use quiet voices, and (5) settle disputes through consensus.

While there are many appropriate ways to implement cooperative learning in your classroom, it is important to remember that just because students are working in groups, they are not necessarily engaged in cooperative learning. A primary component of cooperative learning is the common goal that students have for the group work. The other primary component is that the activity must facilitate collaboration among the students. Every member of the group must have a job to do, and must have an equal voice in coming to the conclusion of the project. Social studies offers a wonderful arena for the use of cooperative learning strategies.

A GLOBAL PERSPECTIVE: CONNECTING TO STUDENTS WITH SPECIAL NEEDS

Cooperative learning strategies are conducive to working with diverse groups of children. By its very nature, cooperative learning encourages heterogeneous ability grouping and cooperation among students with different cultural, racial, linguistic, gender, and socioeconomic backgrounds. Cooperative learning is a powerful tool for enabling children to benefit from the diversity within their classrooms. When properly implemented, cooperative learning can benefit all students in the classroom by promoting respect for and an appreciation of the value of each group member.

Although the IDEA legislation (Individuals with Disabilities Education Act) does not use the term "inclusion," it does state that each student with a disability is entitled to receive a "free and appropriate public education" (FAPE) in the least restrictive environment

(LRE). This means that all students, no matter what their ability levels, are legally entitled to participate to the fullest degree possible with their typically developing peers. Cooperative learning strategies increase the possibilities for inclusion of children with special needs, while offering opportunities for all of the children in the group to make progress with both academic and social skills.

In small groups of three or four, brainstorm the different ability levels and disabilities represented in early childhood classrooms you have visited. Discuss the ways that you might accommodate the different ability levels. Continue your discussion by addressing the benefits and drawbacks that would be demonstrated in these diverse groups. Report to the larger group.

Peer Tutoring

"Peer tutoring is an approach in which one child instructs another child in material on which the first is an expert and the second is a novice" (Damon & Phelps, p. 11). While this definition is not used by all researchers, it gives a general idea about what we're talking about when we discuss "peer tutoring." In some definitions, the peer tutor does not necessarily need to be an "expert."

Young children need to be involved in the learning and to be actively engaged in the lessons presented. Since there are 20+ students in a classroom and (usually) only one teacher, it makes sense to engage the other students in working with one another.

There are many ways that students can be engaged in peer tutoring, and many reasons to do so. There are endless examples of ways to incorporate peer tutoring in your classroom. Something as simple as talking with another child in the classroom about a concept or statement can be considered peer tutoring. Providing partners or small groups for practice of new skills helps to create a bridge between the teacher's demonstration and independence for the learners. Using partners for such activities as flash cards or practice of other factual information is another way to use peer tutoring effectively.

It is important that you understand and communicate with the parents and administrators that peer tutoring is beneficial not only to the student being "tutored" but to the tutor as well. Consider the reason for using peers, why students will be working together, how they will share the tasks, and what provisions will be made for effective grading. Careful planning is needed to ensure appropriate implementation of peer tutoring. While this is an effective strategy, it is not appropriate in all instances and can be overdone.

Project Approach

A project is defined as "an in-depth study of a particular topic that one or more children undertake" (Katz & Chard, 1991, p. 2). Projects offer individual children or groups of children opportunities to do research in the social studies and to apply what they have learned in various ways: dramatic play, construction of products, painting, drawing, songs, poetry, and so forth.

Project work gives children opportunities to engage in discussion and decision-making and in creative expression of what they have learned; it also encourages them to evaluate their own work in an ongoing way.

The Important Book by Margaret Wise Brown

Obtain a copy of *The Important Book* by Margaret Wise Brown. This classic encourages children to think about the critical elements of several different common items—the sun, spoons, and so forth. Use this structure, in groups of two or three, to explore the critical elements of the teaching and planning strategies presented in this chapter. For instance, your group may say...Projects come in many different shapes and sizes. They may be done by individual children or by groups of children. The most important thing about the project approach is that it is an in-depth study of a particular topic. This book lends itself to use in almost every social studies topic. One teacher used *The Important Book* to introduce and close every social studies theme explored over one year. While literally hundreds of children's books were looked at throughout that school year, *The Important Book* set the structure for developing a library of class books on each social studies unit studied that year. These student-made books gave the children pleasure throughout the school year, as they looked at them over and over again. This also served as a kind of distributed practice, in which the students revisited the important information they had learned throughout the school year.

Sylvia Chard (1998, pp. 7–8) outlines the five structural features of the project approach: (1) discussions, (2) field work, (3) representation, (4) investigation, and (5) display. For further insight into this exciting strategy for social studies instruction, see Chard's guide, *The Project Approach: Managing Successful Projects*.

Independent Research

Independent research is exactly what it sounds like. Students feel empowered when they are allowed to make choices concerning their learning. While you, as the teacher, will always be in the lead and set parameters for their learning, allowing students to make choices for their research is an effective motivational strategy. Working cooperatively with the school librarian, while making provisions for students to use the library and/or computer lab for their individual research projects, will ensure successful implementation of independent research.

The displayed food pyramid helps children make educated choices.

Research projects do not have to be huge, multiweek ordeals. Once students have been taught to use the library, computer, and other resources for their research, they are free to engage in research projects throughout the school year, as particular topics interest or excite them.

When using independent research as a strategy in social studies instruction, it is important to plan for ways that the students can share their work with classmates, the greater school community, and their parents. Such options as a social studies research fair, in which students share their work in seminar fashion, oral reports, class newspapers, or cross-age tutoring are ways that students can share their important work.

THEORETICAL BASES FOR PLANNING IN EARLY CHILDHOOD CLASSROOMS

When planning for effective social studies instruction, it is important for the early childhood teacher to revisit the theoretical bases for instruction. While a variety of methods and strategies are available to the classroom teacher, ultimately, the decisions about *what* to teach and *how* to present the information to children will be based on the teacher's theoretical beliefs and understandings.

Constructivism

A misconception about constructivist education is that because it embraces play, it does not include academics. On the contrary, constructivist teachers are very serious about encouraging children to learn about literacy, numeracy, science, and social studies. Constructivists believe that children construct knowledge. They construct knowledge through repeated experiences involving interaction with people and materials (Piaget, 1954).

The work of the Swiss psychologist Jean Piaget advocated that children constructed their own knowledge through interaction with the total environment. He suggested that as children mature, they pass through four stages of cognitive development. Piaget's work under-girds much of the appropriate social studies curriculum. His work concerning a young child's conception of the world, time, and space gives us a theoretical base for the work that we do with young children in social studies.

Social and Cultural Influences

The work of the Russian theorist Lev Vygotsky indicated that the child's social and psychological worlds are interconnected. He believed that child–adult interaction is imperative for cognitive development.

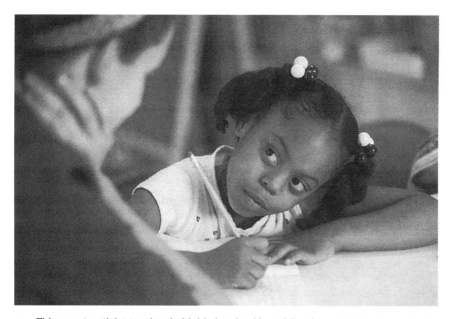

This constructivist teacher is highly involved in guiding her students to academic understandings.

Vygotsky wrote that the capacity of children to regulate thought and action is the source of conscious mental life and that social experience is of utmost importance. He believed that teaching must be geared toward the zone of proximal development (ZPD). That is, the instruction provided for each child must be presented at a level just above his or her level of independent work. Teachers must use their knowledge of child development, and of individual students and the understanding of their culture, and teach to a level just above what is already known.

Developmentally Appropriate Practice

While developmentally appropriate practice (DAP) has been addressed in Chapter 1 of this text, it is important to reiterate its importance as teachers plan. In every activity of every lesson of every day, teachers must address the three tenets of DAP when planning for students' instruction. Keeping in mind what is known about child development, the individual child's ability, and the cultural context of each child, the teacher can effectively plan for appropriate instruction (Bredekamp & Copple, 1997; Bredekamp & Rosegrant, 1992).

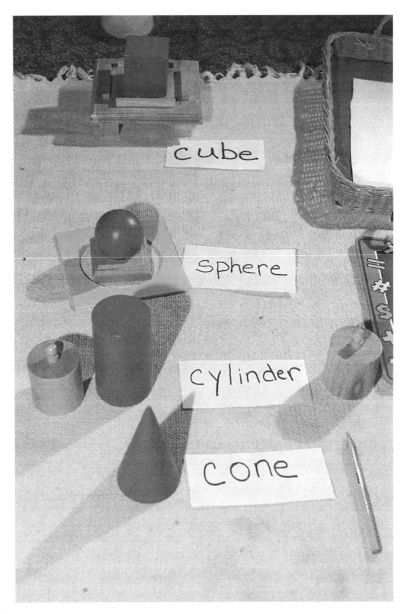

A great deal of planning and preparation has gone into this active lesson.

To plan effectively for individual students, teachers must have a firm understanding of child development. These understandings of a child's sequence of growth must be addressed in long- and short-range planning. Planning must use DAP as a basis for everything that is done in the early childhood classroom. While DAP are addressed in several places in this text, it is important to revisit DAPs when beginning to plan for social studies instruction.

DEVELOPMENTALLY APPROPRIATe PRACTICe

Remember that:

- DAP is not a curriculum with a rigid set of expectations. It is a framework, a philosophy.
- DAP is based on what we know about child development, about individual children, and about the cultural context in which children live.
- DAP supports allowing children ample time to make choices for learning from those experiences offered by the classroom teacher.

- DAP supports allowing ample time for children to explore and experiment with concrete learning experiences.
- DAP supports methods that enhance all areas of growth of the child, including intellectual, physical, and socioemotional skills.
- DAP supports the respect for families.
- DAP recognizes the social nature of learning.

(Bredekamp & Copple, 1997)

Planning exciting and effective social studies lessons for young children can be challenging. Providing adequate time for social studies instruction, assembling interesting and stimulating materials, and incorporating teaching methods and strategies to meet the needs of each child are at the core of good teaching.

Take time to tell the parents and administrators about the lessons you are presenting to the students. It is important to keep them informed about the purposes of the active lessons in which your students are engaged (Bodrova, Paynter, & Leong, 2001).

MAKING A PLAN

Author Gail Godwin says that "good teaching is one-fourth preparation and three-fourths theater." While it is not the job of classroom teachers to entertain children on a daily basis, it is also not our job to bore them to death! Planning can be one of the most exciting aspects of classroom teaching. It is enjoyable to think through all of

CONNECTING TO ADMINISTRATION

INVITING THE PRINCIPAL TO VISIT

Imagine the following scenario:

You are a Kindergarten teacher. You have been teaching for only one year, and your principal is new this year. He was a very successful biology teacher and basketball coach at the high school before being promoted to the position of elementary school principal this school year. The principal is a bright man, well liked and respected in the district, and very pleasant to talk with. However, his experience has been only at the secondary level and he has never taken any child development or early childhood education courses.

One day, early in the school year, he walks down the Kindergarten hall and stops at your classroom door. Your children are actively engaged in a number of learning centers, from the art center, where they are painting at easels, to the nature center, where they are feeding the classroom rabbit. The classroom is active and noisy, though not at all out of control. You, the teacher, are sitting on the floor, working with math manipulatives with a small group of students.

The principal is concerned about the amount of noise and activity in the classroom and asks you to come to his office during your conference period to explain what was going on in the classroom. What do you do?

Talk to your principal! Let him know what you are doing in your classroom and, most importantly, let him know *why*. Take an article or two with you that will help you explain the importance of active participation in the classroom. Explain the standards that are being met in each of the classroom centers and discuss with him the ways that you are assessing the students.

In the future, make a particular effort to have the children invite the principal for special events in your classroom. Invite him down for the students' oral reports or the Reader's Theater presentations that the children have written.

Make it a point to give the newsletter or lesson organizer that you send home to parents to the principal as well. Invite the principal to visit often, and take every opportunity provided to talk with him concerning your classroom goals. Keep him in the loop! By talking with the teacher and visiting the early childhood classroom on a regular basis, the principal can become familiar with best practices for young children and will become the best advocate for young children.

the possible materials and strategies that are available. This creative outlet is one reason that good teachers stay in the classroom.

Planning and scheduling are important aspects of an effective classroom for young children. Planning is especially important when developing a social studies curriculum, since there is so much information from which to choose. Even the most intelligent, well-read teacher cannot know all there is to know in the area of social studies. In this current era of high-stakes testing, often the social studies are ignored completely in favor of spending more time on reading and mathematics. Careful planning allows the classroom teacher to address the social studies effectively within the context and time frame of the rest of the curriculum. Effective planning ensures a well-rounded and effective curriculum.

When developing a plan for the classroom, begin with the underlying philosophy that you have concerning children and learning. A good reference for this is *Developmentally Appropriate Practice in Early Childhood Programs* (1997) by Sue Bredekamp and Carol Coppell. It is important to have a firm philosophical base from which to work when developing plans for students, whatever their ages.

Take some time to review the work of Jean Piaget and Lev Vygotsky. Think about the other theories and theorists you have studied in your foundations courses. Which pieces of these important works resonate with you as a person and as a teacher? As your experience with young children grows, revisit your theoretical background and evaluate why you are teaching the way that you are. What is working? What needs to be revamped?

Keep current with research being done in the area of early childhood education. Three excellent journals for teachers of young children are: (1) *Social Studies for Young Learners* (the National Council for Social Studies), (2) *Young Children* (the National Association for the Education of Young Children), and (3) *Childhood Education* (the Association for Childhood Education International). Reading these journals on a regular basis will help you to keep abreast in terms of research being done with young children in all curricular areas, particularly that of social studies.

Scheduling

A **schedule** lists the times of the school day during which various subjects are explored and various set events take place. The schedule will outline the components of the school day. The schedule can include: (1) set times for lunch, recess, specials (music, art, physical education); (2) times and duration of large-group and small-group activities; (3) free-choice center times; (4) outdoor time; and (5) individual times with teacher and child.

Daily scheduling presents many challenges to the early childhood teacher. The lack of sufficient time is frequently cited by teachers as a major limiting factor in effective teaching. But developing an appropriate and flexible schedule is an important step in developing an effective social studies curriculum. Developing a schedule with appropriate flow and balance of activities is imperative. Child development knowledge tells us that young children learn best through active engagement and hands-on, concrete experiences. Young children have difficulty sitting and focusing for long periods of time, so a balance of active and quiet activities must be taken into account in the daily schedule.

When developing an effective schedule for social studies instruction, there are several important considerations:

1. Include teacher-directed activities for both large-group and small-group times.

2. Provide an approximately equal balance of child-initiated and teacher-directed time.

3. Include time for the teacher to work with individual children.

4. Include ample time for child-initiated and free-choice time for children in centers.

5. Alternate active and quiet times.

6. Include outdoor activities whenever possible.

7. Include time for hands-on, concrete experiences.

8. Include time for skill-focused lessons.

9. Include time for concept-development lessons.

10. Integrate learning whenever possible. This expands the amount of time available for social studies instruction.

11. Allow for "overflow" time when students are particularly engaged in a specific activity.

Gathering Materials for Planning

Armed with a firm understanding of young children and how they learn, a background of strategies for delivering instruction, and the standards for which your students will be responsible, you are ready to assemble the materials necessary for developing an effective plan for your school year. Before sitting down to begin your year-long plan, it is important to gather the materials and information that will guide your planning. The following list with be discussed in detail as the chapter unfolds:

1. District school year calendar
2. State standards for your grade level and the grades before and after yours
3. Teachers' manuals for each subject you will be teaching
4. Daily schedule for your class (things you cannot change, such as lunchtime, conference period, music/physical education times, library schedule, recess schedule, etc.)
5. List of children's books and other materials from your own collection and/or the school library
6. Blank calendar pages
7. List of holidays, celebrations, "weeks" (e.g., Children's Book Week), and so forth
8. Blank paper
9. Lesson plan book or three-ring binder for finalized plans
10. An uninterrupted block of time for work

Developing the Year-Long Plan

State and district curriculum standards, along with the voluntary standards created by individual disciplinary organizations, create the framework from which to build a year-long plan for the early childhood classroom. These documents provide the information about the important curricular areas that must be addressed during each school year. By reviewing the standards for the grade level being taught, as well as the grade level before and after, the classroom teacher can develop an overview of skills and concepts to be studied through the social studies lessons.

Many teachers do not develop a year-long plan, going through the school year, week by week, making decisions about what will be taught next. The danger of this kind of planning is that the school year frequently passes by and the teacher has not addressed important skills and concepts for which he or she and the students will be held accountable. In much the same way that a person maps out the route that he or she will take on a cross-country trip, it is important for the classroom teacher to make a tentative plan for the entire school year, making sure to address all of the important skills and concepts to be taught. Just as on a cross-country trip side trips and detours make for a more exciting and memorable trip, changes along the way in the year-long plan allow the teacher to mold the instruction to the needs and interests of the students. The teacher has a roadmap for the year, knowing exactly where the students need to end up, but the plan is flexible enough to accommodate the individual needs of class members.

Since there are many ways to develop a plan, your plan will be unique, and your strategy for developing it will probably change every year. One way to develop a year-long plan is discussed in this chapter. Again, there are many ways to do this, and your strategies will change each year, as your experiences and knowledge grows.

A helpful first step is the development of a spreadsheet which will be used to check off the standards as they are addressed. Of course, each standard will be addressed many times throughout the course of the school year. Leave plenty of room on the spreadsheet to record the many times that you will focus on a specific skill.

On careful study of the standards for your grade level, whatever your state of residence, you will find fairly broad topics to be covered. It is important to read and reread the standards several times, jotting down overriding themes and specific topics for your grade level. For instance, perhaps a group of fourth graders will be focusing on state history. While other grade levels may touch on state history, through study of the state standards, you will know that it is the responsibility of the fourth-grade teacher to build concepts and a knowledge base for state history during the fourth-grade year. While most of the standards are fairly generic, there are usually some specific topics that are required for each grade level. Jot those down on a blank piece of paper. You will revisit this list throughout your planning.

After listing topics to address, your next task is to revisit the standards and list specific skills to be taught at your grade level. For instance, a simple outline might be introduced in the second-grade standards. You would want to make sure that you plan several opportunities throughout the second-grade school year for your students to learn and practice simple outline-making.

Choosing a Theme for the Year

A theme is an overriding thrust for the whole school year. By choosing topics such as, for example, "Exploration," "Discovery," and "Adventures" for overriding themes, it is possible to connect all of the standards, topics and units that are to be learned during the school year. Look at the skills and topics that will be covered during the school year and choose the theme to encompass those. This process is ongoing, based on what is known about child development, reinforcing the child's current stage of development and encouraging his or her progress toward the next stage of development.

Using the Calendar

Begin planning with a copy of the district calendar. Keep a copy of this calendar in your lesson planning book. Using this calendar, transfer the beginning dates, reporting period dates, early dismissals, parent conferences, school holidays, and so forth to the blank calendar pages. This will allow you to see, at a glance, the constraints of the year's schedule, from which the year-long plan will be developed.

Next, take a look at a list of special days. This might include such dates as the summer solstice; National Vegetable Week, Mother's Day, and so forth. Pick and choose the important events that you would like to include in your plan, those that naturally fit into the standards being studied and the overriding theme that has been chosen for the year. A multitude of these special calendars can be found online or in books designed for this purpose. While you will not want to use a *holiday approach* to the social studies curriculum, this is an effective way to use special days and events to make the curriculum relevant to the students and to tap into their interest in celebrations. This strategy will help to engage students and to tie their social studies lessons to their real-world experience.

Units

Using the list of topics that have been generated during the review of the standards, prioritize the topics, and then decide on the amount of time that will be needed for each topic. Keeping in mind the sequential nature of learning, decide if one topic needs to be addressed first in order to build on that for another topic. Then, tentatively place the topics into the blank academic calendar. Index cards are particularly useful for this kind of planning, as they can be moved around easily.

Write each topic and the number of weeks that you think will be needed to complete the **unit** effectively on a single card. Using colored pens to write the name of the school month (blue) and then putting the number (usually 1–4) for each week of the month (yellow) is a strategy that works for many teachers. Distribute the month-and-week cards on the floor, then "deal" the unit topic cards, into the appropriate weeks. This is an effective way to begin this process because it is easy to move the cards when reviewing the school year topics. An alternative to this hands-on, manipulative planning strategy would be completing a similar process using the computer.

After reviewing the distribution of the cards, take up the cards, in order, and wrap them with a rubber band. Then transfer this information to the paper/pencil planning calendar. The yearly plan always changes, based on the level of interest and development of the students. Remember, this work will have been done the summer before you even meet the children. Many things will change. This is just a starting point!

A similar review of specific language arts and math skills will need to be done, making note of the sequence of skills to be addressed. Make note of any out-of-the-ordinary skills that might need to be taught at a specific time of year, for example, outlining.

Finally, look at objectives for Science, Health, Physical Education, Music, and Fine Arts and integrate those objectives into what is being done in Social Studies.

Some topics and objectives simply do not integrate and must be taught in separate units. It is important to integrate when it makes sense, but it is just as important to *not* make unnatural connections in the curriculum. This weakens the overall flow and impact of a well-integrated program.

While this is just a suggestion of one way to develop a year-long plan, the purpose of this portion of the text is to emphasize the importance of developing a plan for the year. Many seasoned teachers have never completed such a document. It is not surprising that they often get to the end of the school year with "too much book left." You would not embark on a cross-country trip without developing a route for the journey. Along the way, you might decide to take a detour to visit a beautiful farm or an engaging museum, which just serves to enhance the trip that you originally planned. The same can be said for the year-long plan. You will begin with a well-designed map, with the final destination well defined. Along the way, you will probably take some detours to explore specific interests expressed by the children. You may go a little slower or a little more quickly through some parts of the plan, based on the ability level of the students, and you may take a totally unmarked road for a while. The important thing is that you will have had a plan. You will know where you needed to go and where you needed to end up.

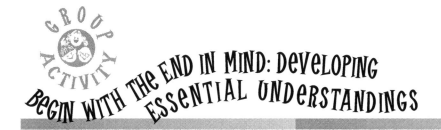

BEGIN WITH THE END IN MIND: DEVELOPING ESSENTIAL UNDERSTANDINGS

Essential understandings are "big ideas" that go beyond standards or objectives. Essential understandings are what teachers want their students to come away with after a unit of study. They are such big ideas as: "There are positive and negative consequences to exploration" or "How did geographic variables affect the course of history?"

Choose an objective from your state or district learning standards. With a partner, develop a list of "big ideas" that could be taught during a study based on that standard. Be ready to share with the large group.

CURRICULUM DEVELOPMENT

The National Association for the Education of Young Children (NAEYC) defines curriculum as "an organized framework that delineates the content children are to learn, the process through which children achieve the identified curricular goals, what teachers do to help children achieve these goals, and the context in which teaching and learning occur" (Bredekamp and Rosegrant, 1992). In addition to knowledge of child development, curriculum involves a knowledge base of the disciplines you are teaching.

Curriculum encompasses what happens in your classroom every minute of every day. Your curriculum reflects your philosophy, which expresses the principles, attitudes, and beliefs of you and your school. As classroom teachers, everything we do in our classrooms reflects what we value. For our children to flourish, we must value each child's cultural background, interests, and abilities.

Allowing children to participate in planning is important. Many times, the children will come up with better ideas than our own! The vision of children planning with their teacher exemplifies the very meaning of cooperation. Only through this kind of cooperation can true and optimal learning occur. Children's participation in planning is most often informal. Much of the child-initiated planning takes the form of choice—choice of reading material, centers, or activities. Sometimes, however, more formal planning can occur with the children. Encouraging involvement in the planning process for units in the social studies can take a form as simple as asking the students what they would like to learn about a topic.

A more formal way of doing this might be the use of the **KWL chart** (Ogle, 1986). In this very effective activity, a teacher may gather the students around him or her at the beginning of a unit. At this point, he or she might ask the students what they already **K**now about the topic at hand. After the students are allowed to explore their current understandings and knowledge of the topic, a classroom discussion would follow, concerning what students **W**ant to learn about the topic. At the end of the unit, a wonderful closure involves revisiting the chart made at the beginning of the unit and listing what the students have **L**earned. Not only does this strategy give students a sense of ownership in their learning, but it also offers a wonderful opportunity for the teachers and students to assess their success in terms of the goal and objectives developed at the beginning of the unit (Ogle, 1986).

Incorporating Individual Differences and Spontaneity Into Planning

While it is very important to develop an overall plan for the school year, it is equally important to maintain flexibility. When developing the year-long plan in the summer, prior to even meeting the students, the teacher will incorporate national standards, state and district requirements, specific thematic possibilities, and skills to be addressed throughout the school year. At this point, however, it is important to note that the teacher has not even met the students!

Cooperative planning among the teacher and students, and even the parents, is an effective way to customize the curriculum to meet the needs and interests of the individual children in the classroom. Some of this planning is very informal. Simply asking students about their interests is one of the most effective ways of customizing instruction in the classroom. It is also very effective to observe children in their play, to see what kinds of interests they already have. The teacher can build on these interests and those explored through read-alouds to generate additional topics of study.

The Teachable Moment

The "teachable moment" involves the teacher giving a spontaneous lesson based on a question or an expression of interest by a student (Diffily, 2002; Goodrow, 2000). This kind of diversion from the planned curriculum is healthy, and many times more beneficial, than the planned curriculum. These "moments" are usually brief and may or may not have anything to do with the topic being discussed. An encouraging remark and a plan to revisit the question and topic are most important in maintaining the interest and enthusiasm of a student making a connection between something that is being discussed in class and his or her spark of interest. A well-developed plan allows for and encourages the teachable moment.

WEEKLY LESSON PLANS

The weekly lesson plan is a natural outgrowth of a teacher's child development knowledge, his or her philosophy of education, thematic choices, and the standards (Peterson, 1996). Weekly planning becomes much easier and more effective when a year-long plan and appropriate materials (as identified earlier in this chapter) are completed and assembled.

Using the year-long plan and specific skills that need to be taught, the classroom teacher can easily plug in specific objectives for students on a weekly basis. Further development of the plan through the listing of read-alouds, writing activities, materials, projects, and so forth makes the social studies lessons and activities relevant, appropriate, and meaningful for young students.

Questions When Designing Lessons

When developing weekly lesson plans, you are already miles ahead because of the year-long plan, the materials list that you have assembled, your knowledge of child development, and the standards with which you have familiarized yourself. As you begin to make the weekly plan, ask yourself the following questions:

1. What do students need to know and be able to do?
2. How does this relate to national, state, and district standards?
3. How will they demonstrate what they know?
4. What prior knowledge do students bring to the lesson?

5. How will I present the lesson?

6. What activities, materials, and assignments will I use to introduce and practice the skills or knowledge introduced in the lesson?

7. How will I differentiate instruction? How will I re-teach for those students who do not "get it" the first time?

8. How will I extend student understanding and apply higher-order thinking skills?

9. What is the timeline for my lesson? What will the sequence of instruction be?

10. How can I make instructional links to the home during this lesson?

An excellent plan is the first and most important step in providing an excellent learning opportunity for your students. On occasion, a talented and experienced teacher may be able to effectively "wing it." This does not happen often or predictably. A good plan is imperative for good teaching.

GROUP ACTIVITY — The Year-Long Plan

Long-term assignment: With a small group of students, who are interested in teaching the grade level you are interested in, develop a skeleton year-long-plan. What materials do you need? How will you structure your curriculum? What will guide your planning? Gather the materials listed above and spend some time developing your strategy.

Share your year-long plan with the other members of the class. There is no right answer to this assignment. Your class members will benefit from learning about the process you used to complete your plan. Bring in examples of the materials you used, Web addresses, and other materials to share. Each summer, when you complete your plan for the next school year, the process will be a little different. The important part of this assignment is the *process*, not the final product.

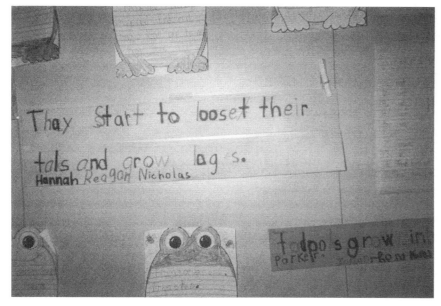

Using tadpoles as a unit of study.

Examples of Appropriate and Inappropriate Lessons for Young Children

Following are two examples of units of study that might take place in an early primary classroom. The two lessons address the very same subject matter, but have very different emphases and outcomes for the students.

Tadpoles

In a first-grade classroom, the teacher chooses to teach a unit on tadpoles. This unit meets the standards for several subject areas. The teacher who understands and embraces child development would develop a unit based on hands-on experiences. In this case, the teacher might plan to introduce the unit by having students take a walking field trip to the pond at the end of the road. She might plan to have tadpoles in the classroom for observation, and she might have students make written observations on the changes taking place with the tadpoles. Students might keep a journal of the days that it takes for the tadpoles to become frogs, might graph the days the process takes, or make a chart indicating their observations. Students could hone their prediction skills as well, through this plan.

In a first-grade classroom across the hall, the teacher also chooses to develop a unit on tadpoles. Again, this unit will address standards in many subject areas.

Tadpoles

This teacher introduces the unit on tadpoles by having the students sit at their desks and listen to a lecture on the stages of a frog's life. The teacher has a great deal of information about the life cycle of frogs and is well versed on the standards. Students read about tadpoles in their science textbooks and complete a page in their workbooks, placing the stages of tadpole development in order.

The standards addressed are the same as in the first example and the teacher is as knowledgeable about the subject matter. The unit, however, will not be nearly as successful as the previous example, since the teacher has not taken into consideration the specific developmental needs of the students.

BLOOM'S TAXONOMY

In 1948, following the Convention of the American Psychological Association, B. S. Bloom took the lead in developing a classification of the goals of the educational process. Three domains were identified, the first of which was the Cognitive Domain, which involved knowledge and the development of intellectual skills. While we will deal only with the Cognitive Domain, it is important that you are aware that the others are the Affective Domain and the Psychomotor Domain.

Benjamin Bloom and his co-workers developed a hierarchy of educational objectives, which we know now as **Bloom's Taxonomy**. This taxonomy divides the cognitive objectives into subdivisions ranging from the simplest (knowledge level) to the most complex (evaluation level). Of course, the divisions are not absolutes and the divisions between the levels can be interchangeable. This excellent representation gives guidance for making delineations between different kinds of learning.

While the upper levels of Bloom's Taxonomy are areas that we strive for, it is important to realize that each level of the taxonomy is important. It is impossible to reach the evaluation level without having first given students the information needed at the knowledge level, from which they will synthesize and evaluate.

The divisions of Bloom's Taxonomy are not absolutes, but they do offer an easily understood guide for teachers, as we develop lessons and questioning strategies. Many teachers keep a copy of the taxonomy, with a chart of appropriate verbs to use with each level, in the back of their lesson planning notebook. Refer to the taxonomy as you begin to write objectives each week, making sure that you are addressing the appropriate levels of complexity in the lessons.

Knowledge

Knowledge is defined as remembering learned material. This represents the lowest level of learning outcomes in Bloom's Taxonomy. Examples of knowledge level material are learning the multiplication tables, reciting states and capitals, or memorizing geographic terminology.

Comprehension

Comprehension is defined as the ability to gain meaning from material. This may be done by summarizing or interpreting material, finding the main idea of a selection, or answering questions concerning the read material. This goes a step beyond the knowledge level and represents the lowest level of *understanding* on Bloom's Taxonomy. Some examples of comprehension level objectives are interpreting graphs and maps or estimating future outcomes based on current data.

Application

Application is defined as the ability to use learned material in new situations. This requires a higher level of understanding than the comprehension level. Examples of application level objectives would be solving mathematical problems, constructing charts and graphs, or demonstrating a procedure for finding a location using longitude and latitude.

Synthesis

Synthesis is defined as the ability to put parts together to form a new whole. Learning outcomes involve creative production. Some examples of learning objectives at this level include writing an original poem or theme, developing a plan for an experiment, or developing a plan for solving a problem

Evaluation

Evaluation is defined as the ability to judge the value of material for a given purpose, based on specific criteria. Learning outcomes are at the highest level of the cognitive hierarchy because the learner must use all of the other elements and then make a judgment based on specific criteria. Examples of learning objectives at this level are judging a work of art, judging the appropriateness of proposed solutions to problems, and developing and applying a rubric to evaluate the work of other students.

A chart representing Bloom's Taxonomy is shown in Table 4-1. This table includes verbs that can help guide the teacher in developing learning objectives and examples of products that students may produce at each level of the taxonomy. This can serve as a handy guide when developing lessons at various levels within a unit of study.

Some Taxonomy Sample Questions

Developing a questioning strategy is an important aspect of effective teaching. Appropriate questions can help students extend their understanding of the material that has been presented. When developing a lesson plan, it is effective to think through some sample questions, at different levels of Bloom's Taxonomy, to use before, during, and after the lesson. Some examples of questioning at different levels of Bloom's follow.

Knowledge

1. Name the main characters in the novel.
2. Where does the story take place?
3. Describe the main character in the story.

Comprehension

1. In your own words, tell what the chapter is about.
2. Tell why the author chose the title.
3. Illustrate one of the main events in the novel.

Application

1. Think about a situation encountered by the main character in the story. Write about how you might have reacted to the situation.

TABLE 4-1
Bloom's Taxonomy Chart With Suggested Learning Objective Verbs

LEVEL OF COMPLEXITY	MEANING	SOME THINGS THE STUDENT MAY DO	SOME THINGS THE STUDENT MAY PRODUCE	SOME VERBS TO USE IN YOUR OBJECTIVES	EXAMPLE OF PRODUCT
Knowledge	Recognition of specific information	Respond Absorb Remember Recognize	Name List Label Definition	Define Repeat List Name Label Record Recall Relate Reproduce Match Memorize	Completion of worksheet naming Southern states
Comprehension	Understanding of information given	Explain Translate Interpret	Explanation Fact Reproduction Answer on an objective test	Re-state Identify Describe Explain Discuss Review	Writing a paragraph describing the geographic features of an area
Application	Use methods, concepts, theories, and principles in new situations	Solve problem Demonstrate use of knowledge Construct	Illustration Diagram Diorama Model Diary Map	Translate Apply Illustrate Use Practice Employ Interpret Make Demonstrate Dramatize	Development of a diorama based on a historical novel
Analysis	Break down information into its constituent elements	Discuss Uncover Dissect	Questionnaire Survey Chart Graph Summary Report Outline Plan	Classify Diagram Compare Contrast Research Criticize Examine Analyze Categorize Debate Distinguish Investigate	Development of a graph of cities where class members were born
Synthesis	Put elements together to form a whole that reflects original, creative thinking	Generalize Compare Contrast Abstract Relate	Invention Story Poem Art product Project Media production	Imagine Combine Estimate Invent Forecast Design Formulate Create Organize Infer Hypothesize	Composition of a song based on information learned in the study of their state
Evaluation	Develop and apply standards by which to judge ideas, materials, or methods	Judge Dispute Develop criteria	Recommendation Investigation Survey Opinion Editorial Verdict Judgment	Evaluate Assess Appraise Predict Judge Select Choose Verify Editorialize Rate Dispute Decide	Development and application of criteria to judge classmates' projects for the social studies fair

Adapted from Bloom, B. S. (Ed.) (1956) *Taxonomy of educational objectives: The classification of educational goals. Handbook I: Cognitive domain.* New York: Longmans, Green.

2. What would you do if you could visit the place where the main character lives?

3. If you met the main character from the book, what would you talk about?

Analysis

1. What part of the story was the most exciting?

2. List three things from the story that could not happen in real life.

3. Find five words in the story with the same root word.

Synthesis

1. Rewrite the selection from the Native American's point of view.

2. Make a collage of the main characters in the story.

3. Write a poem about an event in the story.

Evaluation

1. Which character from this story would you like to spend a day with? Why?

2. Compare two characters in the story. Which one did you like best? Why?

3. If you had an opportunity to visit the setting of this story, would you? Why or why not?

CONNECTING TO DIVERSE POPULATIONS

Planning for Diversity

Children often find themselves in diverse communities and classrooms. Today, other countries in the world are more familiar to children than in the past. Children travel and move to different areas of the country and the world; media images link young children to different parts of the world more than ever before. When planning the early childhood program, it is important to celebrate diversity, discard stereotypes, and include anti-bias and multicultural awareness activities throughout the school day.

SUMMARY

For many years,"teachers believed that knowledge was something to be transmitted to students, and so they relied on teaching methods that treated children as passive learners" (Sloane, 1999, p. 76). When planning instruction for a diverse group of young learners, it is important to keep in mind the general expectations for the entire group, while looking for ways to appropriately challenge each individual in the group.

   With all learners, but especially with young children, it is important to keep child development principles and learning theory in mind when planning for instruction. It is important to make the learning come alive for young students, making the goal *understanding,* rather than the acquisition of information. Planning for effective instruction involves a paradigm shift from the teacher as "transmitter of facts" to "facilitator."

   Learning should be fun. While it is not the job of the classroom teacher to entertain the students, it is the teacher's job to model the joy of learning. There is a willing audience, in the form of young children, who are anxious and excited about learning. It is important to plan effectively in order to maintain their enthusiasm. The effective teacher chooses to teach knowledge and skills that are in each child's Zone of Proximal Development (Vygotsky, 1978). These skills should form the basis of each child's individual plan.

▶ THEMATIC STRANDS AND FOCUS QUESTIONS

Culture

1. How can the early childhood teacher plan effectively for the cultural diversity in the classroom?

2. How does the developmentally appropriate classroom address cultural diversity?

Individual Development and Identity

1. Which teaching strategies and methods meet the individual needs of the students in an early childhood classroom?

2. How can the early childhood teacher guide the individual development of the students in the classroom, while meeting the curricular demands of the school district?

► KEY TERMS

anticipatory set
application
Bloom's Taxonomy
closure
comprehension
constructivist learning
cooperative learning
discovery method
distributed practice
evaluation
formal lesson cycle
guided practice
independent practice
input
inquiry teaching
knowledge
KWL chart
modeling
objectives
re-teach
schedule
sponge activity
synthesis
topic
unit
wait time

► REFERENCES

Bloom, B. S. (Ed.). (1956). *Taxonomy of educational objectives: The classification of educational goals. Handbook I, cognitive domain.* New York: Longmans, Green.

Bodrova, E., Paynter, D., & Leong, D. (2001). Standards in the early childhood classroom. *Principal, 80*(5), 10–15.

Bredekamp, S., & Copple, C. (1997). *Developmentally appropriate practice in early childhood programs.* Washington, DC: NAEYC.

Bredekamp, S., & Rosegrant, T. (1992). *Reaching potentials: Appropriate curriculum and assessment for young children* (Vol. 1). Washington, DC: NAEYC.

Chard, S. (1998). *The project approach: Managing successful projects.* New York: Scholastic.

Diffily, D. (2002). Classroom inquiry: Student-centered experiences. *Social Studies and the Young Learner, 15*(2), 17–19.

Goodrow, M. (2000). The teachable moment. *Young Children, 55*(4), 42–43.

Humboldt State University (2002). The taxonomy of educational objectives. http://www.humboldt.edu/~tha1/bloomtax.html (Accessed May 30, 2004).

Hunter, M. (1982). *Mastery teaching.* El Segundo, CA: TIP.

Johnson, D. W., Johnson, R. T., and Smith, K. (1991). *Active learning: Cooperation in the college classroom.* Edina, MN: Interaction Book.

Katz, L., & Chard, S. (1991). *Engaging children's minds: The project approach.* Norwood, NJ: Ablex.

NCSS (National Council for the Social Studies) (1994). *Curriculum standards for social studies.* Washington, DC: National Council for the Social Studies.

Ogle, D. M. (1986) K-W-L—A teaching model that develops active reading of expository text. *The Reading Teacher, 39*, 564–570.

Peterson, E. (1996). *A practical guide to early childhood planning, methods and materials.* Boston: Allyn & Bacon.

Piaget, J. (1954). *The construction of reality in the child.* New York: Ballantine Books.

Sloane, M. (1999). Engaging primary students: Learning resource centers. *Childhood Education, 75*(2), 76–82.

Vygotsky, L. (1978). *Mind in society: The development of psychological processes.* Cambridge, MA: Harvard University Press.

▶ SUGGESTED READINGS

Chard, S. (1998). *The project approach: Managing successful projects.* New York: Scholastic.

Fayden, T. (1997). Children's choice: Planting the seeds for creating a thematic sociodramatic center. *Young Children,* November, 15–20.

Hannigan, K. (2004). *Ida B . . . and her plans to maximize fun, avoid disaster, and (possibly) save the world.* New York: HarperCollins Children's Books.

Johnson, D. W., &Johnson, R. T. (1989). *Cooperation and* competition: Theory and research. Interaction Book.

Johnson, D. W., & Johnson, R. T. (1995). *Creative controversy: Intellectual challenge in the classroom.* Interaction Book.

Johnson, D. W., Johnson, R. T., & Johnson Holubec, E. (1994). *The nuts and bolts of cooperative learning.* Interaction Book.

Katz, L., & Chard, S. (1991). *Engaging children's minds: The project approach.* Norwood, NJ: Ablex.

American Holidays and Observances

http://www.timeanddate.com/
Click on "Calendar."

Social Studies Trade Books

http://www.ncss.org/
Click on "Your Classroom." Click on "Download the latest book lists."

CHAPTER 5
Civics and Government

OBJECTIVES

After reading this chapter, you should be able to:

➤ Identify key elements of a civics curriculum for young children.

➤ Design a lesson focused on character development.

➤ Evaluate the key elements of citizenship set forth by the National Council for the Social Studies (NCSS) as they relate to young children.

➤ Create a model for a class meeting that encourages democracy in the early childhood classroom.

➤ Discuss the importance of teaching children about war and peace.

Character, in the long run, is the decisive factor in the life of an individual and of nations alike.

Theodore Roosevelt, 26th American President

Patriotism begins at an early age.

INTRODUCTION

The fundamental purpose of public schools is to teach children their moral and intellectual responsibilities for living and working in a **democracy**. Public education is built on the premise of preparing an informed citizenry for our democracy. Thomas Jefferson said, "Whenever the people are well-informed, they can be trusted with their own government." Where will the greatest proportion of the people in a democracy be likely to learn about these conditions?

The public schools are, of course, the institution where the greatest majority of children will be exposed to these all-important democratic principles (Cuffaro, 1995). The civic nature of education strives "to prepare informed, rational, humane, and participating citizens committed to the values and principles of American constitutional democracy" (Center for Civic Education, 1994a, p. 1).

The early childhood years are an ideal time to introduce children to **democratic principles** such as cooperation, the need for rules, and the concept of justice. Political attitudes begin to be formed in early childhood, and the process of learning to be effective citizens begins at birth. Children are not born with an innate sense of how to be good citizens. It is our responsibility, as teachers of young children, to introduce them to the important principles of our democratic society.

Teaching democratic principles helps children become effective citizens later in life.

A primary goal of constructivist education is to develop children's autonomy (DeVries et al., 2002; Piaget, 1932/1965). Constructivist teachers encourage children to reflect on their own thinking (Dewey, 1916). The social studies, all day, every day, are the ideal place in the curriculum in which to engage in this important task.

DEMOCRACY

Winston Churchill said, "It has been said that democracy is the worst form of government except all those other forms that have been tried from time to time." "Because democracy is an idea that requires continuous construction and nurturance, the necessity for teaching democratic principles, especially to young citizens, is an ongoing process, and the principles are therefore important curricula for pre- and inservice teachers" (p. 339). As we prepare to work with young children in developing an understanding of democratic principles and laying the foundation for civic responsibility, it is important to look at the conditions necessary for a democracy to survive. Within the framework for the greater democracy, teachers can examine the ways these principles are carried out in the classroom.

Conditions for Democracy

Teachers of young children have a unique opportunity and responsibility to contribute to the continuation of the United States of America and the democracy we enjoy. By setting up the early childhood classroom in a way that introduces young children to the basic principles of a democratic society, we are allowing them to learn, from an early age, their rights and responsibilities as citizens. This process of political socialization begins early in a child's education. To develop into a citizenry able to continue the democracy, children need to know and understand several conditions (Dewey, 1916).

CONNECTION TO CHILDREN'S LITERATURE

America: A Patriotic Primer

Obtain a copy of *America: A Patriotic Primer* by Lynne Cheney. This wonderfully illustrated ABC book outlines the principles on which our country was founded. It offers an excellent focus for discussion of democratic principles.

"A is for America,
the land that we love.
B is for the Birthday
Of this country of ours..."

In small groups, take an assigned letter of the alphabet. Make a class ABC book (or chart) on ways to teach democratic principles to young students. This activity can be easily transferred to the elementary classroom, offering a structure for development of many important concepts.

ABC books abound! Use them as you introduce each of your units in the social studies. Children develop a fondness for and understanding of the structure of the ABC books and are able to glean main ideas and important elements from them easily. Students can make their own ABC books, either as an end-of-unit activity or as an ongoing project throughout the course of the unit. These projects offer an opportunity for students to review the units in a pleasant and appropriate fashion, throughout the school year.

Encouraging children to be helpful can be a first step in establishing trust.

Trust

People must have trust if they are to allow themselves to enter into long-term relationships, which are necessary for political and social interaction in a democracy. How does this play out in our classrooms? From the first day of school, we must establish a climate of trust and respect for all students. Children are very intuitive and can spot a phony immediately! We must set up our classrooms as models of a trusting environment.

As the teacher and the model for appropriate behavior in your classroom, it is important to treat each child respectfully, to model respect for fellow teachers, administrators, and parents. Holding students accountable for their behavior, in an equitable way, is also important. Students need to learn that equitable does not always mean equal, or exactly the same.

Some students have specific needs in terms of behavior, academics, medical conditions, or other aspects of classroom life. In a truly democratic society, everything is not exactly the same. Some children in our classrooms need extra time to complete work, or need to be able to stand or wiggle when our expectations for the greater group is to sit still. Helping young children to understand the differences in others' needs is a cornerstone to creating a working classroom democracy.

Social Capital

People must have social and political skills in order to problem-solve together, as opposed to simply accepting orders. This condition speaks to us in terms of discipline management and teaching strategies. Students must be *allowed* to work together, in order to *learn* to work together. This does not happen in isolated work, on individual assignments. Cooperative learning strategies are excellent ways to help students develop their social capital.

In addition, we must give students an opportunity to develop an internal locus of control. If we have harsh and authoritarian discipline plans in place in our classrooms, students become used to accepting orders rather than thinking for themselves and behaving well because it is the right thing to do.

Respect for Equal Justice Under Law

In a democratic society, we must have a belief in justice. We must believe that justice will be administered equally to all in our society.

Young children are quick to point out an unfair situation. Our challenge, as teachers of young children, is to always treat children fairly, though not always in exactly the same way. If we have been successful in building trust with our students, they will be accepting of the need to work with all students in an independent and appropriate fashion. They will understand that one student may need to work on 5 spelling words, when they will have a list of 20. Children watch carefully for equal treatment in terms of discipline. They are the first to notice when the teacher disciplines one student for an infraction of the rules while ignoring the same infraction in another.

Respect for Civil Discourse

Democratic societies need a positive climate of people talking to each other, advancing ideas and considering different options and opinions without resorting to physical and verbal violence.

In a classroom, it is often difficult for teachers to let go of the reins of power and encourage discourse among the students. This is vitally important if we are to teach students to value the freedom and responsibility that we have in this country for participation in civil discourse. Students must be encouraged to think critically and to learn to speak their minds in a courteous and forceful way.

Recognition of the Need for E Pluribus Unum—"Out of Many, One"

Our democracy depends on the diversity represented by our many peoples. Children must be taught to respect individual and group differences. The most effective way to do this is by modeling respect. As teachers of young children, everything we do is observed and mimicked by our students. They pick up on the way that we treat other people, both the adults and the children in our schools. We can encourage an understanding of other cultures by providing multi-cultural, anti-bias literature, bulletin boards, materials, and supplies for our students. Whenever possible, we should provide opportunities for students to explore people of different cultures, religions, ethnicities, and abilities.

Free and Open Inquiry—Central to a Democracy

People must have an inclination to inquire into all aspects of the workings of society. We can help our students to develop this propensity for inquiry by encouraging thought and by using effective questioning strategies. We must develop lessons with extensions and open-ended possibilities in mind. Open inquiry must be encouraged and valued in early childhood classrooms if our students are to mature into good citizens who value inquiry.

Knowledge of Rights

Children need to be aware of their rights, in the classroom and in the nation. As important as their understanding of the rights that they have as citizens is the coupling of rights with responsibilities. Children must be taught that, along with the rights that they have as American citizens, there are corresponding responsibilities.

George Washington spoke of the need to teach "the people themselves to know and to value their own rights; to discern and provide against invasions of them; to distinguish between oppression and the necessary exercise of lawful authority" (First Annual Address to Congress).

Freedom

Children must have the power to exercise freedom and the insight to value it. For those of us who have lived only in the United States, freedom is something that we frequently take for granted. For our students, for whom the concept of *not being free* is totally foreign, allowing them to explore different cultures, where freedom is not a normal part of daily life, is an important aspect of teaching students about what freedom *is*.

Recognition of the Tension Between Freedom and Order

Children need to learn that a balance must be reached between enjoying freedom and maintaining order. This delicate balance can be demonstrated in the classroom by setting up an environment in which students are allowed freedom to choose center work, cooperative group members, and so forth, within the bounds of order and effectiveness. Only by helping students to *live* the balance can we teach them the principles of living in a democratic society.

Recognition of the Difference Between a Persuaded Audience and a More Thoughtful Public

Giving students multiple opportunities to practice critical thinking and problem-solving skills is important in helping them become effective members of a democratic society. In all areas of teaching, the early childhood professional can build in opportunities for the students to make decisions based on good information. Through these ongoing practices, children are able to construct a foundation for effective decision-making.

Ecological Understanding

John Goodlad said, "The only way for democracy to survive is for the larger environment to survive." In order for our democracy to continue, teachers must help students understand the importance of taking care of the environment. Integrating ecological responsibility into the curriculum is an important aspect of teaching students to be good citizens. Later in this text, we will explore specific ways that ecological concerns can be integrated into the everyday social studies curriculum. Students need to learn that taking care of our world is an important aspect of their global citizenship.

GROUP ACTIVITY — CONDITIONS FOR DEMOCRACY

- Divide into pairs or triads, depending on the size of your university class.
- Take one of the "Conditions for Democracy."
- Brainstorm ways that you can model that condition in your early childhood classroom.
- Report out to the class.

TEACHING FOR EFFECTIVE CITIZENSHIP

"Educators must seize every opportunity to teach, nurture, and develop in students the traits of 'good citizenship' and a deep commitment to the nation's shared values" (Pohan, p. 372). According to the National Council for the Social Studies, "citizens in the twenty-first century must be prepared to deal with rapid change, complex local, national, and global issues, cultural and religious conflicts, and the increasing interdependence of nations in a global economy" (NCSS, 2001b, p. 1).

According to this Position Statement of the National Council for the Social Studies, an effective citizen:

- Embraces our core democratic values.
- Accepts responsibility for the well-being of oneself and of one's family and community.
- Has knowledge of people, history, and traditions that have shaped our democracy.
- Has knowledge of founding documents, civic institutions, and political processes.
- Is aware of issues and events that impact people at all levels.
- Seeks information from varied sources to develop informed opinions and creative solutions.
- Asks meaningful questions and is able to analyze and evaluate information and ideas.

- Uses effective decision-making and problem-solving skills.
- Has the ability to collaborate effectively.
- Actively participates in civic and community life (NCSSa, 2001).

If we understand the conditions of democracy in the greater society, it is a simple extension to embrace the conditions in our own classrooms. It is only through practice and modeling that young children come to understand the importance of the gift they have been given, that of living in a democracy.

CONNECTING TO ADMINISTRATION

MODELING DEMOCRACY

Early in the school year, meet with your principal and discuss your interest in modeling democracy in your classroom. Suggest that the school community might meet at the flagpole once a week, to sing, share patriotic stories and poetry, and to demonstrate the correct usage of the American flag. You might suggest developing a schedule of classrooms to lead these weekly meetings (you might even volunteer to develop that schedule yourself). This weekly get-together encourages a sense of community, while giving students an opportunity to learn more about the traditions of their country.

CIVICS TODAY

Thomas Jefferson said, "If we think the people not enlightened enough to exercise the power with a wholesome discretion, the remedy is not to take the power from them but to improve their discretion through education." The National Council for the Social Studies believes that the primary goal of public education is to prepare students to be engaged and effective. Preparing young children for citizenship in a democracy is a difficult task.

How do we help children to become adults who are capable of making informed decisions? This question was pondered by our founding fathers in the very infancy of our country. Throughout history, the

These classmates are using effective decision-making and problem-solving skills.

answer has been: education. Giving students opportunities to engage in critical thinking and make informed decisions is the most important task in teaching citizenship skills for life in a democracy.

Social studies topics, explored in an ongoing, "all day, every day" fashion, are excellent vehicles for helping students learn to make informed decisions and to practice problem-solving strategies—both absolutely necessary skills in furthering the democracy.

Civic Dispositions

The National Standards for Civics and Government (Center for Civic Education, 1994b) describes **dispositions** that enhance "citizen effectiveness and promote the healthy functioning of American democracy" (Center for Civic Education, 1994b, p. 37). Dispositions are defined as beliefs that guide behavior and include such things as self-discipline, individual responsibility, honesty, respect for the law, patriotism, and compassion, to name a few. These civic dispositions fit within the conditions for democracy previously discussed.

Dispositions cannot be taught through workbook pages and multiple-choice tests! By modeling, encouraging, and holding students responsible for their own behavior, we can begin to help students develop positive dispositions. Children's daily experiences in the classroom environment can help them to understand how to be responsible citizens in a classroom community. Involvement in social studies topics—all day, every day—is a most effective way to integrate encouragement of positive dispositions in early childhood classrooms.

GROUP ACTIVITY
PROFILE OF A CITIZEN

To be effective teachers of citizenship, we need to develop our own definition of what it means to be a good citizen. What does one look like? What markers of citizenship will we identify to try to instill in our students? How do we know when we have been successful?

Divide into small groups of three or four. Brainstorm your goals for teaching citizenship in the early childhood classroom.

What would your ideal citizen look like? How do you want your students to turn out? What should involved citizens be able to do? What should involved citizens know?

As you answer the questions, make suggestions of how you might introduce these dispositions to young children.

The Democratic Classroom

Creating a democratic classroom is one of the most important tasks of the social studies teacher (Hutchinson & Hunt, 2001). Through modeling the aspects of a democratic society in the classroom, the early childhood teacher can help students develop an understanding of the democratic process as a whole.

There are several important components of a democratic classroom setting. First, a democratic classroom holds students accountable for their own work and behavior. These expectations serve to strengthen the classroom community. Democratic classrooms value student thought by emphasizing interactive discussion and problem-solving over autocratic discipline and instruction. They encourage students to create a support structure with classmates, increasing interaction, and ultimately increasing student autonomy (Alter, 1997).

THE CLASS MEETING

One of the most impressive strategies for creating a democratic atmosphere in the early childhood classroom is the implementation of regular, daily class meetings. Beginning with very young children, and maintaining its effectiveness throughout the school experience, the class meeting is a mainstay of civics instruction in the primary grades. From the very first day of school, students begin to form a community, working on projects, settling disagreements, and learning from one another (Logan, 1998).

When the class meeting is implemented appropriately, it creates a caring community in which children participate in rule- and decision-making, discoveries about their own learning, and friendship-building activities (Ashton, 2002). The teacher is responsible for gentle guidance in this process, maintaining a delicate balance between too much teacher-directed instruction and mayhem.

The class meeting is a time of shared rituals, which can also provide structure for the day ahead (McClurg, 1998). This ritual provides an atmosphere that helps children establish a sense of safety and belonging. Kriete (1999) suggests having children share thoughts and ideas during this morning time. Children practice speaking clearly and listeners practice attending to what is said and responding appropriately.

There are several ways to structure the class meeting. One first-grade teacher prepares a "morning message" written in marker on a piece of adding machine tape to begin each morning meeting. In dramatic fashion, the teacher unrolls the message each morning, following school-wide announcements and opening exercises. The message usually lets the students know about a special activity that will be occurring that day and poses a question or challenge for the students to ponder.

The first portion of the morning meeting, as described by Bondy and Ketts (2001), is the *Greeting*. The greetings help each student in the class to gain a sense of belonging in the classroom environment. This portion of the meeting gives students an opportunity to practice communication skills that are central to building community as school children and as citizens.

The second component of the class meeting is *Sharing*. This portion of the class meeting was designed to simulate face-to-face conversation. This daily activity gives students an opportunity to practice listening, taking turns, asking questions, and looking at issues from different perspectives. The sharing portion of the class meeting might look something like this:

CLASS MEETING

Jack: My dad took me fishing yesterday. I'm ready for questions and comments.

Sarah: Did you catch any fish?

Jack: Yes, I caught two.

Brandon: Where did you go fishing?

Jack: We went to the lake out by the cement plant.

Megan: Did you fish from the pier or from a boat?

Jack: We don't have a boat. We fished from the pier.

Through this process, Jack, the speaker, was given an opportunity to practice presenting orally to a group. The listeners were given the opportunity to practice their skills of active listening, reflection on a topic, formulation and asking relevant questions, and making thoughtful comments. These skills are foundations for building an effective and ongoing democracy.

The third portion of the Morning Meeting involves a pair-and-share activity, in which students sit, knee-to-knee, eye-to-eye, and discuss a topic suggested by the teacher. The students take turns asking and answering questions surrounding the topic.

The fourth and final component of the Morning Meeting is the *News and Announcements*. In this portion of the meeting, students refocus on the teacher's daily message. This can be done by having a single student reread the message, or by having the group read in unison. There may be a related writing activity, or a storybook reading that relates to the work for the day. Whatever the activity, the class meeting serves as a transition point from the arrival of students to school and the rest of the day.

The class meeting can set the tone for the entire day and can have great payoffs for student learning and development over the course of the school year (Harris & Fuqua, 2000). To make the most of the class meeting, teachers must guide young students to learn to care for one another and to be in control of their own learning. The class meeting serves to help focus students on the learning at hand, as well as offering an opportunity to practice important skills necessary for building a caring classroom community.

COMPONENTS OF THE CLASS MEETING

Greeting	Pair-and-Share
Sharing	News and Announcements

Rule-Making and Democracy in the Classroom

Teaching democratic principles in the early childhood classroom involves both giving students a knowledge base about democracy and allowing them to *experience* democracy in action. Children must experience the effects of a democratic society in order to understand the knowledge-level information they are being taught (Cartwright, 2004). One effective way to help children experience democracy is to encourage them to develop and reinforce the rules of their classroom.

Because children live as members of groups in society, it is important for them to understand how rules help groups to function effectively (Clayton & Wood, 1995). Children want and need boundaries. A few well-thought-out rules, developed by the students themselves, help to create a safe and secure classroom environment. Encouraging students to create rules for the classroom sets the stage for the entire school year. Encouraging children to develop their own rules and consequences models the democratic process for young children, from the very beginning of the school year.

When the teacher creates an environment in which students solve classroom problems through collaboration, the democratic process is modeled as a process for young students. Rightmyer (2003) suggests the implementation of a Book of Solutions. The Book of Solutions is used for students to record decisions about resolving problems in the classroom. When a problem arises in the classroom, record the problem in the Book of Solutions. Brainstorm possible solutions as a whole class, and then record them in the class book. This provides a year-long record of challenges that have faced the students, as well as the solutions to those problems. This process empowers children as they learn to get along in a group situation and grow in their knowledge and understanding of the democratic process.

POLITICAL CONCEPTS

Children learn about political concepts in an informal fashion. Most children come to school already acquainted with the American flag, patriotic songs, and the Pledge of Allegiance. Children also come to school familiar with ideas about voting, war and peace, and the importance of laws. Once children enroll in school, formal study of these symbols and concepts helps them to clarify their understandings. The ways in which teachers introduce and reinforce these concepts are important for developing deep understanding and appreciation of the symbols and concepts in our democracy.

The Flag and the Pledge of Allegiance

By the time children start school, most have had some experience with the American flag. They usually have some concept of the importance of the flag as a symbol of our country, though they rarely understand exactly what it means. Study of the history of the flag is a great way to help students understand the importance and meaning of the flag. Children's literature offers a vast selection of books, both fiction and nonfiction, that can help the young student to understand the meaning of the American flag and the history behind it.

In 1940, the U. S. Supreme Court ruled that states could require all children to salute the flag. This ruling was reversed in 1943, stating that the previous ruling violated religious beliefs. Students should not be compelled to recite the pledge. Beyond the legalities of having young children recite the pledge, there are some very critical developmental implications.

Recital of the Pledge of Allegiance is generally meaningless for young children, as they do not understand the words or concepts

CONNECTION TO CHILDREN'S LITERATURE

Children's Literature Selections

Stars and Stripes, Our National Flag by
Leonard Everitt Fisher

Fireworks, Picnics and Flags by James Cross
Giblin

The Story of the Liberty Bell by Natalie Miller

Will You Sign Here, John Hancock by Jean
Fritz

A More Perfect Union by Betsy and Giulio
Maestro

Shh! We're Writing the Constitution by Jean
Fritz

Our Constitution by Linda Johnson

involved in the pledge. Rather than having children mindlessly recite the pledge, it is more meaningful to discuss the concepts represented by the flag. While it is important for children to learn what the pledge is, and to have recognition of the pledge, allowing them to construct their own knowledge of the symbols of our country is much more meaningful for young children. Children's literature offers an excellent introduction to the concepts represented by the American flag, giving insight into the history and proper care of the flag, as well as other symbols of America.

Patriotism

Many Americans become emotional as the National Anthem is played and the American flag is raised. This feeling cannot be mandated or taught. Students must be introduced to the feeling of pride that comes from being a part of a unique community, and this begins in the classroom. Through appropriate experiences, encouraging pride in being a part of a classroom and school community, students are able to begin to understand the importance of being a part of the larger, national community. Through these kinds of experiences, seeds of national pride and patriotism are sewn.

A GLOBAL PERSPECTIVE

CONNECTING TO TOLERANCE IN THE PATRIOTIC CLASSROOM

While the public schools in the United States of America were designed to further the American democracy, the very ideal of America demands that we celebrate and value the diversity within those classrooms. Chances are, in your early childhood classroom, you will have several children who are not American citizens.

Discuss with your neighbor the value of introducing children to patriotism and the dilemma this course of instruction offers as we embrace children from other nations and cultures in our social studies classrooms. How can early childhood teachers balance the important task of developing patriotism while embracing the diverse cultures in our classrooms?

NATIONAL STANDARDS FOR CIVICS AND GOVERNMENT

Understanding what government is and what it does can begin in the early grades, by having students examine their own families and classrooms as examples of government. Abstract concepts, such as citizenship and government, are not understood by young children and should not be introduced in the abstract. Children do, however, have an excellent grasp of the concept of family structure and the structure of the classroom. (It is important here to recognize the different kinds of family structures represented in your classroom and to honor that diversity). The following standards have been developed by the Center for Civic Education, funded by the U. S. Department of Education in 1994 to guide our instruction in civics education.

CHARACTER EDUCATION IN SOCIAL STUDIES

American essayist, philosopher, and poet Ralph Waldo Emerson (1803–1882) said, "The true test of civilization is not the census, nor the size of cities, nor the crops—no, but the kind of man the country

STANDARDS FOR CIVICS EDUCATION

What is government and what should it do?	What is the relationship of the United States
What are the basic values and principles of	to other nations and to world affairs?
American democracy?	What are the roles of the citizen in American
How does the government established by the	democracy?
Constitution embody the purposes, values,	
and principles of American democracy?	

turns out." Emerson, as well as our founding fathers, understood that the ideal of America required a virtuous citizenry. "**Character** education is as old as education itself. Down through history, education has had two great goals: to help people become smart and to help them become good" (Lickona, 1993, p. 6.). Social studies teachers play an important role in preserving this American ideal. "Our founders and early educational pioneers saw in the very diverse, multicultural American scene of the late 18th and 19th centuries the clear need for a school system that would teach the civic virtues necessary to maintain our novel political and social experiment. They saw the school's role not only as contributing to a person's understanding of what it is to be good, but also as teaching the enduring habits required of a democratic citizen (Ryan, p. 16). It is an important obligation of the early childhood program to teach democratic principles and to inspire civic virtue.

Bronfenbrenner (1979) wrote: "No society can long sustain itself unless its members have learned the sensitivities, the motivations and the skills involved in assisting and caring for human beings" (p. 53). Character formation is a complex process. Schools must be places where adults model good character and where children have an opportunity to practice good citizenship. Teaching academics and teaching character can be mutually reinforcing. To develop their dispositions for virtuous behavior, students must be given many opportunities to practice virtuous living. Schools should be places where the behavior of teachers and students is informed by basic democratic principles. For instance, if fairness is modeled and reinforced in every facet of the early childhood classroom, children learn to be fair. By observing the teacher's respectful and kind interaction with parents, faculty, and students, young children learn to be respectful and kind. Character education is central to the curriculum of early childhood classrooms.

While the early American public schools were built on a premise that character education was a mainstay of the curriculum, through the decades, character education declined. In the 1960s a rise in the emphasis on individual rights and freedom from responsibility undermined the teaching of values in the American public school (Lickona, 1993). The growing diversity and secularism in the United States became barriers to character education, as educators struggled with *which* values to teach and concerns about crossing the line between church and state.

In recent years, a resurgence of character education has been noted. Some reasons for this renewed interest in character education are noted by Likona. The first factor noted is the decline of the family. While the family traditionally has been the primary morality teacher of children, many believe that this guidance is lacking in the lives of many children today. Second, the researcher cites the troubling trends in youth character. Suggested as possible reasons for this are poor role models, sex and violence portrayed in the media, and peer pressure. Finally, there has been a renewed awareness that adults must "promote morality by teaching children such values as respect, responsibility, trustworthiness, fairness, caring, and civic virtue" (Likona, p. 9)

Character education involves more than simple lectures about the virtues of being virtuous! As teachers, it is our responsibility to model acceptance and to embrace all members of the school community—not just tolerate them.

In creating a moral community for young students, early childhood teachers model respect and help students to feel a valued membership in the group (Wallace & Knotts, 2003). By involving students in decision-making and rule-making, the teacher can help to create a democratic classroom environment. Finally, by teaching effective conflict resolution strategies, young students can acquire the essentials necessary to solve conflicts fairly and peacefully.

Characteristics of a Good Citizen

The development of good citizens is the most important goal of public schools, particularly of social studies instruction. Democratic classrooms are the basis of modeling a greater democratic society for young children (Allerman & Brophy, 2002). The teacher establishes and maintains principles of democracy in the classroom; by following the principles of democracy, children develop an understanding of democratic values, and through experience they begin to develop important political concepts.

WAR AND PEACE

Modeling acceptance and tolerance are important ways that early childhood teachers can teach children about peace. Unfortunately, terrorist attacks in America and the horrors of war are realities for children and adults alike. As adults, it is our job to help children feel safe in a dangerous world.

War

Unfortunately, young children are affected by war and violence. Television images of war and of domestic violence bombard children's minds on a daily basis. These electronic-media images have caused young children to become increasingly fearful about war, terrorism, and crime. The classroom is a most appropriate setting for teaching children the truth about war and ways to facilitate peace.

Since the attacks on America on September 11, 2001, explaining war and terrorism to children has become a necessity. By creating an open environment where children can feel free to ask questions and express their feelings, early childhood teachers can lay the foundation for effective discussion of these difficult topics. When talking about terrorism in response to student questions, it is important for the teacher to be honest. Be reassuring, but don't make unrealistic promises. While it is appropriate to tell children that they are safe in their homes and at school, children can't be promised that there will be no more plane crashes or that no one else will be hurt.

Children do not understand the politics of war. As they watch television and listen to friends talk about parents being deployed and leaving their children behind, they may wonder if their own parents will have to leave as well. When they hear news of the deaths of soldiers, they may become particularly upset and worried.

Children have difficulty coming to terms with conflicting information given about fighting. They are told that fighting with classmates is wrong, but then are told about the necessity of war to protect innocent people (Kreidler, 1995). Offering children an opportunity to discuss their feelings and talk through the confusing inconsistencies is an important step in assuaging their fears and confusions.

TALKING TO CHILDREN ABOUT WAR

Be honest.

Listen.

Encourage children to talk about their concerns.

Don't deny the seriousness of the situation.

Let children draw, use dramatic play, or writing to express their concerns.

Help children to keep from stereotyping people from specific cultures or countries.

Create a safe environment.

Put the event in perspective. Children need to know that the world is generally a safe place.

Experts offer some suggestions for talking to children about war (Levin, 2003; Farish, 2003). First, it is important to tell the truth. In addition, it is important to listen to children as they talk about war. Let them take the lead in terms of the amount of information they want. Finally, encourage children to talk about their concerns. They may feel more comfortable drawing a picture, using blocks to act out their thoughts, or writing in a journal. The role of the teacher is to give accurate information at the appropriate level, and to guide the children to ask questions and talk through their concerns.

Excellent children's books are available on topics related to war. Following are some titles that may help explain the concept of war to children in an early childhood classroom:

Gleam and Glow by Eve Bunting

The Roses in My Carpet by Rukhsana Khan

The Knight and the Dragon by Tomie dePaola

I Dream of Peace: Images of War by Children of Former Yugoslavia by James Grant

It's Mine! By Leo Leonni

The Pig War by Betty Baker

Six Crows by Leo Lionni

Let's Be Enemies by Janice May Udry

The Quarreling Book by Charlotte Zolotow

Matthew and Tilly by Rebecca Jones

The Hating Book by Charlotte Zolotow

The Wall by Eve Bunting

The Breadwinner by Deborah Ellis

All the Secrets of the World by Jane Yolen

Several national organizations offer support and materials for teaching about war and peace with young children. The organizations' Web sites offer links to publications, conferences, and experts to help guide the early childhood professional in helping young children to understand the meaning of war. Some of these are listed in the box entitled "Organizations for Peace."

Peace

"It is easy to teach children about war," says Joan Almon, U. S. Coordinator of the Alliance for Childhood. "It is much more challenging to teach them how to create peace." The Association for Childhood Education International (ACEI) issued the following statement in March, 2003: "Peace education is not simply favoring the absence of war. Children must be guided to think clearly, analyze penetratingly, and challenge fearlessly. The next generation of children must reject killing as an uncivilized and unproductive way to deal with human conflict. The citizens of the world deserve future leaders who will be able to face and solve problems with diplomacy and dialogue."

Since world is the way that it is—violent—we must actively teach children to engage in peaceful resolution of their problems (Carter, 1993). Several simple, but important, steps can be taken by teachers to encourage peaceful resolution of conflicts in the early childhood classroom. Most importantly, model the behaviors you would like to see your students emulate. Teach kindness by being kind. Teach patience by being patient. Teach nonviolence by being nonviolent. In addition, praise appropriate behavior. Pointing out appropriate ways that students solve conflicts among classmates is one effective way to encourage continued appropriateness in student interaction.

Teach students to use appropriate words to express anger, frustration, or fear (Carllson-Paige & Levin, 1998). By encouraging children to use their words instead of their fists to solve conflicts, they will see the possibilities of nonviolent resolution of their problems. Finally, think about what kind of adult you would like for your students to become (Miller, 2001).

ORGANIZATIONS FOR PEACE

ACT Against Violence
c/o National Association for the Education of
    Young Children
http://www.naeyc.org
(202) 232-8777

Action Alliance for Children
1201 Martin Luther King Way
Oakland, CA 94612
(510) 444-7136
http://www.4children.org

Children's Defense Fund
PO Box 90500
Washington, DC 20090
202-662-3652
http://www.childrensdefense.org

Educators for Social Responsibility
23 Garden Street
Cambridge, MA 02138
1-800-370-2515
http://www.esrnational.org
PeaceBuilders
http://www.PeaceBuilders.com
(877) 473-2238

Peace Education Foundation
2627 Biscayne Blvd.
Miami, FL 33137-4532
1-800-749-8838
http://www.peaceeducation.com

Teaching for peace emphasizes communication and collaborative problem-solving. Well-designed conflict-resolution programs can have a significant impact on young children. It is not enough to tell them what *not* to do; we need to teach young students the skills and strategies for dealing with conflict effectively (McDermott, 1999). Talk to the students about the value of peacefulness. Look for the "teachable moment" and be ready to discuss peaceful resolution of problems that arise in the classroom

There are many children's books that address the issue of peace. Some of the many titles available follow:

The Big Book for Peace by Lloyd Alexander

Somewhere Today: A Book of Peace by Shelly Thomas

The Story of Ferdinand by Munro Leaf

A Million Visions of Peace: Wisdom from the Friends of Old Turtle by Jennifer Garrison

Peace and Bread: The Story of Jane Adams by Stephanie McPherson

Peacebound Trains by Haemi Balgassi

September Roses by Jeanette Winter

If Peace Is . . . by Jane Baskwill

War Play

Through the ages, children have integrated violent themes into their play (Levin, 2003). Banning war play rarely works, so the early childhood teacher must redirect student play to involve creative themes, rather than the violent ones that children first employ. By maintaining a high profile during recess time, and observing and interacting with children as they work and play in learning centers, teachers are able to redirect students' play.

In our society today, children are exposed to a great deal of violence—in television and video games, as well as in their neighborhoods and homes. The most effective way to reduce violent play is to reduce the violence that children see. While the classroom teacher does not have ultimate control over this aspect of the child's life, he or she does maintain control over six or seven hours of each school day. Maintaining a stance against violent media and literature in the classroom can be a first step in reducing the amount of violent material that students see.

When the curriculum calls for the inclusion of violent material, such as a study of war or civil unrest, the teacher is in an excellent position to lead the students to an understanding of other ways that might have been employed to solve the problems presented. Mahatma Gandhi said, "If we are to reach real peace in this world and if we are to carry on a real war against war, we shall have to begin with the children." It is the responsibility of the early childhood teacher to lead that charge.

Helping Children Cope in a Time of Tragedy

Since the tragic events of September 11, and the ensuing war in Iraq, violence and fear are a very real part of the lives of the young children in the public schools. It is impossible to turn on the television or radio and not have details of the war all across the airwaves. Children are affected at differing levels by these images and reports, but almost all are affected in some way.

As we continue to learn more about those responsible for the September 11 attacks, it is important to help young children understand that making assumptions about entire groups of people based on race, ethnicity, or religious background is not appropriate or accurate. Many teachers have a void in their understanding of the Arabic world and Islamic culture as well, making it important to spend some time researching and developing an understanding of those cultures before presenting information to children.

Using children's literature and building on the ongoing anti-bias curriculum already in place in the classroom are excellent beginnings for helping young children understand that while tragedy did strike the United States on September 11, 2001 and that our country is suffering from the effects of the ensuing war, individual people were responsible for the attacks, not the entire Arabic and Islamic world.

SUMMARY

"A democracy that works depends on educated, forthright, responsible citizens" (Cartwright, 2004, p. 108). The freedoms that we cherish did not appear without a struggle. In light of the events of September 11, 2001, it is clear that these freedoms will not be maintained without a struggle.

Children take for granted the freedoms that we do have, not understanding that people in many other nations do not enjoy the freedom to speak freely, to disagree with government officials, or to practice the religion of their choice. It is part of the job of the teacher to help children understand the gift of freedom. As educators, we have a responsibility to equip our students with the tools necessary to carry on our democracy, and indeed, to improve it.

Citizenship in a democracy is not easy. Along with the awesome rights that come with citizenship in America come equally awesome responsibilities. Public schools were established to inform a democratic citizenry. Throughout the history of our country, public schools have educated students to become informed, thinking, and virtuous citizens.

We can teach children about democracy only by actually "doing democracy." It is not a spectator sport. Children have to experience democracy in order to understand it. The principles of democracy must be taught, by modeling, in order for those principles to become a part of the child's worldview. It is incumbent upon the teacher of young children to begin the process of teaching children to be problem-solvers, analytical thinkers, and participants in this great democracy of ours. "A social context of building the future with children who understand how important it is to live together happily in a pluralistic society is vital to the teacher's role" (Hunt, 1999, p. 41). Our job is to prepare our young students to sustain the democratic ideals of America.

▶ THEMATIC STRANDS AND FOCUS QUESTIONS

Culture

1. How can the early childhood teacher embrace the diverse cultures in the classroom, while teaching about American ideals and patriotism?

2. What are the routines and activities that contribute to the development of an effective early childhood classroom culture?

Individuals, Groups, and Institutions

1. How does the early childhood teacher introduce the importance of national institutions to young children?

2. How can young children learn to identify with different groups within the United States of America, while holding on to their individuality?

Power, Authority, and Governance

1. How does the early childhood teacher introduce the structure of government and its importance to the day-to-day lives of young children?

2. How does the class meeting help young children to understand the importance of democratic governance?

Civic Ideals and Practices

1. How does the early childhood teacher introduce and reinforce the important civic ideals of the United States of America?

2. How does the structure of the classroom itself model the civic ideals and practices of a democracy?

▶ KEY TERMS

character
class meeting
democracy
democratic principles
dispositions

REFERENCES

ACEI (Association for Childhood Education International). (2003). ACEI statement on children and war/peace education. from www.acei.org/press25 mar03.htm (Accessed October 15, 2004).

Allerman, J., & Brophy, J. (2002). How government rules and regulations affect a young student's life. *Social Studies and the Young Learner, 15*(1), 9–10.

Alter, G. (1997). The emergence of a diverse, caring community: Next steps in responsive curriculum design for elementary social studies. *Social Studies and the Young Learner, 10*(1), 6–9.

Ashton, L. A. (2002). Teaching the importance of government to third grade students. *Social Studies and the Young Learner, 15*(1), 21–23.

Bondy, E., & Ketts, S. (2001). Like being at the breakfast table: The power of classroom morning morning. *Childhood Education, 77*(3), 144–149.

Bridges, L. (1995). *Creating your classroom community.* York, ME: Stenhouse.

Bronfenbrenner, U. (1979). *The ecology of human development: Experiments by nature and design.* Cambridge, MA: Harvard University Press.

Carllson-Paige, N., & Levin, D. (1998). *Before push comes to shove: Building conflict resolution skills with children.* St. Paul, MN: Redleaf Press.

Carter, J. (1993). *Talking peace: A vision for the next generation.* New York: Dutton.

Cartwright, S. (2004). Young citizens in the making. *Young Children, 59*(5), 108–109.

Center for Civic Education. (1994a). National Standards for Civics and Government.

http://www.civiced.org/stds_toc_preface.html (Accessed April 17, 2005).

Center for Civic Education. (1994b). National Standards for Civics and Government. Calabasas, CA: Author.

Clayton, M. L., & Wood, C. (1995). Rules grow from our hopes and dreams. *The Responsive Classroom, 7*(2), 1–3.

Cuffaro, H. K. (1995). *Experimenting with the world: John Dewey and the early childhood classroom.* New York: Teacher's College Press.

DeVries, R., Zan, B., Hildebrandt, C., Edmiaston, R., & Sales, C. (2002). *Developing constructivist early childhood curriculum: Practical principles and activities.* New York: Teacher's College Press.

Dewey, J. (1916). *Democracy and education.* New York: Macmillan.

Farish, J. (2003). *When disaster strikes: Helping younger children cope* (Brochure 533). Washington, DC: National Association for Education of Young Children.

Harris, T., & Fuqua, J. (2000). What goes around comes around: building a community of learners through circle times. *Young Children, 5*(1), 44–47.

Hunt, R. (1999). Making positive multicultural early childhood education happen. *Young Children, 54*(5), 39–42.

Hutchinson, J. N., & Hunt, J. A. (2001). Living democracy in the classroom. *Democracy and Education, 13*(4), 2–6.

Kreidler, W. (1995). *Teaching conflict resolution through children's literature*. New York: Scholastic.

Kriete, R. (1999). *The morning meeting book*. Greenfield, MA: Northeast Foundation for Children.

Levin, D. (2003). *Teaching young children in violent times: Building a peaceable classroom* (2nd ed.). Cambridge, MA: Educators for Social Responsibility.

Lickona, T. (1993). The return of character education. *Educational Leadership, 51*(3), 6–11.

Logan, T. (1998). Creating a kindergarten community. *Young Children, 53*(2), 22–26.

McClurg, L. G. (1998). Building an ethical community in the classroom: Community meeting. *Young Children, 53*(2), 30–35.

McDermott, K. (1999). Helping primary school children work things out during recess. *Young Children, 54*(4), 82–84.

Miller, C. (2001). Teaching the skills of peace: More elementary and preschools are going beyond "conflict resolution" to teach positive social behavior. *Children's Advocate*, May/June, 9.

NCSS (National Council for the Social Studies). (2001a, May). Position Statement of the NCSS—Creating effective citizens. www.socialstudies.org (Accessed on March 1, 2004).

NCSS (National Council for Social Studies). (2001b, May). Creating effective citizens. www.socialstudies.org (Accessed March 1, 2004).

Piaget, J. (1965). The moral judgment of the child. New York: Free Press. (Original work published 1932)

Pohan, C. (2003). Creating caring and democratic communities in our classrooms and schools. *Childhood Education, 79*(6), 369–373.

Rightmyer, E. (2003). Democratic discipline: Children creating solutions. *Young Children, 58*(4), 38–45.

Wallace, M., & Knotts, C. (2003). An unlikely pair. *Childhood Education, 80*(3), 134–146.

SUGGESTED READINGS

Khan, R. (1998). *The roses in my carpets*. Markham, Ontario: Stoddart Kids.

Leaf, M. (1936). *The story of Ferdinand*. New York: Viking.

Lionni, L. (1988). *Six crows*. New York: Knopf Books for Young Readers.

Lionni, L. (1986). *It's mine!* New York: Books for Young Readers. McPhearson, S. (1993). *Peace and bread: The story of Jane Adams*. Minneapolis, MN: Carolrhoda Books.

NAEYC (National Association for the Education of Young Children) Helping children cope with disaster. http://www.naeyc.org/coping_with_disaster. htm.

Southern Poverty Law Center. *Teaching Tolerance* (biannual magazine available at no charge to educators), 400 Washington Avenue, Montgomery, AL 36104.

Thomas, S. (1998). *Somewhere today: A book of peace*. Morton Grove, IL: Albert Whitman.

Winter, J. (2004). *September roses*. New York: Farrar, Strauss, & Giroux.

Udry, J. (1988). *Let's be enemies*. New York: HarperTrophy.

Yolen, J. (1991). *All the secrets of the world*. Boston: Little Brown.

Zolotow, C. (1982). *The quarreling book*. New York: HarperTrophy.

Zolotow, C. (1989). *The hating book*. New York: HarperTrophy.

CHAPTER 6
Children's Literature in Social Studies Instruction

OBJECTIVES

After reading this chapter, you should be able to:

➤ Develop criteria for selection of children's literature in the early childhood classroom.

➤ Model a think-aloud while reading a piece of children's literature.

➤ Develop a lesson plan for social studies instruction, using children's literature as a base.

➤ Describe the appropriate use of children's literature in developing positive multicultural dispositions with young children.

➤ Develop a list of children's literature for use in teaching social studies topics.

Until I feared I would lose it, I never loved to read.
One does not love breathing.

Harper Lee, *To Kill a Mockingbird*

169

Effective teachers provide a variety of literature.

INTRODUCTION

As we struggle to make reading across the curriculum a reality, it is important to access an array of materials—magazines, the World Wide Web, and
children's literature—both fiction and nonfiction. Children's literature provides an engaging focus for thematic instruction, while offering endless
opportunities for modeling reading, thinking, and problem-solving skills
(Johnson & Janisch, 1998).

Children's picture books have had a significant place in early childhood classrooms for a long time. Their use in recent years has transformed classroom instruction in all areas of the curriculum. Fiction, nonfiction, and poetry offer young children many opportunities to gain information about the world around them. The beautiful illustrations, easy-to-read format, and varied topics engage the child's imagination.

Using literature to teach social studies is not a recent innovation. Stories about the triumphs of people of good character and those embodying civic virtue were at the core of nineteenth-century common school curricula. The increasing interest among teachers in using literature as a basis of the social studies curriculum has been enhanced by the growing number of appropriate books for young children.

The increasing importance of children's literature may be seen in the growing numbers of children's books published per year. In 1940, 984 books for children were published in the United States. In 1997, the number was 5,353 (Huck, Hepler, Hickman & Kiefer, 2001). Children's literature has found its way into classrooms as daily read-alouds, content for reading programs, and as supplements or alternatives to textbooks in content areas.

OVERVIEW OF CHILDREN'S LITERATURE IN SOCIAL STUDIES INSTRUCTION

Fiction has long held a position of prominence in elementary classrooms. Fiction encompasses all forms of imaginative writing including novels, short stories, plays, and so forth. Traditionally, the primary purpose of fiction has been to entertain. On the other hand, the primary purpose of nonfiction has been to explain, demonstrate, or provide information.

While many teachers of young children are quite adept at using fiction in the classroom, the use of nonfiction, informational books is an underutilized source of instructional material. Informational texts are defined as texts written with the primary purpose of conveying information about the world—typically by someone more knowledgeable on the subject. Features commonly found in **informational texts** include graphic elements, such as diagrams and photographs; text structures, such as compare/contrast and cause and effect; and access formats, such as headings and an index. These kinds of books lend themselves beautifully to enrichment of the social studies curriculum. Many of the features inherent in informational texts, such as charts and graphs, represent skills presented in the social studies standards.

Young children are naturally curious about the world around them. Early childhood educators have an important role to play in increasing the availability of informational texts for young children. Inquiry or thematic units are popular ways to organize instruction in social studies. Nonfiction books are ideal for use in these kinds of studies.

The great selection of children's literature available today offers an exciting starting place for meaningful social studies instruction. Children's literature is a powerful tool for linking social studies learning and literacy development in the early childhood classroom. Literature can serve several purposes, "some of which are aesthetic, psychosocial, and informative/instructive (Mendoza & Reese, 2001, p. 2). Picture books offer children exposure to ways of thinking about other human beings. Literature can transport children to another time or place, can give them an insight into the points of view of people they would never meet, and provide them with vicarious experiences.

When used effectively in the classroom, picture books can help children to learn about the world around them. Rather than providing a breadth of information, the way a textbook does, a picture book is likely to focus on a single topic or on a single character. By using a number of books throughout the course of a unit of study, students are exposed to a number of perspectives on a single topic.

For students who have difficulty in reading the more difficult text in the social studies book, children's literature offers a greater level of accessibility and the pictures offer support for English language learners (Allington, 2002). Use of children's literature in social studies instruction is an excellent way to ensure that our students are exposed to social studies, all day—every day.

WHY USE CHILDREN'S LITERATURE IN SOCIAL STUDIES INSTRUCTION?

Many classroom teachers are frustrated by the lack of readable, child-friendly materials for social studies instruction (D'Arcangelo, 2002). Many teachers remember endless afternoons of directions from their own social studies teachers to "read the chapter and answer the questions at the end of the chapter." Unfortunately for many students, the social studies textbooks are often written at a level of readability inaccessible to many class members.

The social studies are rich with possibilities for teaching all subjects. Many successful teachers arrange the entire year's curriculum around the social studies. Students frequently gain academic ground in all areas of instruction, from reading level to mathematics achievement—all because of their fascination with the topics presented in social studies themes. Children's literature is an effective basis for social studies instruction. A vast array of beautiful and easy-to-read literature is available to entice the reluctant social studies student.

There are several strategies for obtaining just the right book to illustrate the social studies standards and skills that are to be introduced in each thematic unit. Many teachers begin by looking at the electronic card catalog in the school library. Unfortunately, the selections are usually limited at first (but librarians are often happy to provide titles requested by teachers as funds become available). Then, teachers can search online for literature lists provided by other teachers and read countless online lesson plans on the topics to be presented. Many teachers report that their most efficient strategy is to log onto one of the prominent online booksellers and search the topic that will be presented. This strategy provides an immediate supply of appropriate books, along with a very useful summary of each book and links to related literature. When not purchasing the selections from the online bookstores, teachers can take the information gained from this kind of online research to the local public library, and check out many of the titles obtained online.

An appropriate goal for effective teaching in the social studies is the use of at least six read-alouds each day. This will be very difficult at first, but after a few weeks, you will not know how you taught any other way.

Rereading selections that students enjoyed is not only acceptable; it is also advisable. In fact, early childhood teachers should reread books and poems that the students found interesting. Another layer of meaning is always gleaned from a second and third reading of the same material. Choose related poetry, articles from the newspaper, paragraphs from the textbook, selections from the Internet, encyclopedia entries, diary entries, and so forth as well as children's literature books for read-alouds. Through these multiple readings, the teacher is able to model for students fluency as well as the use of different genres while getting the knowledge-level information to them on a regular basis. Then, make read-aloud material available to the students—whether in the form of books, laminated newspaper articles, or Internet selections.

CONNECTION TO CHILDREN'S LITERATURE

Criteria for Selection of Children's Literature for Social Studies Instruction

Materials selection is an important part of the effective teacher's job. A variety of methods can be used to choose the children's literature for a social studies lesson. While you will, ultimately, develop your own system for making selections, following are some things to consider as you begin to build your library of children's books for social studies instruction.

1. Is the information in the book accurate? Who wrote the book, and what qualifications do they have for writing it? When was the book written? Is the information still current and accurate in light of current research?
2. Is the book pleasing? Are the illustrations or photographs illustrative of what you are trying to convey in your lesson?

3. Does the book lend itself to "thinking aloud?" If so, which teaching points might you choose to model for the students?
4. Can you use the book for more than one concept or topic? Children benefit from multiple readings of a book. How many different ways could you use that one piece of literature in your teaching?
5. Is the book fun? Is it thought-provoking? Is it engaging? If not, don't buy it.

Your children's literature library will have a personality all its own. You may be attracted to historical fiction, or you may prefer a particular kind of illustration. Be careful, though, to offer a wide variety of material for your students. Augment the books you choose to purchase with a selection from the school or public library.

GENRE

Genre is defined as a category of language that is used to classify its form and content. Numerous genres are appropriate for use in the social studies, including fairy tales, tall tales, fables, poetry, historical fiction, adventure stories, recipes, menus, lists, nonfiction books and passages, invitations, journals, diaries, and notes, to name a few. It is important for children to explore and experience a wide variety of literacy materials. As they explore, children build schemas for the many functions and forms of written language. Introducing children to all genres of literature is an important step in helping students make meaning from text.

Knowledge of genre is important in developing good readers and good thinkers. Most teachers of young children are very competent users of the story genre. Extensive and appropriate use of story reading in early childhood helps children learn about and make sense of the world. Through stories, children experience new ideas, environments, and ways of looking at the world. A wide array of storybooks related to the topics and skills that are being taught in social studies are available and should be used to highlight specific concepts. Children understand the story genre because they have had many opportunities to explore it. It is important that students are given an opportunity to develop an understanding of the other genres as well.

Expository Text and Social Studies Instruction

Reading **expository text** is an important part of a child's literacy development and a wonderful way to expose students to information inherent in the social studies. Expository text is defined as text written by authors to inform, explain, describe, present information, or to persuade. Expository text is subject oriented and contains facts and information. It uses little dialogue (Tonjes, Wolpow, & Zintz, 1999). Children can build **schema** for social studies content through the use of books. They learn important information from expository text that they may not be exposed to in other genres of text. Several very good series of expository text are available in libraries and bookstores and are quite useful in getting knowledge-level information to students about a variety of topics in the social studies. Tables, graphs, charts, and photographs in these kinds of books are generally very helpful in making the information accessible to all of the students in the classroom.

There are many engaging types of expository works. ABC books, biographies, brochures, recipes, interviews, journals, lists, and maps are just a few of the excellent materials available for use in the early childhood social studies classroom. These materials bring a different perspective to the students' study of a variety of themes and allow them to see different aspects of the theme. For instance, during a study of colonial life in a second- or third-grade classroom, the teacher might introduce the theme with a storybook. He or she then might follow up with expository text, illustrating the games played by children of the era, modes of transportation, or foods and traditions of the colonial period. The storybook would have served to engage the children in the era to be studied, while the expository follow-up gives more in-depth information for children to build on as they develop a conceptual framework for the colonial period of history.

Many teachers use at least one ABC book during every thematic unit, to emphasize important aspects of the theme, and then follow up with a biography of a child of the time being studied. Cooking with students is a wonderful way to bring in other modalities of learning, so authentic recipes and the use of authentic utensils, if available, is another way to extend and deepen the understanding of the theme.

Use of a wide variety of books and other written materials during each unit helps students connect more readily with different kinds of materials. Students develop a growing understanding and enjoyment of expository text as the school year progresses and as they are exposed more and more to this kind of writing. After using a book or other piece of reading material (book, chart, recipe, list) place it on the chalk tray at the front of the classroom, for student use. Students frequently choose those books that are used in read-alouds for their independent reading.

Several factors contribute to the difference between narrative and expository style writing (see Table 6-1). Both external and internal factors are involved. The external factors include format, typographical aids, and graphic features. The internal factors include the author's style, language, and explanation.

Helping Children Access Expository Text

Young children are very familiar with narrative text, but have less experience with expository text. To help children understand this genre, teachers need to give them lots of experience with these kinds of books. Make expository reading a regular part of classroom activities. When reading expository text, point out the aids given by the author that help the reader access information in the text (headings, graphs, photographs). Take advantage of young children's natural curiosity by providing expository books to match the interests expressed by the students. Use expository text in read-aloud sessions, and then make those books available to the students for independent reading.

While reading, use metacognitive strategies (think-alouds) to model appropriate use of expository text. As you read aloud, also *think aloud*. Talk to students about what a graphic might be telling

There are many ways a teacher can encourage reading.

TABLE 6-1

Differences Between Narrative and Expository Text

TEXT FACTOR	NARRATIVE	EXPOSITORY
Purpose	Tells a story.	Gives information.
Text pattern	Predictable story line Beginning, middle, and end	Variety of text patterns. Time order, compare/contrast, cause–effect, problem–solution
Use of illustrations/graphics	Use of illustrations to support storyline	Use of graphics, illustrations, photographs to deliver information
Vocabulary	Use of familiar vocabulary, with a few new terms, vocabulary words introduced	Introduction of new vocabulary, relevant to content
Purpose in social studies instruction	Provides context. Provides background information. Provides hook to interest students in topic.	Provides introduction to new vocabulary and concepts. Gives introduction to new themes. Explains concepts, answers questions.

Adapted from the work of Bamford & Kristo (2000).

them about the information in the book. Talk it out to yourself (out loud) and invite the children to model that metacognitive procedure.

Use multiple copies of appropriate expository books in reading groups. Small-group instruction provides a perfect opportunity to

model effective use of expository text. Reading groups can be organized by using student interest in a particular topic to be explored in the expository text.

Provide opportunities for students to participate in research projects. Model appropriate use of expository text in research, and then allow students to practice these skills. Provide ample and varied resources within the classroom through the use of the school and public libraries, accessing the campus budget, and participation in book clubs, which provide inexpensive or free books.

Use ABC books to provide a simple, easy-to-understand introduction to the effectiveness of expository text. There are excellent ABC books on just about any topic you might use with young children. Follow up the reading of ABC books by having students create their own. They can construct the template for the book at the beginning of a thematic unit, and fill in the "letter pages" as they gain information throughout the study.

GROUP ACTIVITY
USING EXPOSITORY TEXT

1. Before coming to class, select a standard from your state or district standards in social studies.
2. Select and bring to class a nonfiction book from the library or bookstore.
3. With a partner, develop two lesson plans using the nonfiction books you have brought with you to class.
4. Share with the rest of the class.
5. Be sure to take note of the books brought in by other members of the class. This will be a great start to your own bibliography of children's literature to use in social studies instruction.

With the wide variety of children's literature available to highlight various social studies topics in the early childhood classroom, it becomes important for the early childhood teacher to organize the instructional classroom library. One effective way is to create a system that will allow the teacher to access each appropriate book in the children's literature library. One example of such a spreadsheet is seen in Table 6-2.

TABLE 6-2
Example of Literature Spreadsheet

TITLE	AUTHOR	TOPIC NO. 1	TOPIC NO. 2
A, B, C's: The American Indian Way—paperb	Red Hawk, Richard	Native Americans	Alphabet
A, My Name is Alice (big book)	Bayer, Jane	Alphabet	Names
A, You're Adorable	Kaye, Buddy	Alphabet	Song
Aaugh! A Dog Ate My Book Report—paper	Schultz, Charles	Book Report	Excuses
ABC's of Crawlers and Flyers	Ryden, Hope	Alphabet	Bugs
Accidental Zucchini, The	Grover, Max	Alphabet	
Albert's Thanksgiving—paperback	Tyron, Leslie	Thanksgiving	
Alligator Arrived with Apples—hardback/signed	Dragonwagon, Crescent	Alphabet	
Alligator Arrived with Apples—paperback	Dragonwagon, Crescent	Alphabet	
Alpahbet Parade, The	Chwast, Seymour	Alphabet	Wordless book
Alphabet from Z to A	Viorst, Judith	Alphabet	
Alphabet Tree	Lionni, Leo	Alphabet	
Alphabet Tree, The paperback	Lionni, Leo	Alphabet	Trees
Amadeus Mozart	Lepscky, Ibi	Mozart	Biography
Amanda Bean's Amazing Dream	Burns, Marilyn	Marh	
Amos: The Story of an Old Dog and His Couch	Seligson, Susan	Dogs	
And Then What Happened Paul Revere?	Fritz, Jean	Revolution	Biography
Animalia	Base, Graeme	Alphabet	
Animals Born Alive and Well—signed	Heller, Ruth	Mammals	Science
Animals, Animals—signed	Carle, Eric	Animals	Poetry
Annie and the Wild Animals	Brett, Jan	Snow	Animals
Apple Picking Time—paperback	Poploff, Michelle	Apples	Fall
Arrow to the Sun: A Pueblo Indian Tale	Isadora, Rachel	Native Americans	Legends
Aunt Nancy and Old Man Trouble	Root, Phyllis	Trickser Tale	

If you are not ready to begin an extensive library of your own, a spreadsheet based on books checked out from the school library or public library can be developed. An additional column can be added to remind the teacher of the location of the selected books Teachers can code the list for easy reference when the unit is taught in subsequent years.

Each teacher will develop a strategy to organize his or her individual children's literature list. Some choose to use a three-ring binder, or to have the children write annotated bibliographies for each selection, or to organize the list according to the unit in which the book was introduced. Whatever your ultimate format or style, be sure to make note of what you used the book to teach and where you found the book! You'll be glad you did when you teach that unit again in subsequent years.

READING ALOUD

One of the most effective things that parents and teachers can do to help children become readers is to read aloud to them (Trelease, 2001). Read-aloud time is an enjoyable part of the school day for children, and offers an excellent opportunity for the introduction of concepts and characters in the social studies curriculum. While teachers of very young children spend a great deal of time reading aloud, as students grow older and move into the upper grades, read-aloud time diminishes. It is important and very effective to read aloud with older students as well (Forte, 1995; Miller, 1998; Sanacore, 1992). Making time for multiple read-aloud sessions throughout the school day is an important part of curriculum building in the early childhood classroom.

The Interactive Read-Aloud

The **interactive read-aloud** is quite different from the traditional teacher-directed read-aloud (see Table 6-3). The most important difference is the practice of encouraging children to interrupt and participate during the reading. Instead of the teacher reading through the text uninterrupted, students are encouraged to ask questions and to make connections to their own lives and experiences.

For many teachers, the interactive read-aloud is somewhat uncomfortable at first. Knowing how to guide students through the interactive read-aloud and keeping a focus on the learning at hand while encouraging participation demands a delicate balance. Thinking about possible situations during the read-aloud sessions ahead of time can help the teacher to respond appropriately when working with children. The Group Activity below gives real-life examples of situations that can occur during an interactive read-aloud.

Letting children see that reading is important to the people who are important to them is an important way to encourage them to become active readers. Make it a practice to invite people important to the lives of your students to read in the classroom. The guest may

TABLE 6-3
Read Aloud

TRADITIONAL READ ALOUD	INTERACTIVE READ ALOUD
Teacher reads/children listen.	Teacher reads/children respond and Question.
Teacher shows pictures at end of page.	Teacher holds book to show pictures throughout reading.
Children in desks	Children on floor/chairs around teacher
Read book once.	Multiple rereadings
Read straight through.	Practice metacognitive strategies.
Read in isolation.	Read as a part of a thematic unit.

GROUP ACTIVITY

WHAT DO YOU DO WHEN...

Divide into pairs. Discuss the following situations that may occur during a read-aloud session with young children. How would you handle these situations, keeping in mind the value of the *interactive* read-aloud?

1. A child calls out, "I've already read this book!" Several others then respond that they, too, have read the book.
2. Children call out details that they notice about the illustrations.
3. Children begin to mumble a repetitive phrase as the teacher reads the book.
4. A child interrupts the teacher's reading to relate a personal experience.
5. A child talks about a character from the book.
6. A child interrupts the teacher's reading to connect a scene in the book being read to a book she has read before.
7. A child interrupts the teacher's reading to point out a rhyming pattern in the book.
8. A child interrupts the teacher's reading to make a prediction about the ending of the book.
9. Two children begin to talk about the book with one another.
10. Children call out "Read it again!" when the teacher finishes reading the book.

have favorite books that he or she would like to share, or you can offer suggestions of specific titles that would contribute to the overall development of the themes that students are working with at the time.

Reading aloud is one of the most important things teachers can do to help students develop complex social studies concepts.

INVITING A GUEST READER

Invite your principal in to be a guest reader. Meet with him or her before the session, to discuss the objectives you will be addressing on the day of the visit. Offer a variety of books from which to choose, or the principal may have a favorite to share.

Encourage the children to participate in interactive read-alouds with the principal, asking questions, clarifying, making connections to other text and to real life. Through this guest reading, the principal will gain an understanding of the way that you are using children's literature to meet the standards in your classroom.

Reading centers invite children to read.

STRATEGIES TO USE WITH CHILDREN'S LITERATURE IN THE SOCIAL STUDIES

Children's literature is a powerful tool to use to engage students in social studies instruction (Button, 1998). A variety of techniques and strategies are available to deepen the literature experience for children. Several are discussed below.

Story Maps

The use of story maps is a great introduction to mapping skills with young children. As with most activities we do with young children, there are multiple purposes and outcomes of this activity. In story mapping, not only are children getting a relevant introduction to cartography, but we are also giving them strategies for increasing comprehension of a story, of understanding story elements (particularly setting), of using multiple modalities to learn and show what they have learned, and, frequently, to work cooperatively with other students. By having students share their maps with the teacher and other students, we are also encouraging oral language development and allowing students to speak in front of a group from an early age.

While some stories obviously lend themselves to this strategy more readily than others, most stories can be mapped. This strategy can be used with children as young as kindergarten age.

In a recent lesson, a second-grade teacher allowed different groups of students to read and map several versions of fairy tales, such as *Cinderella, Little Red Riding Hood,* and *Hansel and Gretel.* In small groups, students read (or reread, because in most cases, the teacher had read the stories aloud before giving the assignment) and mapped the stories. This is an easy and effective way for students to see, in a very graphic way, how the different versions of these fairy tales compare in terms of setting and specific characters, while maintaining the same overall story structure.

INTRODUCING STORY MAPPING TO YOUNG CHILDREN

1. Begin with a book with which the children are familiar. It could be one that you have read to them before or it could be one that represents a specific genre, such as *Little Red Riding Hood.*
2. Discuss and chart the different places that Little Red Riding Hood visited. For instance, she started at her own home, and then followed the forest path, passing several landmarks along the way, and ended up at grandma's house. She then escaped back into the forest and, in the version I'm reading, she ends back at home, in her kitchen.
3. Have students, either individually or in pairs or small groups, illustrate the locations listed.
4. Give each child or group a large piece of manila or chart paper.
5. Cut out and label each picture.
6. Glue, in an orderly configuration, the location pictures, onto the larger paper.

Students can broaden this experience by acting out the story, using the story map as a guide.

Many excellent books are available for use in introducing story mapping to young children. The best books for this purpose are those that have several location changes, making it easy for children to see the movement of the characters.

Some suggestions for children's literature to use in story mapping are:

Rosie's Walk by Pat Hutchins

Little Red Riding Hood by Tina Schart Hynman

If You Give a Moose a Muffin by Laura Numeroff

The Rainbow Fish by Marchs Pfister

A Visit to the Zoo by Aliki

Grandfather's Journey

Obtain a copy of Allen Say's beautifully illustrated book, *Grandfather's Journey*. This wonderful book tells the story of the author's grandfather, who travels to the United States from Japan, then returns to Japan to be with his family. He tells of the beauty of California and how he longed for Japan when he was in America, then longed for America when he returned to Japan. This is a wonderful book to use when studying immigration in the upper primary grades. It also lends itself to story mapping, allowing students to explore the various locations represented in the text. These kinds of stories offer opportunities for students to reflect on their own experiences.

Think-alouds

A think-aloud is just what it sounds like—the teacher models effective text reading by thinking out loud about the way she is processing the book. Through thinking aloud, the teacher models those thought processes that make an effective reader. For example, as the teacher approaches a vocabulary word, she can model the thought process of a good reader, as that reader comes to a new word. She might break the word into syllables, looking at the root or endings. She might model the use of a glossary or dictionary at this point, thumbing to the end of the book to access the glossary or setting the book aside and picking up the dictionary. This models what good readers do when they come to a word they do not know.

As she reads aloud, the teacher might relate the text to a book or film previously explored in the classroom. She might talk about how a particular piece of the text reminds her of something that has happened in her own life or a television show that she knows the children might be familiar with. Again, this strategy models for children what we as good, mature readers do to access information in a text.

SOME EXAMPLES OF A "THINK-ALOUD"

1. "I always try to make a picture in my mind when I read. I have a picture of a dolphin, jumping in the waves right now."
2. "I don't understand that paragraph. I'm going to reread it."
3. "This reminds me of the movie Finding Nemo. It particularly reminds me of the part of that movie when the pelican lands on the dentist's window."
4. "I was at the ocean just before school started this year. I saw many dolphins jumping as I rode the ferry out to the island."
5. "That word is unfamiliar to me. I know the root word, though. I think I'll look in the glossary. Oh yes, that's what I thought it might mean."
6. "This Venn Diagram will help me to see the differences and similarities between whales and dolphins."
7. "I didn't realize there were so many different kinds of whales! These photographs help me to see the differences."
8. "This is an expository text. It is nonfiction and gives factual information about sea life. I have read lots of storybooks about the ocean. Storybooks tell a story, while this kind of book gives information in a different way."
9. "I've read several books by this author. I like the way she writes and explains new information. I know that we have several of her books on our classroom library shelves."
10. "I love to learn about the ocean. I think that I'll use 'dolphins' as the topic for my research paper."

Sequencing

Sequencing is a cornerstone skill for developing historical concepts with young children. Sequencing requires students to put the events of a story or historical selection into the order in which they occur.

Using children's literature as a basis of this skill development is an interesting and tangible way to help young children understand the meaning of first, middle, last, and sequential ordering. Sequencing lessons provide perfect opportunities to teach the concept of chronology and can also be used to teach a series of events in a circular formation. Eric Carle's *Very Hungry Caterpillar* is a great book to use to help students practice skills of chronology. The wonderful series of books by Laura Numeroff, which includes *If You Give a Mouse a Cookie*, *If You Give a* Moose *a Muffin*, *If You Give a Pig a Pancake*, and so forth offer interesting storylines to illustrate events in circular formation.

Venn Diagrams

Venn Diagrams are excellent, visual ways for children to learn and reinforce their skills in comparing/contrasting. This simple tool lends itself to a wide range of uses. It can be used effectively with students as young as kindergarten and is very effective with older children as well. The Venn Diagram is made up of two or more overlapping circles. In mathematics, it is used to show relationships between sets. In language arts and social studies, the Venn Diagram is useful in examining similarities and differences in characters, stories, poems, events, and so forth. The Venn Diagram can be used as a prewriting activity to help students organize thoughts or as an assessment tool to help evaluate student understanding of the topics presented.

A SAMPLE INTRODUCTORY LESSON WITH VENN DIAGRAMS

1. Read *Town Mouse Country Mouse* by Jan Brett with the students.
2. Using two hula hoops, make a Venn Diagram on the floor and have students sit in a circle around the diagram.
3. Use tagboard to label student answers as you lead a brainstorming session about the characteristics of the city mouse and the country mouse.
4. Place the tagboard labels of characteristics on the appropriate side of the Venn Diagram.
5. Place the tagboard labels of characteristics that apply to both the city and country mice into the intersection of the Venn Diagram.

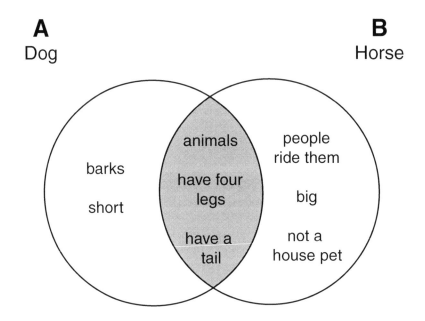

FIGURE 6-1. Venn Diagram.

When using the Venn Diagram, the teacher needs to lead the discussion by asking the following questions:

1. What do you want to compare?
2. What characteristics do the items (people, events, ideas) have in common?
3. How are the items different?

The Venn Diagram can be used with the youngest of our students. Many teachers use hula hoops as effective tools in introductory lessons using the Venn Diagram. Simply overlap the hula hoops and place them on the floor, with students making a circle around the hula hoops. Write the names of the items to be compared on tagboard, and for very young children, illustrate the labels (e.g., Dog and Horse in Fig. 6-1). Then ask students to call out characteristics of the two items to be compared, and write those on tagboard, placing the labels in the correct portion of the Venn Diagram.

Through this demonstration, young children are able to see, first hand, the process for developing a Venn Diagram. It is always effective to have several whole-group demonstrations of a strategy before having students complete an activity independently.

KWL Chart (Know—Wonder—Learn Charts)

KWL charts are graphic organizers that help students organize what they know and what they want to learn about a topic in social studies before and after the unit research is done. The KWL chart can be used before, during, and after a new unit in social studies. This excellent large-group activity allows you, as the teacher, to access prior knowledge that students have about a topic. The "K" column, which allows students to tell what they already know about the topic at hand, will help you to plan instruction at the appropriate level of difficulty for the students in your class. The "W" or "wonder" column allows students to request specific information that they have about a specific topic. Again, this allows the teacher to plan appropriately and target specific interest levels of the students in the classroom. The "L" or "learned" column of the chart offers an excellent opportunity for whole-group assessment of learning at the end of the unit. This is generally done as a whole group, but can also be done individually, if you would like more specific assessment on learning objectives from individual children.

This graphic organizer has been used a great deal in early childhood classrooms in recent years. Many teachers begin and end each unit in social studies with this technique, then laminate each KWL chart and add a page to a student-made big book. This big book is then placed in the reading center. Students tend to go back to those books on a regular basis and enjoy reviewing what has been learned in their social studies instruction throughout the year. This also serves as an excellent artifact for parents and administrators to review when visiting the classroom.

A Variation of the KWL Chart—KWHL Chart

K stands for what you already KNOW about a topic.

W stands for what you WONDER about that topic.

H stands for HOW you will learn more about the topic.

L stands for what you LEARNED during the unit of study.

This version, of course, works exactly as the KWL chart, with the added benefit of having children identify different ways that they might explore the topic.

Biography Organizer

Whether your students are studying history, geography, economics, or any of the other fascinating disciplines in the social studies, the study of the important people involved in the events of those disciplines may be the most interesting aspects of the study. A biography organizer can be used to help students identify important aspects of the person's life.

This can be done in a variety of ways. Modeling this technique by drawing a series of simple rectangles on a large piece of chart paper is effective. Students can help outline the important aspects of a person's life, including birth date, birth place, family background, childhood adventures, education, adult life (marriage, children, etc.), major accomplishments, and how those accomplishments impacted the area of study, then their death date and place. When possible, find a photo of the person being studied and add the photo to the chart paper.

Laminate each page and make a big book for the reading center. Students will spend hours reading and rereading these self-made books, reinforcing the factual information they gain about people important in the social studies. This activity also reinforces the importance of biographical and factual information.

Timelines

Timelines are used to represent data in chronological or sequential order. For example, give students an assignment, early in the school year, to create a timeline of their own lives. Children can interview parents and other family members, and then create a timeline, filling in the pertinent information for a simple timeline.

Create the base of a timeline all around the classroom. The time markers depend on the grade level being taught. When working with very young children, you may begin by marking the months of the year. When working with older students, begin with the earliest era to be studied in the grade-level social studies curriculum.

As social studies lesson take children into different periods in time, students can help place those events in the corresponding spot on the timeline by placing labels or drawings under the appropriate time markers. This technique offers an excellent visual aid for students by helping them begin to think of historical events in terms of sequence and chronology. This is another ongoing graphic organizer that helps to build an understanding of complex historical concepts with young children.

Fact/Opinion Graphic Organizer

The important skill of discriminating between fact and opinion is one that takes a great deal of practice and instruction with young children. Facts are statements that can be proven to be true. **Facts** can be looked up in the encyclopedia, or seen for ourselves. **Opinions** express how people feel about something. They do not have to be based on truth or even logic.

When working with students in developing an understanding of historical events, of theories in economics, or biographies of famous people, we can help them to develop an understanding of "fact" and "opinion" by modeling ways that we make that determination. This is a very useful tool in helping students develop critical thinking skills.

Cause–Effect Diagrams

These diagrams are very valuable tools for developing critical thinking skills with young children. They are particularly useful when working in the social studies, as most of what we study lends itself to looking at causes and effects. These diagrams describe how events affect one another in a process. Use of this diagram requires that students are able to identify and analyze the cause and effect of an event or process. As they examine the event, they come to realize and identify how one step affects the other.

This can (and should) be done at a very rudimentary level at first, allowing students to observe simple events in the classroom, and then identify the causes and effects in that action. These can be charted and referred to as studies become more complex. Students need to practice this skill over and over to truly understand that there is a cause-and-effect sequence to every event.

T-Chart

Another excellent graphic organizer to use with young children is the T-chart. This simple chart helps students to examine two facets of a topic or decision. For instance, students could list the pros and cons of getting a classroom pet. It can also be used when introducing a new unit of study, getting students' inputs on what they know and what they feel about a particular topic. One example of the T-chart was used in a fourth-grade classroom, when introducing a year-long unit on people with disabilities. In this unit of study, the teacher was working with a group of fourth graders who would be mentors to a small group of early childhood special education students. These fourth graders had never worked with people with disabilities, and in most cases had never met a person with a disability. This T-chart helped the students to voice their concerns about the project that they would be embarking upon.

T-CHART: WHAT I KNOW AND FEEL ABOUT PEOPLE WITH DISABILITIES

Some look different.	How I Feel About People With Disabilities
Some have learning problems.	Sorry
They are brats.	Sad
It can be caused by injury, prenatal problems, or genetics.	I feel like helping them learn to read
	Really bad and melancholy
Some can't walk.	Scared
They need lots of help.	Angry
Some people make fun of them.	Happy that they are not in our class

USING CHILDREN'S LITERATURE TO ADDRESS ISSUES OF DIVERSITY AND ACCEPTANCE

Anthropologists refer to **cultural universals,** which are domains of human experience that have existed in all cultures, past and present—food, clothing, shelter, family, transportation, communication, occupations, and recreation (Brown, 1991). While not all of these have the same form or meaning in each culture, they do exist in all cultures. Looking at these universals with young children creates an effective framework for building appreciation for all cultures.

Using children's literature is an essential way to help young children learn about the world outside their own experience. Picture books can be used as focal points of social studies lessons and units. Siu-Runyan (1996) suggests that the use of children's literature about moral issues is an effective way to promote children's moral development. Giving young children opportunities to examine the differences and similarities among groups of people and individuals is a good first step in helping them develop positive attitudes and acceptance of others.

The growing need to educate children about different races, abilities, and genders has led teachers to seek out literature that addresses the diverse world in which young students are living and growing (Boutte, 1999; Derman-Sparks and the ABC Task Force, 1989; Mosley, 1997; Siu-Runyan, 1996). By focusing on common bonds of all children, while honoring their differences, early childhood teachers can choose appropriate books that will help students develop a pride in themselves, while learning to understand and appreciate those who differ from them.

Excellent illustrations are an extension of the written text and are particularly important when portraying culture in picture books for young children. Illustrations are very important when selecting books that present multicultural images. The artist's style conveys messages that guide young children's understanding of multicultural information.

Using Children's Literature to Support Gender Equity in Early Childhood Classrooms

"Children's understanding of themselves as male or female and what that means in their particular environment is influenced by biological, social and cognitive factors" (Couchenour & Chrisman, 2004, p. 31). Consideration of gender roles is an important element in the early childhood classroom. "For girls and boys to have equal access to the benefits and responsibilities of citizenship, they must have the opportunity to learn in educational environments that support learning in all academic areas and that foster the development of those skills that are necessary for adult employment and family life" (Marshall, Robeson, & Keefe, 1999, p. 9).

Research has examined the depiction of gender stereotypes and their influence on the development of gender identity in young children (Fox, 1993). "Children's literature has been cited for promoting gender inequity by depicting males as strong and assertive and females as passive and nurturing" (Charlesworth, 2004, p. 453). Picture books provide role models for children and nonsexist books can produce positive changes in self-concept, attitudes, and behavior (Evans, 1998; Narahara, 1998; Roberts & Hill, 2003). Examining literature used in the classroom for sex-role stereotypes, and balancing images of males and females in traditional and nontraditional roles in that literature, is one effective way to encourage gender equity in the early childhood classroom (Trepanier-Street & Romatowski, 1999; Wellhousen, 1996).

USING CHILDREN'S LITERATURE TO SUPPORT MULTICULTURAL UNDERSTANDING IN THE EARLY CHILDHOOD CLASSROOM

The United States is a culturally diverse society, and is becoming more so every day. Children are influenced by the images they encounter at an early age. The growing role of children's literature in education is evidenced by the number of books published each year. In 1940, 984 books for children were published in the United States. In 1997, there were 5,353 (Huck, Hepler, Hickman, & Kiefer, 2001).

Sims Bishop (1997) describes multicultural children's literature as both a "mirror and a window." Good multicultural literature can benefit children in early childhood classrooms by helping them to build understanding and empathy. Books that accurately portray the cultural backgrounds of the children represented in the classroom help to extend children's awareness of the significant groups in their community and the wider world (Derman-Sparks and the ABC Task Force, 1989, p. 12).

When gathering a classroom library of multicultural literature for young children, it is important to assemble many books concerning each ethnic group. It is incorrect to think that a single book could adequately portray the overall experience of an entire group of people. Within every cultural group, a huge range of attributes and experiences is evident. It is important to make a wide variety of books available, depicting the range of human experience within each group. Learning to recognize and share good multicultural literature with children is "a process, as is learning about people different from oneself" (Mendoza & Reese, 2001, p. 15).

When selecting appropriate books for multicultural study, teachers may choose to employ a technique known as *reading against the grain*. Reading against the grain is "a way to examine the unexamined, question the unquestioned, and hold up to scrutiny the unspoken assertions the text is making about the way lives are lived in society" (Temple, Martinez, Yokota, & Naylor, 1998, p. 43). By examining the literature and asking questions such as the following, teachers can select books that depict a variety of attributes of the

SOME CHILDREN'S LITERATURE SELECTIONS MULTICULTURAL UNDERSTANDING

Abuelita's Heart by Amy Cordova
Tomas and the Library Lady by Pat Mora
My Father's Boat by Sherry Garland
Father's Rubber Shoes by Yumi Heo
Two Mrs.Gibsons by Toyomi Ignus

Dumpling Soup by Jama Kim Rattigan
Umbrellas by Taro Yashima
So Far From the Sea by Eve Bunting
Sachiko Means Happiness by Kimiko Sakai

groups represented: (1) Are the characters stereotypical? (2) Who has the power in the story? Who has the wisdom? (3) Who has written and illustrated the story? (4) What do the words and pictures say about race, gender, age? (Mendoza & Reese, 2001). There are no perfect books. It is up to the early childhood professional to examine and present the salient points represented in each book.

Developing a Multicultural Classroom Library for Young Children

When choosing literature to share with children, as read-alouds and as a part of the library center, it is important to keep in mind several important guidelines:

1. Choose books that represent various ethnic groups, religious groups, both genders, different socioeconomic levels, individuals with disabilities, different age groups, various lifestyles, and differing family structures within the larger cultural groups represented.

2. Choose books that describe holidays from many different cultural traditions.

3. Provide fairy tales from different cultures.

4. Provide books that depict males and females in traditional and nontraditional roles.

5. Choose books that show people from different cultures working together.

6. Choose books that reflect diversity.

7. Choose books that do not promote stereotypes (Boutte, 1999).

Using Children's Literature to Support Understanding of Disabilities in the Early Childhood Classroom.

Children's literature is an effective tool for teaching young children about disabilities and illness (Blaska, 1996). While the numbers of accurate and appropriate books on these topics are increasing, it is important to preread the books carefully to make sure that the message given in the book is the one you want to pass along to the students. When choosing books to support the understanding of disabilities in an early childhood classroom, the teacher should choose books that:

- Promote understanding, not pity
- Promote positive images of people with disabilities.
- Give accurate information about people with disabilities and the disabilities themselves
- Address the abilities as well as the disabilities of the characters
- Demonstrate respect and acceptance of people with disabilities.
- Emphasize the person first, the disability second
- Give accurate images of adaptive equipment.

(Based on the work of Blaska, 1996; Blaska & Lynch, 1998; National Dissemination Center for Children with Disabilities, 2001)

SOME SUGGESTIONS FOR LITERATURE TO SUPPORT UNDERSTANDING OF DISABILITIES

Someone Special, Just Like You by Tricia Brown

Rolling Along: The Story of Taylor and His Wheelchair by Jamee Riggio Heelan

Elana's Ears, or How I Became the Best Big Sister in the World by Lowell & Brooks.

A Very Special Critter by Mercer Mayer

Views From Our Shoes: Growing Up With a Brother or Sister With Special Needs by Donald Meyer.

What's Wrong With Timmy? By Maria Shriver

We'll Paint the Octopus Red by Stephanie Stuve-Bodeen

Don't Call Me Special: A First Look at Disability by Pat Thomas

Andy and His Yellow Frisbee by Mary Thompson

My Brother, Matthew by Mary Thompson

Susan Laughs by Jeanne Willis

Using Children's Literature to Support Intergenerational Understanding

"It's important for children to learn to appreciate the diverse contributions to society made by older people just as they learn to value diversity in race, religion, and gender. Positive attitudes are not learned quickly; they develop over time, and attitudes that children adopt early in life affect behavior throughout their lifetime" (Jame & Kormanski, 1999, p. 32). Most families these days are nuclear and many children do not get an opportunity to spend time with their grandparents. Intergenerational books can help young children to value the contributions of the elderly and can serve to eliminate stereotypic thinking about older people (Seefeldt & Warman, 1990).

It is important to provide a variety of books representing intergenerational relationships (Yahres & Kormanski, 1999). Young children need to be exposed to the individuality of the elderly through books that illustrate the differences among older people, as well as the attributes they share. Young children need to see that aging is a natural and lifelong process (McGuire, 1993). Older people should be

SOME SUGGESTIONS FOR INTERGENERATIONAL BOOKS

Oma's Quilt by Paulette Bourgeois

Sweet Dried Apples: A Vietnamese Wartime Childhood by Rosemary Breckler

The Wednesday Surprise by Eve Bunting

Bigmamma's by Donald Crews

Nana Upstairs & Nana Downstairs by Tomie dePaola

Now One Foot, Now the Other by Tomie dePaola

Abuela by A. Dorros

The Old, Old Man and the Very Little Boy by Kristine Franklin

Family Pictures/Cuadros de familia by Carmen Garza

My Family/En mi familia by Carmen Garza

Goodbye Curtis by Kevin Henkes

Amazing Grace by Mary Hoffman

When I am Old With You by Angela Johnson

Beginnings and Endings With Lifetimes in Between by Bryan Mellonie

A Birthday Basket for Tia by Pat Mora

Always Gramma by Vaunda Nelson.

Betty Doll by Patricia Polacco

The Keeping Quilt by Patricia Polacco

Chicken Sunday by Patricia Polacco

The Relatives Came by Cynthia Rylant

The Grannyman by Judith Schachner

Mei-Mei Loves the Morning by Margaret Tsubakiyama

Our Granny by Margaret Wild

I Know a Lady by Charlotte Zolotow

represented as capable, productive individuals and intergenerational books should show positive relationships between children and elders.

Topics such as illness, the need for assistance as people age, and death should be portrayed with respect and honesty. Children's literature that presents elderly people in a variety of relationships, settings, life situations, and roles can help children to develop understanding and sensitivity toward the elderly and toward the natural aging process.

Using Children's Literature to Support Understanding of Gay and Lesbian Parents

Like families headed by heterosexual parents, lesbian and gay parents and their children are a diverse group When young children ask questions about gay and lesbian families, we can give age-appropriate answers. Particularly when there are students in the classroom who have gay or lesbian parents, it is important to help classmates learn about different kinds of families. Using children's literature is an effective and appropriate way to begin the conversation.

SOME SUGGESTIONS FOR LITERATURE TO SUPPORT UNDERSTANDING OF GAY AND LESBIAN PARENTS

How My Family Came to Be: Daddy, Papa and Me by Andrew Aldrich

ABC A Family Alphabet Book by Bobbie Combs

123 A Family Counting Book by Bobbie Combs

Emma and Meesha My Boy: A Two Mom Story by Kaitlyn Considine

Molly's Family by Nancy Garden

All Families Are Different by Sol Gordon

Heather Has Two Mommies by Leslea Newman

Felicia's Favorite Story by Leslea Newman

The Family Book by Todd Parr

Who's in a Family by Robert Skutch

Daddy's Roommate by Michael Willhoite

CONNECTING TO DIVERSE POPULATIONS: MULTICULTURAL PICTURE BOOKS

Children deserve to see positive images of children like themselves in the books they read. Children's books have a significant place in early childhood classrooms. All genres offer children vast opportunities to enhance a child's self-esteem, to gain information about other cultures, and to experience perspectives other than their own. Children's books that depict a variety of ethnic, racial, and cultural groups allow children to gain an understanding of others, while affirming their own cultural identity. There are increasing numbers of excellent children's books on the market that encourage children to reach beyond their immediate life experience and consider the lives of others.

FINDING THE RIGHT BOOKS

Many excellent children's books currently on the market have relevance to the social studies curriculum. Finding the right book for the right lesson can be difficult, however. Several strategies and materials can be employed by the early childhood teacher to sift through the many titles available. One effective way to discover good books and ideas is to read the publisher's catalogs and reviews of children's books in professional journals.

In journals such as *Young Children*, the journal of the National Association for the Education of Young Children, *Childhood Education*, the journal of the Association for Childhood Education International, and *Social Studies for Young Learners*, a publication of the National Council for the Social Studies, relevant titles are listed and discussed. In these journals, there are an abundance of articles on ways to use children's books in the social studies classroom. These are excellent resources for information about new publications, as well as the application of older children's books.

Reference books such as *The Best Books for Children: Preschool – Grade 6* (7th ed.) by John Gillespie or *Great Books About Things Kids Love: More than 750 Recommended Books for Children 3–14* by Kathleen Odean are excellent sources of detailed information about specific titles relating to units of study presented in the early childhood classroom. School librarians have other printed resources to help guide selection of read-alouds for the early childhood classroom.

The National Council for the Social Studies publishes a list each year, in cooperation with the Children's Book Council, entitled "Notable Trade Books for Young Children." This annotated book list represents books that are evaluated and selected by a book review committee appointed by the NCSS. In Notable Trade Books for Young Children, the titles are arranged by broad subject categories and subthemes and indicate the related thematic strand from Expectation of Excellence: Curriculum Standards for Social Studies. Archived lists are available on the NCSS Web site, at www.socialstudies.org. Follow the links to publications, then to the Notable Books List.

Other helpful tools for finding appropriate books for social studies themes are the reviews of children's books from the online bookstores. The teacher can simply type in the topic to be studied, and a multitude of titles then come up on the screen. A positive feature of this resource is the list of related books that are listed on the review page.

Alongside these printed resources, the early childhood teacher's best source of information about good books is a knowledgeable, enthusiastic, and helpful school librarian. School librarians love books and are happy to share their knowledge and enthusiasm with the classroom teacher. Many times, librarians are pleased to include titles requested by the classroom teacher as they prepare the budgets and orders for the school library. Make friends with this powerful resource.

SUMMARY

Using children's literature to facilitate social studies instruction is an interesting and effective strategy. Each year, teachers are responsible for more and more curriculum content in the early childhood classroom. There is simply not time in the day to add yet another thing. Incorporating children's literature into the social studies curriculum and using social studies concepts and topics as a basis for the reading program can significantly increase the amount of time available in the early childhood classroom, for both reading and social studies instruction.

By helping students construct meaning from the text, to activate their prior knowledge, and to focus on the big ideas in a reading selection, teachers set the stage for more in-depth conceptual development. Children's literature offers interesting and varied ways to introduce new information and to reinforce previously explored information.

Literature also offers a way to meet the needs and interests of students who are just being introduced to a concept, while extending and deepening the understanding of the concept for those students who have more experience with a particular topic. This is one effective strategy to use in "leveling the playing field" for students being introduced to a social studies concept.

By reading both narrative and expository text with young students, teachers are able to activate students' prior knowledge on a subject, while providing much-needed background information for those with no prior knowledge on a particular topic. Use of children's literature also offers an excellent opportunity for teachers to model reading and thinking strategies, through think-alouds and through the use of graphic organizers based on specific pieces of children's literature.

As teachers consider ways to maximize the instructional "bang for the buck," the use of children's literature is undoubtedly a most effective tool.

A large number of high-quality children's books, on a variety of appropriate topics, are readily available and affordable. By working with the school librarian and school administration, teachers can provide a wide variety of literature selections, appropriate for young children and for extending the social studies curriculum.

▶ THEMATIC STRANDS AND FOCUS QUESTIONS

Culture

1. How can children's literature be used to expand children's understanding of different cultures?
2. How can children's literature be used to help young children develop an understanding of *perspective*?

Time, Continuity, and Change

1. How can the use of expository text encourage the development of a sense of time with young children?
2. What are some strategies to use with children's literature to help young children understand the concept of *change*?

People, Places, and Environments

1. How can the use of children's literature in the social studies curriculum help children to apply a geographic view to a current or historical event?
2. How can children's literature be used to help young children to develop an understanding of the people in history?

Individuals, Groups, and Institutions

1. How can the use of children's literature help young children to understand the differences and similarities among people with disabilities and themselves?
2. How can the use of children's literature help young children to understand the institutions represented in history and current day America?

Global Connections

1. How can the early childhood teacher choose effective multicultural literature for use in the early childhood classroom?
2. How can the early childhood teacher employ children's literature to expand children's ethnocentric thinking?

Librarians are a great resource for teachers.

KEY TERMS

cultural universals
expository text
fact
genre
informational text
interactive read-aloud
opinion
schema

REFERENCES

Allington, R. (2002). You can't learn from books you can't read. *Educational Leadership*, November, 16–19.

Bamford, R., & Kristo, J. (2000). *Checking out nonfiction K–8: Good choices for best learning*. Norwood, MA: Christopher-Gordon.

Blaska, J. (1996). *Using children's literature to learn about disabilities and illness*. Moorhead: MN: Practical Press.

Blaska, J., & Lynch, E. (1998). Is everyone included? Using children's literature to facilitate the understanding of disabilities. *Young Children, 53*(2), 36–38.

Boutte, G. (1999). *Multicultural education: Raising consciousness*. Atlanta, GA: Wadsworth.

Brown, D. (1991). *Human universals*. Philadelphia, PA: Temple University Press.

Button, K. (1998). Linking social studies and literacy development through children's books. *Social Studies and the Young Learner, 10*(4), 23–25.

Charlesworth, R. (2004). *Understanding child development* (6th ed.). Clifton Park, NY: Thomson Delmar Learning.

Couchenour, D., & Chrisman, K. (2004). *Families, schools, and communities: Together for young children* (2nd ed.). Clifton Park, NY: Thomson Delmar Learning.

Council on Interracial Books for Children. (1980). Guidelines for selecting bias-free textbooks and storybooks. New York: Author.

D'Arcangelo, M. (2002). The challenge of content-area reading: A conversation with Donna Ogle. *Educational Leadership*, November, 12–15.

Derman-Sparks, L., & the ABC Task Force (1989). *Anti-bias curriculum: Tools for empowering young children*. Washington, DC: National Association for the Education of Young Children.

Evans, K. (1998). Combating gender disparity in education: Guidelines for early childhood educators. *Early Childhood Education Journal 26*(2), 83–88.

Forte, F. (1995). Reading aloud to fourth grade students. ED379 640.

Fox, M. (1993). Men who weep, boys who dance: The gender agenda between the lines of children's literature. *Language Arts, 70*(2), 84–88.

Huck, C., Hepler, S., Hickman, J., & Kiefer, B. (2001). *Children's literature in the elementary school*. New York: McGraw-Hill.

Jame, J., & Kormanski, L. (1999). Positive intergenerational picture books for young children. *Young Children, 54*(3), 32–38.

Johnson, M., & Janisch, C. (1998). Connecting literacy with social studies content. *Social Studies and the Young Learner, 10*(4), 4–8.

Marshall, N., Robeson, W., & Keefe, N. (1999). Gender equity in early childhood education. *Young Children, 54*(4), 9–13.

McGuire, S. (1993). Promoting positive attitudes toward aging. *Childhood Education, 69*(4), 204–210.

Mendoza, J., & Reese, D. (2001). Examining multicultural picture books for the early childhood classroom: Possibilities and pitfalls. *Early Childhood Research and Practice, 3*(2), 1–32.

Miller, T. (1998). The place of picture books in middle-level classrooms. *Journal of Adolescent and Adult Literacy, 41*(5), 376–381.

Narahara, M. (1998). Gender stereotypes in children's picture books. ED419248 CS216343.

National Dissemination Center for Children with Disabilities (2001). *Children's literature and disability*. Washington, DC: author.

Odean, K. (2001). *Great books about things kids love: More than 750 recommended books for children 3–14*. Ballantine Books.

Roberts, L., & Hill, H. (2003). Come and listen to a story about a girl namec Rex: Using children's literature to debunk gender stereotypes. *Young Children, 58*(2)39–42.

Sanacore, J. (1992). Reading aloud: A neglected strategy for older students. ED 367971.

Seefeldt, C., & Warman, B., with Jant, R., & Galper, A. (1990). *Young and old together*. Washington, DC: NAEYC.

Sims Bishop, R. (1997). Selecting literature for a multicultural curriculum. In V. J. Harris (Ed.). *Using multiethnic literature in the K–8 classroom* (pp. 1–20). Norwood, MA: Christopher-Gordon.

Siu-Runyan, Y. (1996). Caring-courage, justice, and multicultural literature. *Journal for a Just and Caring Education, 2*(4), 420–429.

Temple, C., Martinez, M., Yokota, J., & Naylor, A. (1998). *Children's books in children's hands: An introduction to their literature*. Boston: Allyn & Bacon.

Tonjes, M. J., & Wolpow, R., & Zintz, M. (1999). *Integrated content literacy*. New York: McGraw-Hill.

Trelease, J. (2001). *The read-aloud handbook* (5th ed.). New York: Penguin Books.

Trepanier-Street, M., & Romatowski, J. (1999). The influence of children's literature on gender role perspectives. A reexamination. *Early Childhood Education Journal, 26*, 155–160.

Wellhousen, K. (1996). Girls can be bull riders, too! Supporting children's understanding of gender roles through children's literature. *Young Children, 51*(5), 79–83.

Yahres, J., & Kormanski, L. (1999). Positive intergenerational picture books for young children. *Young Children, 54*(3), 32–38.

▶ SUGGESTED READINGS

Aldrich, A. (2003). *How my family came to be: Daddy, papa and me*. New Family Press.

Aliki. (1999). *A visit to the zoo*. New York: HarperTrophy.

Bamford, R., & Kristo, J. (2000). *Checking out nonfiction K–8: Good choices for best learning*. Norwood, MA: Christopher-Gordon.

Bourgeois, P. (2001). *Oma's quilt*. Tonawanda, NY: Kids Can Press.

Breckler, R. (1996). *Sweet dried apples: A Vietnamese wartime childhood*. Boston: Houghton Mifflin.

Brett, J. (2003). *Town mouse country mouse*. New York: Putnam.

Brown, T. (1995). *Someone special, just like you*. New York: Henry Holt & Company.

Button, K. (1998). Linking social studies and literacy development through children's books. *Social Studies and the Young Learner, 10*(4), 23–25.

Combs, B. (2001a). *ABC A family alphabet book*. Ridley Park, PA: Two Lives Publishers.

Combs, B. (2001b). *123 A family counting book*. Ridley Park, PA: Two Lives Publishers.

Considine, K. (2004). *Emma and Meesha my boy: A two mom story*. Philadelphia: Xlibris.

DePaola, T. (1981). *Now one foot, now the other*. New York: Trumpet.

DePaola, T. (2000). *Nana upstairs and nana downstairs*. London: Puffin.

Dorros, A. (1991). *Abuela.* New York: Trumpet.

Franklin, K. (1992). *The old, old man and the very little boy.* New York: Antheneum.

Garden, N. (2004). *Molly's family.* Farrar, Straus and Giroux.

Garza, C. (1993). *Family pictures/cuadros de familia.* San Francisco: Children's Book Press.

Garza, C. (2000). *In my family/en mi familia.* San Francisco: Children's Book Press.

Gordon, S. (2000). *All families are different.* Amherst, NY: Prometheus Books.

Heelan, J. (2000). *Rolling along: The story of Taylor and his wheelchair.* Atlanta: Peachtree Publications.

Henkes, K. (1995). *Good-bye curtis.* New York: Greenwillow.

Hoffman, M. (1991). *Amazing grace.* New York: Dial.

Hutchins, P. (1971). *Rosie's walk.* New York: Aladdin.

Hynman, T. (1982). *Little red riding hood.* New York: Hyman House.

Johnson, A. (1993). *When I am old with you.* London: Orchard Books.

Johnson, M., & Janisch, C. (1998). Connecting literacy with social studies content. *Social Studies and the Young Learner, 10*(4), 4–8.

Kupetz, B. (1993). Bridging the gap between young and old. *Children Today, 22*(2), 10–13.

Lowell, G., & Brooks, K. (2000). *Elana's ears, or how I became the best big sister in the world.* Washington, DC: Magination Press.

Maaka, M., & Lipka, A. (1997). I used to think reading sucked! Promoting positive literacy habits and attitudes in the elementary classroom. Paper presented at the Annual Meeting of the American Educational Research Association (Chicago, IL: March 24–28, 1997).

Mayer, M. (1993). *A very special critter.* New York: Golden Books.

Mellonie, B. (1983). *Beginnings and endings with lifetimes in between.* London: Paper Tiger.

Meyer, D. (1997). *Views from our shoes: Growing up with a brother or sister with special needs.* Bethesda, MD: Woodbine House.

Moen, C. (2004). Ten to-do's for successful read-alouds. *Book Links, 13*(4), 10–13.

Mora, P. (1997). *A birthday basket for Tia.* New York: Aladdin.

Mosely, J. (1997). Multicultural diversity of children's picture books: Robert Fulton elementary school library. Master's research paper, Kent State University. ED413926 IR056758.

Nelson, V. (1988). *Always gramma.* New York: G.P. Putnam's Sons.

Newman, L. (2000). *Heather has two mommies,* 10th anniversary edition. Los Angeles: Alyson Publications.

Newman, L. (2002). *Felicia's favorite story.* Ridley Park, PA: Two Lives Publishing.

Numeoff, L. (1985). *If you give a mouse a cookie.* New York: Geringer.

Numeroff, L. (1991). *If you give a moose a muffin.* New York: Geringer.

Owocki, G. (1999). *Literacy through play.* Portsmouth, NH: Heinemann.

Parr, T. (2003). *The family book.* Boston: Megan Tingley.

Pfister, M. (1992). *Rainbow fish.* New York: Nord Sud Verlag.

Polacco, P. (1992). *Chicken Sunday*. New York: Scholastic.

Polacco, P. (1998). *The keeping quilt*. New York: Simon & Schuster.

Polacco, P. (2001). *Betty doll*. New York: Philomel.

Rudman, M. (1995). *Children's literature: An issues approach*. White Plains, NY: Longman.

Rylant, C. (1993). *The relatives came*. New York: Aladdin.

Say, A. (1993). *Grandfather's journey*. Boston: Houghton Mifflin.

Schachner, J. (1999). *The grannyman*. New York: Dutton.

Shriver, M. (2001). *What's wrong with Timmy?* Boston: Little, Brown.

Skutch, R. (1997). *Who's in a family?* Berkeley, CA: Tricycle Press.

Spitz, E. (1999). *Inside picture books*. New Haven: Yale University Press.

Stuve-Bodeen, S. (1998). *We'll paint the octopus red*. Bethesda, MD: Woodbine House.

Thomas, P. (2002). *Don't call me special: A first look at disability*. Barron's Educational Series.

Thompson, M. (1992). *My brother, Matthew*. Bethesda, MD: Woodbine House

Thompson, M. (1996). *Andy and his yellow Frisbee*. Bethesda, MD: Woodbine House.

Trelease, J. (1989). *The new read-aloud handbook*. New York: Penguin Books.

Tsubakiyama, M., & Van Wright, C. (1999). *Mei-Mei loves the morning*. Morton Grove, IL: Albert Whitman.

Wheeler, R. (1996). *Teaching the ten themes of social studies*. New York: McGraw-Hill.

Whitin, D. J., & Wilde, S. (1995). *It's the story that counts*. Portsmouth, NH: Heinemann.

Willhoite, M. (1991). *Daddy's roommate*. Los Angeles: Alyson Publications.

Willis, J. (2000). *Susan laughs*. New York: Henry Holt & Company.

Zolotow, C. (1972). *William's doll*. New York: HarperCollins.

Zolotow, C. (1984). *I know a lady*. London: Puffin.

CHAPTER 7
Geography and the Environment

OBJECTIVES

After reading this chapter, you should be able to:

➤ Define and describe the discipline of **geography**.

➤ Design a lesson based on one of the five themes of geography.

➤ Brainstorm ways in which geography can be incorporated into the "social studies—all day, every day" curriculum in early childhood classrooms.

➤ Develop a unit on cartography, based on the use of building blocks.

➤ Discuss the importance of **environmental education** in early childhood classrooms.

I may not have gone where I intended to go, but I think I have ended up where I intended to be.

Douglas Adams, *The Hitchhiker's Guide to the Galaxy*

Teaching geography in an early childhood setting.

INTRODUCTION

The study of geography can be fascinating! Geography can be easily integrated into the core subjects of language arts, mathematics, science, and fine arts, making it an interesting focus of any lesson. Jay Leno's "Jaywalking" segments, based on his travels around the streets of Los Angeles, highlight the appalling state of geographic knowledge in our country. These funny episodes highlight the need for a more effective geographic curriculum in the public schools.

Geography is the study of the location and spatial arrangements of the things on Earth. It is "the study of people, places, and the environments and the relationships among them" (National Geographic Joint Committee, 1994, p. 1). The study of geography helps students to understand the relationship between humans and our planet. Initial experiences in geography provide building blocks for geographic concepts that will be introduced later in a child's education.

From infancy, children explore and learn about their world (Bredekamp & Copple, 1997). Young children learn about major geographic concepts such as space, place, distance, time, and representations naturally, by using their senses. Their innate curiosity makes teaching geographic concepts a natural fit in the early childhood classroom.

The "expanding communities" model of social studies instruction encourages us to foster an understanding of geography by having children study themselves, their families, and then their neighborhoods and larger communities. In this model, students study what they know best, themselves, first. Then as they progress through the curriculum, they expand from their own lives to those of their families, school, neighborhood, state, nation, and then the larger world. Helping children see beyond themselves and empathize with other people can be accomplished in appropriate ways by making connections between the child and similar characteristics of people in other lands. Guiding children to compare and contrast their own lives with situations in different geographic regions helps them to connect familiar experiences to related situations in unfamiliar settings.

Environmental studies have an exciting and relevant place in the early childhood curriculum (Dighe, 1993; Fenton, 1996; Olds, 1989; Rivkin, 1995). Connecting the disciplines of geography and environmental studies gives the early childhood teacher a perfect opportunity to help young children connect to the greater world and to see themselves as integral to the global community.

GEOGRAPHY INSTRUCTION FOR YOUNG CHILDREN

For young children, it is important to introduce concepts of the different ways that land formations and climate affect people's lives. By studying people in different lands, students develop an interest in and appreciation for other cultures. Through appropriate study of geography, students also begin to understand how location, land formations, and climate affect the ways that people eat, dress, work, and live. By studying people in different geographic regions, young children learn that people all over the world have the same basic need for food, shelter, and clothing. Although these needs are consistent, the ways that the needs are met are dependent on the land and climate in which people dwell.

Geography takes us to places we've never been and exposes us to people and places we've never seen. Through geography, teachers are able to help children connect to the larger family of humankind. Geography helps children to understand the world in an organized way, by looking for relationships and patterns. The study of geography gives young students the foundation for the tools they will need to become responsible citizens.

Recent History of Geographic Instruction

As a result of the educational goals set forth by presidents George H. W. Bush and William Clinton in the 1980s and 1990s, educators established national standards for social studies, "Expectations of Excellence: Curriculum Standards for Social Studies" (National Council for the Social Studies. Expectations of Excellence: Curriculum Standards for Social Studies, 1994). Standards were also established for the different disciplines, including geography (Geography Education Standards Project, 1994).

Later in the 1990s, the standards were developed into content-specific learning objectives for geographic education through a grant from the National Geographic Society. The subsequent document, *Path Toward World Literacy,* divided the national standards for geography into six essential grade clusters, or Geography Education Standards:

1. The World in Spatial Terms
2. Places and Regions
3. Physical Systems
4. Human Systems
5. Environment and Society
6. The Uses of Geography

Developing Geographic Understanding

"First, geographic understanding must become a process of lifelong learning that forms a seamless connection between formal preschool through college education and into adult life. Second, geographic understanding must be set into life contexts of family, school, society, and occupation" (Freese, 1997). The early childhood educator Lucy Sprague Mitchell believed that geographic knowledge started "unofficially at birth" (Mitchell, 1934/1991, p. 21). This complex understanding must be first explored experientially, using concrete objects and a well-designed environment. Children must be given multiple opportunities to explore the space in their environment, and then be helped to make connections to the geographic information they are to learn.

The six Geography Education Standards describe the knowledge, skills, attitudes, values, and dispositions of a geographically informed person (National Council for Geographic Education [NCGE], 1994).

SIX GEOGRAPHY STANDARDS

Element 1: The World in Spatial Terms
Use of maps and other geographic representations to understand spatial perspectives.

Element 2: Places and Regions
The physical and human characteristics of place and how culture and experience influence perceptions of places and regions.

Element 3: Physical Systems
Physical processes that shape the Earth's surface and the ecosystems of the Earth.

Element 4: Human Systems
The characteristics, distribution, and migration of human populations and patterns of economic interdependence.

Element 5: Environment and Society
How human actions and physical systems affect the environment. The distribution and importance of resources.

Element 6: The Uses of Geography
How to apply geography to interpret the past and present and plan for the future. (NCGE, 1994)

Geography takes us to places we have never been and introduces us to people and cultures and landscapes we've never met. Geographic literacy can and should begin as soon as children enter school.

The Guidelines for Geographic Education (Natoli, 1989) identify five fundamental themes for geography: location, place, human–environment interactions, movement, and regions. Using these themes as a framework lays a foundation for the understanding of geography.

USING MAPS IN EARLY CHILDHOOD CLASSROOMS

Maps are the most important tool used by geographers. Maps define and describe space symbolically. Cartographers are the people who make maps. Children's literature, again, offes an excellent introduction to cartography (Hartman & Giorgis, 2003).

According to the National Geographic Joint Committee (1994), maps have five basic elements:

1. Perspective: looking at objects from various positions

FIVE GEOGRAPHY THEMES

Theme 1: Location
Description: The position of people, places, and objects on the Earth's surface

Concepts and Topics: Identifying one's absolute position, identifying one's relative position, using maps, building models, estimating distance

Theme 2: Place
Description: Unique human, cultural, and physical traits that distinguish a place

Concepts and Topics: Recognizing natural or physical characteristics such as land forms, water forms, vegetation, animal life, and climate of an area. Also includes identification of human characteristics including cultures, language, transportation, communication, and so forth

Theme 3: Relationships Within Places
Description: Relationships between people and their environment

Concepts and Topics: Locations where people live, animal habitats, use of environmental resources, environmental protection

Theme 4: Movement
Description: Movement of people. How they interact with each other in their new location

Concepts and Topics: Immigration, transportation, communication, movement of goods to market

Theme 5: Regions
Description: Change in humans and land areas

Concepts and Topics: Natural areas, human habitats, animal habitats, land use

(NCGE, 1996)

2. **Scale:** representation of the sizes of real objects in proportion to other objects on the map

3. Position and Orientation: relationships between objects. Position tells where and orientation tells the specific location of an object, using the cardinal points (north, south, east, west)

4. Symbols: Representations of the elements and objects depicted on a map.

5. Content and Purpose: The purpose of a map is defined by its content.

Even very young children enjoy using and drawing maps. Beginning with directional concepts, by reading such books as *Rosie's Walk* by Pat Hutchins, or by teaching the old standard,

DEVELOPING PERSPECTIVE

For young children, perspective is a very difficult concept (Liben & Downs, 1993). It is important to give them many opportunities to see objects from different perspectives before we try to teach the abstract concept. Many good geography teachers encourage children to stand on their desks, to lie on the floor, and to climb on top of the play apparatus on the playground to get a different perspective on the way things look. One excellent first-grade teacher introduces the concept of "birds-eye view" from the top of the jungle gym. *George Shrinks* by William Joyce is a great book to use for introducing the concept of perspective. In this tale, George wakes up one morning to find he is smaller than his toy soldiers. The illustrations give students an opportunity to think about what the world would look like from a different perspective.

"Going on a Bear Hunt," young children begin to develop important concepts of "over, under, around, through." These simple activities give the teacher an opportunity to introduce and reinforce concepts that will be used in an abstract way later in a child's mapmaking education.

In the Home Living or Drama center, have **orienteering** props, such as maps, binoculars, and compasses. By playing with these geographic tools from a very young age, students are able to gain an understanding of their use. As children grow cognitively, the perceptive early childhood teacher will be able to increase the complexity of their interaction with these tools.

Linking photographs of familiar places, such as the school, to mapmaking is an effective step between the concrete experiences suggested above and the abstract exercise of mapmaking on paper. Have photographs of community buildings, such as the post office, fire department, and grocery store available. This allows even the youngest child to begin to make connections between the two-dimensional model and the real thing.

Given the appropriate experiences and encouragement, even the youngest child can begin to develop a good sense of location and space. Movement, manipulatives, stories, songs, and active involvement can make geography a favorite area of study for all young students.

GROUP ACTIVITY
TAKE A WALK!

Divide into small groups of three or four. Take a clipboard, graph paper, and a pencil for each group and take a walk! The university campus is just full of wonderful places that many students never see. On one university campus, students found a beautiful courtyard outside of the Architecture building that none of them had seen before. Look for these hidden spots as you take your walk.

Make a map of the new area that you found. Using the concepts you will be teaching in geography, develop a map to help the rest of the class members find the new spot.

Mapmaking as Play

Even very young children are able to understand simple cartographic images (Trifonoff, 1998). Well-designed and developmentally appropriate activities foster the development of cartographic abilities. One of the most appropriate ways to introduce cartographic understandings and skills is through the use of blocks.

Block Play and Cartography

Piaget noted long ago that symbolic play moves through stages leading to increasing realism. Representation through blocks allows children to examine the world around them. Use of blocks to depict spatial arrangements engenders a greater awareness of a child's environment. In the primary grades, children can begin mapmaking with blocks. Beginning with their classroom, the playground, or their own rooms at home, children can construct maps representing the geography of that area.

Early elementary school-age children are in the concrete operational stage of thinking (Piaget, 1969). They understand the world by actively engaging with their world. Vygotsky's work underscores the importance of social interaction among children as they work together to solve problems. These theories on learning are a foundation for the

Block play is a first step in developing spatial awareness.

use of block play in early childhood and the continuation of that play through the early elementary years.

Children in the elementary school years are able to build schema when they have opportunities to represent their ideas and

DIALOGUE BETWEEN FIVE-YEAR-OLDS IN THE BLOCK CENTER

Sarah: Let's make a house.

Caleb: I know how to make a house with these blocks.

Sarah: My house is in the country. Let's make my house.

Caleb: Do you have a barn?

Sarah: Yes. We have two barns—one for the emus and one for the tractors.

Caleb: I love tractors. Let's make your house.

Sarah and Caleb work for a few minutes, putting a block perimeter around the area where the farmhouse will be built.

Caleb: There. Now, everything inside will be your farm.

Sarah: Our house is by the creek. How will we make the creek?

Caleb (Looks through building materials on the shelf): Let's use the blue Legos.

Sarah: That's a good idea. I'm going to make the big barn. You make the little barn.

Caleb continues to work on the creek. He then starts to make a structure in the far corner of the perimeter.

Sarah: That's too far from the house. The barn is close to the house. That way, we don't have to walk so far to feed the emus.

Caleb: Do you have any trees? I'm going to use these little blocks for trees. What do you think we can use for the tractors?

Sarah: There are some little tractors on the shelf, but we could use those blocks (points to a smaller block).

Caleb: Let's use the tractors. I'll put them inside the barn.

The cooperative play between Caleb and Sarah lasts throughout the 25-minute center time before lunch. When the teacher signals, with a song, that it is time to clean up for lunch, Caleb and Sarah both groan. They have been transported into the world of their block play. The teacher responds by telling them that they can leave their blocks in place until after lunch; then they can make a paper reproduction of their "map" to hang on the wall above the block center. Many of the other children have represented their block maps on paper, and this one will join the map gallery.

new concepts in concrete, physical ways. Use of concrete materials and firsthand experiences are essential in learning complex concepts such as mapping. The flexibility and appropriateness of blocks for learning are readily observable as we closely watch children in block play (Hirsch, 1996). Using three-dimensional models built with blocks, children are able to grasp the symbolization and abstractions of mapping.

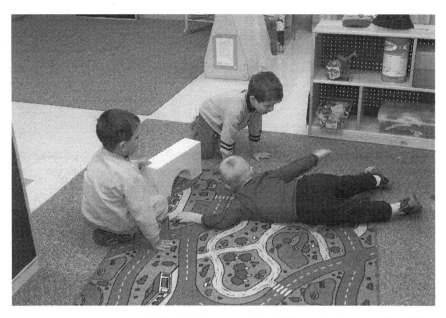

A Block Center may help children develop mapping skills.

With their growing ability to deal with abstractions, elementary-age students can make great intellectual leaps through the use of concrete objects. Contrary to common belief that such use holds children back in terms of abstract thought, the use of these gives a physical form to their developing thoughts. Use of concrete objects enables children to develop sophisticated concepts and solve complex problems with greater success. All mapmaking should stem from the child's own experience and should be introduced on a continuum from the concrete to the abstract.

Use of a well-conceived block center can help children develop mapmaking skills. The following dialogue between five-year-olds illustrates the way that young children begin to make sense of spatial experiences.

Mapping as an Abstract Activity

In her book, *Really Important Stuff My Kids Have Taught Me* (1994), Cynthia Copeland Lewis says, "Getting lost teaches you how to read a map." Through extended experience with concrete objects, children begin to develop mental maps of familiar places. Most appropriate subjects of early mapping experiences are those that are

GROUP ACTIVITY

BLOCKS AND MAPS

1. Using the interaction between Caleb and Sarah, discuss the importance of block play in developing spatial awareness.
2. Compare this activity with the traditional way that many teachers introduce mapmaking—paper and pencil tasks.
3. Design an environment, complete with materials, in which block play is an integral part of the social studies curriculum. Why is this important?

familiar to students, such as their homes, classrooms, or playgrounds. Neighborhood walks and more extensive field trips are wonderful opportunities to expand a child's growing understanding of geography. On an even more abstract level, photographs can be used to help children extend their mapping skills. Maps are abstractions. To develop this abstract concept, students must be exposed to many relevant, concrete experiences that relate to their own personal experiences.

In understanding the abstraction of mapping, there are four fundamentals to be taught: Representation, Symbolization, Perspective, and Scale.

Representation

Representation is the idea that a map represents a place. Use of blocks to foster representation is a concrete experience, which can lead to greater understanding as children transfer their understanding of representation to more abstract forms of mapmaking.

Symbolization

Children must learn that symbols represent a real thing. The use of a map's key is an essential skill to develop as young children move to more sophisticated ways of working with maps.

Perspective

Looking at features from a different viewpoint is a very difficult concept for young children. Through practice and many varied experiences, young children can develop a foundation for building the concept of perspective.

A GLOBAL PERSPECTIVE
CONNECTING TO THE WORLD

Julie Gold's book, *From a Distance*, illustrates the words to her hauntingly beautiful song by the same name. Pairing the book with Bette Midler's version of the song is an effective and motivating introduction to the concept of a global perspective.

"From a distance

You look like my friend

Even though we are at war."

This book also offers a great introduction to the concept of perspective as the illustrator gives several different views of the same scene. Young children see all people as friends, not judging others because of the color of their skin or the religion they practice. The early childhood classroom is a perfect place to celebrate this wonderful attribute.

Scale

The concept that a map shows a real area, in smaller form, is the foundation for teaching scale to young children.

While we don't really know the exact sequence of development as children learn to read maps, we are able to build a foundation for their later map-reading and interpreting skills by planning regular, developmentally appropriate experiences for them to work with maps and mapmaking (Mitchell, 1934/1991). Maps are visual tools which present complex information in an easy-to-understand format. They show the relative size and location of specific geographic areas. There are many different kinds of maps; the two most common types are political maps and physical maps. Political maps show human-made boundaries, such as state and country borders. Physical maps show physical features such as lakes, rivers, and mountains. Both are appropriate for use with young children and offer excellent opportunities for developing cartographic skills (Hinshaw).

There are many ways that the early childhood teacher can help students develop an understanding of *place*. Developing spaces where children can explore the relationships between different areas of their environment is one important step that can be taken by early childhood teachers.

Map Terminology

As with any discipline, learning the terminology is an important part of what we do with young children. Cartography has its own language, and it is exciting for young children to learn the correct terminology for what they are doing. Knowing the terminology will provide a wonderful bridge for them as they move into more abstract map-making activities in later school years.

CONNECTING TO ADMINISTRATION

MAKING A MAP

Talk to your principal about painting a large map on your parking lot or blacktop. Children spend countless hours running from California to Texas, down to Florida and up to Oregon. After several weeks of allowing the students to "just play" on the map, teachers can develop some games for the students to play, giving information about the different states for the children to learn as they move from state to state. Names of the state capitals can be added, giving students an engaging way to learn some of that knowledge-level information that they eventually will need to know.

Your principal is your best ally when you have "great ideas." Most principals will do anything they can to help you reach your instructional goals for your students. Make an appointment and go armed with standards and objectives for your students' learning. Usually, the principal will help make your dreams come true.

SOME SUGGESTIONS FOR INITIAL MAPMAKING EXPERIENCES

1. Maps of the classroom
2. Maps of the child's bedroom
3. Maps of the playground
4. Maps of the route from home to school
5. Maps of the school

MAP TERMINOLOGY

Title: Identification of the area shown on the map and the map's special focus

Legend: Explanation of the symbols on the map

Compass rose: Identification of the directions on the map. Points out cardinal directions.

Scale: A line that indicates the relationship between distances on the map and actual distance

Latitude and longitude: Imaginary horizontal lines

(latitude) that circle the globe from east to west (also called parallels), and vertical lines (longitude) going from north to south (also called meridians)

UNDERSTANDING THE EARTH

Young children's knowledge about the physical world develops gradually. They, understandably, have naïve concepts about the Earth. Lucy Sprague Mitchell, pioneer in early childhood education in the 1930s, identified the developmental stages of geographic or environmental awareness. According to Mitchell, an important beginning to helping a child understand the world is helping him to develop a sense of his own physical characteristics, and then build on this understanding to help him expand and interact with other environments. Active and direct exploration is critical to a child's understanding about the world around him (Mitchell, 1934/1991).

Learning cartography.

It is the responsibility of the early childhood teacher to provide concrete and direct experiences with the child's environment to help guide more mature ideas about the world around him. It is important to begin by accessing current understandings and knowledge of the way the world works. Simply asking children about their world is a great starting place!

Early geographic experiences include helping children to develop an awareness of the Earth. Through the use of globes, photographs, and appropriate children's literature, young children can gain an understanding of the Earth as "round" and as a part of the solar system.

Through personal experiences, children learn about night and day, the changes in the seasons, and the differences in climate and physical features in different parts of the world. Use of children's literature, media, and technology helps to further enhance students' understanding of the Earth.

CONNECTION TO CHILDREN'S LITERATURE

In recent years, the selection of beautiful picture books appropriate for use in geography lessons has exploded! These books offer excellent opportunities to introduce geographic concepts in interesting and engaging ways. In addition, students are more interested in reading about geography when teachers use children's literature as read-alouds in introductory lessons. Reading several selections about a single topic gives students different perspectives of the same information, frequently helping to scaffold their understanding of complex elements of geographic and environmental study. A few favorites are listed below.

Sweet Clara and the Freedom Quilt (1995) by Deborah Hopkinson

If I could only have one book in my classroom, this would be it! I have used it in a variety of units, and my students enjoy it and find something new in it every time. This is the story of a young slave, who is moved from the fields into the "big house" to be a seamstress. She overhears some of the men talking about the different geographic elements of the plantation and surrounding areas, as well as about the Underground Railroad. Clara decides that she can use scraps of fabric to create a quilt, which is a map to freedom. This wonderful book is a perfect vehicle for introducing the concept of map symbols, compass roses, legends, and other elements of mapmaking. This is a must-have for any classroom.

The Scrambled States of America (1998) by Laurie Keller is a visually exciting book, perfect for using to introduce a unit on states. In this fun book, Kansas wakes up in a grumpy mood and encourages the other states to switch places. This book really does make geography fun, and encourages students to pay attention to the U.S. map. Students enjoy going back to this one again and again, long after the unit on states is completed.

(continued)

CONNECTION TO CHILDREN'S LITERATURE

(continued)

Celebrate the 50 States! By Loreen Leedy is a great resource for children interested in the states. The wonderful illustrations engage students and help celebrate the diversity of our country. This is another great one for ongoing perusal by the students.

How to Make an Apple Pie and See the World (1996) by Marjorie Priceman is another favorite. This fun book follows a little girl through her quest to gather the materials for an apple pie. She goes around the world, collecting the ingredients for her pie, using various modes of transportation. Try following the reading of this book with a cooking demonstration (and an eating demonstration!) Fun, fun, fun.

This Land is Your Land (1998) by singer Woody Guthrie is a great one for introducing U.S. geography. Pair this book with Peter, Paul, and Mary's rendition of the song and it becomes one of the staples for singing throughout the school year.

What a Wonderful World (1995) by George Weiss is a beautiful book. Louis Armstrong's beautiful song is illustrated in this vibrant book. Try using it as an introduction to the study of geography in general. Again, pair the book with the song, chart the words, and encourage students to enjoy it over and over again. Throughout the school year, it's not unusual to hear kids "singing the room" as they revisit the many songs and books that have been used to introduce concepts in geography.

Movement

The theme of "movement" involves the movement of people, products, information, and ideas around the world. This theme can be explored with young children by having them expand on a map that they have drawn of the school. Individually, or in small groups, have students describe how they move through their school day. They can point to the different areas of the school as they describe where they move and why they move to that location in the school. What are the purposes of the different areas of the school? This is a great jumping off place for a discussion of movement of people around the globe.

This activity can be extended to help students think about the products that come into the school. For instance, books and magazines in the library come from many different areas of the world.

Older children can find publication information in the books and magazines and locate those places on a map. Furniture, puzzles, and other classroom materials are frequently manufactured in other parts of the country. Students can find the country of origin on the boxes that come with the materials, then trace the path taken by the materials on the classroom map.

TRY THIS WITH CHILDREN...

Set up a "travel agency" center in the classroom. Have students research different destinations and make travel brochures, illustrating the geographic features of the area, as well as items of cultural interest and activities to do while visiting the country. This can be an ongoing center in your classroom, shifting focus as your students study different areas of the state, country, or world.

GEOGRAPHY AND LITERATURE

The study of literature improves comprehension of geography. Research has shown that geographic awareness among students is influenced more by travel experience than by any other factor (Bein, 1990). Most children, however, are not able to travel the world. The challenge for the early childhood teacher is to bring the world to the young child. One of the most effective ways to do this is through the use of good children's literature.

Almost every literature selection describes the setting in some detail. Many selections further link the storyline to the foods, language, home life, and relationships of the characters in the story, giving young children a glimpse into the lives of those characters and the culture of those in the story. The classroom teacher can further extend the geographic impact of the story by encouraging students to locate the setting on a map, perhaps making a permanent mark on the map, giving the title of the book set at that location. Teachers can encourage students to make connections between the literature piece and the geographic study being currently undertaken in the curriculum.

SOME SUGGESTIONS FOR BOOKS ON GEOGRAPHY

From a Distance by J Gold.
This Land Is Your Land by Woody Guthrie
The Block Book by E. Hirsch
Sweet Clara and the Freedom Quilt by Deborah Hopkinson.
George Shrinks by W. Joyce.
The Scrambled States of America by Laurie Keller

Celebrate the 50 States! by Loreen Leedy
How to Make an Apple Pie and See the World by Marjorie Priceman
Somewhere in the World Right Now by S. Schnett
What a Wonderful World by George Weiss

ENVIRONMENTAL EDUCATION IN EARLY CHILDHOOD

Environmental education is education in, about, and for the environment. Young children learn about the environment by interacting with it, but many have limited opportunities for experiences in the out-of-doors. The great majority of Americans live in urban areas, and even those growing up in suburban or rural areas spend much of their time in settings that keep them indoors (e.g., day care) or in activities that keep them from interacting with the natural world (television, organized sports).

Children must develop a sense of respect for the natural environment during their first few years of life or they may be at risk for never developing these attitudes (Wilson). Another rationale for providing environmental education in the early childhood years is based on the belief that positive interactions with the natural environment are an important part of positive child development (Cobb, 1977).

Exploring Nature With Young Children

"Every subject known to humans has its roots in the natural world, so nature must be considered core knowledge and therefore an essential element of every program for children from birth on" (Humphryes, 2000, p. 20). Helping young children to respect life, to

CONNECTING TO DIVERSE POPULATIONS

Understanding that one form of life is dependent upon one another is basic to living in a democracy. Through the study of geography and the environment, young children can develop this most important understanding. Classroom teachers can help students to make these important connections by providing classroom pets and gardens for the students to care for. Through caring for a classroom pet and working in the classroom garden, students can see, first hand, that the ability of living things to thrive depends on a delicate balance of different interactions. The artful early childhood teacher can offer opportunities for children to generalize this understanding to the greater world.

preserve our natural resources, and to care for the Earth begins early in a child's education. "Because children are curious about their surroundings, the environment provides a perfect vehicle for learning to read, write, and make sense of the world" (Kupetz & Twiest, p. 59). "One element of nature-oriented education is teaching young children to respect and care for the natural world" (Woyke, p. 84). When teaching about environmental issues, teachers can begin by giving children an opportunity to use their senses. Help them learn to see, feel, smell, and listen to nature (Callander & Power, 1992). Giving young children an opportunity to observe the world around them helps them to develop a basis for ecological understanding. Taking children for walks through the neighborhood, pointing out examples of litter, or by taking them for walks in the park, pointing out the diverse beauties of nature, are ways to give them first-hand, multisensory explorations of their world.

When developing the curriculum for environmental education in the early childhood classroom, there are several factors to keep in mind. R. A. Wilson (1993) suggests the following guidelines in fostering a sense of wonder during the early childhood years:

1. Begin with simple experiences, with an environment that is familiar to the children. Focus on a tree in the playground or the classroom garden.

2. Provide frequent experiences outdoors. Children learn by doing, so daily experiences in the out-of-doors allow them to experiment and investigate the natural environment.

3. Focus on "experiencing" rather than on "teaching." Because of the nature of early childhood learning, the role of the effective teacher is more that of facilitator than teacher. The effective early childhood teacher will prepare the environment for exploration and investigation by the child.

4. Demonstrate a personal interest in and enjoyment of the natural world. The students take their cues from the teacher. If the teacher is excited and interested in a particular subject, the students will become excited as well.

5. Model caring and respect for the natural environment. The teacher must demonstrate his or her respect for the natural world. This is far more effective than simply *talking* about it. Care can be demonstrated by establishing habitats for wildlife and by recycling and reusing as many materials as possible.

6. Infuse environmental education throughout all aspects of the school program.

7. Focus on the beauty and wonder of nature.

Daily interaction with well-developed environmental themes is an effective way for the early childhood teacher to help young children develop a sense of respect for nature. Giving children an opportunity to observe their surroundings helps to stimulate an interest in their environment and provides an impetus for learning about caring for the Earth.

One way to help children explore environmental themes is through the use of learning centers in the classroom. Some materials and equipment necessary for preparing centers for nature study follow.

Reduce–Reuse–Recycle

An important aspect of the environmental education program in early childhood education is the introduction of the concept of the 3R's: reduce, reuse, and recycle. The 3R's are a simple guide to help children understand how to minimize waste in their lives.

Reduce means living more carefully so that there is less to get rid of. For children in the classroom, this means (1) taking care of classroom books and materials so that they last a long time; (2) using the backs of papers for scratch sheets, rather than wasting a new piece of paper; (3) sharing and borrowing materials, rather than buying new ones; (4) making gifts, rather than buying them; and (5) using disposables sparingly.

CENTER MATERIALS FOR NATURE EDUCATION

Sand and water table: sand tools, containers

Sensory table: Leaves, pinecones, shells, rocks

Music: Background music of nature (ocean, wind, rain, etc.)

Art: natural materials—Pinecones, leaves, sand, grasses, sand, pebbles

Manipulative Center: Puzzles with nature, animal themes

Dramatic play: Equipment for animal hospital, garden shop, zoo

Language/literacy: Nature magazines—*Ranger Rick, Your Big Backyard*

Puppet Center: Animal puppets

Literacy Center: Books about nature, books about recycling, books about interconnectedness

Reader's Theater: Poems about nature, plays with nature themes, plays with environmental themes

Ourdoor play: Magnifying glasses, clipboards for notes/drawings

Reusing means using the same item more than once rather than disposing of it after a single use. This saves energy and resources that would have been used to produce a new product and also means that the product will not go into the landfills. Some ways to encourage reuse in the classroom include (1) borrowing and sharing materials, (2) buying second-hand books for use in the classroom, and (3) using recycled materials for containers and art materials.

Recycling involves returning a waste product to a factory where it's remade into a new item. This saves landfill space and the resources that would have been used to make the product again. Some materials to recycle in the classroom include (1) paper, (2) aluminum cans and foil, and (3) milk and juice cartons.

SUMMARY

Few people cite geography as a favorite subject in school. Many remember geographic instruction as boring and meaningless. Addressed in an appropriate fashion, however, geography can be an exciting and meaningful part of the early childhood curriculum. Young children love to move and explore, and geography offers an exciting and relevant reason to do both.

Geography helps young children develop a way of thinking about and appreciating the Earth. Geographic instruction gives children the tools they need to move throughout the world, to relate to people of other cultures, and to understand the weather and environment.

Integrating environmental education into the early childhood curriculum also helps young children to discover the world around them, and to understand themselves better as well (Wilson). Learning about environmental issues helps children to develop an interest in and concern for the natural environment. Providing stimulating, meaningful, active instruction in both geography and environmental studies helps young children to understand their important roles as global citizens, which is the ultimate goal of the social studies.

▶ THEMATIC STRANDS AND FOCUS QUESTIONS

Culture

1. How can early childhood teachers use geographic study to help children understand people from other cultures?

2. How can environmental studies help children understand the cultural differences of others?

People, Places, and Environments

1. How can young children develop a sense of place?

2. How can young children make a connection between land forms and climate and the ways that people live?

Individual Development and Identity

1. How does an understanding of geographic "place" help children to understand their own place in the larger society?

2. What can the early childhood teacher do to help young children understand their importance in creating an environmentally friendly world?

Science, Technology, Society

1. How can young children become familiar with the physical processes that shape the Earth's surface and the ecosystems of the Earth?

2. How can the early childhood teacher help young children understand the importance of technology as it relates to environmental problems and solutions?

Global Connections

1. How can children's literature be used to help young children begin to understand their connection to the greater world community?

2. How does the "expanding communities" theory of geographic instruction help or hinder young children's understanding of their interconnectedness to the greater world?

▶ KEY TERMS

cartographer
compass rose
environmental education
geography
human–environment interaction
legend
orienteering
perspective
scale

▶ REFERENCES

Bein, F. (1990). Baseline geography competency test: Administered in Indiana universities. *Journal of Geography, 89*, 260–265.

Bredekamp, S., & Copple, C. (1997). Developmentally appropriate practice in early childhood. Washington, DC: National Association for the Education of Young Children.

Callander, G. D., & Power, S. (1992). The importance of and opportunities for wildlife in an urban environment. *Journal of Environmentl Education and Information, 11*(3), 173–180.

Carroll, L. (1867). *Alice in wonderland* (p. 17). London: MacMillan & Co.

Cobb, E. (1977). *The ecology of imagination in childhood.* New York: Columbia University Press.

Dighe, J. (1993). Children and the earth. *Young Children, 48*(3), 58–63.

Fenton, G. (1996). Back to our roots in nature's classroom. *Young Children, 51*(3), 8–11.

Freese, J. (1997). Using the national geography standards to integrate children's social studies. *Social Studies and the Young Learner, 10*(2), 22–24.

Geography Education Standards Project. (1994). Geography for life: The national geography standards. Washington, DC: National Council for Geographic Education.

Guthrie, W. (1998). *This land is your land.* Boston: Little, Brown.

Hartman, K., & Giorgis, C. (2003). Exploring maps through children's literature. *Social Studies and the Young Learner, 13*(3), 14–16.

Hinshaw, C. (1998). It's a flat world. *Social Studies and the Young Learner, 11*(1),30–31.

Hirsch, E. (1996). *The block book.* Washington, DC: NAEYC.

Humphryes, J. (2000). Exploring nature with children. *Young Children, 55*(2), 16–20.

Kupetz, B., & Twiest, M. (2000). Nature, literature, and young children: A natural combination. *Young Children 55*(1), 59–63.

Lewis, C. (1994). *Really important stuff my kids taught me.* New York: Workman Press.

Liben, L. S., & Downs, R. M. (1993). Understanding person-space-map relations: Cartographic and developmental perspective. *Child Development, 29,* 739–752.

Miller, J. (1985). Teaching map skills: Theory, research, and practice. *Social Education, 49,* 30–33.

Milson, A. (1998). Mental mapping: Today my home, tomorrow the world! *Social Studies and the Young Learner, 11*(1), 1–2.

Mitchell, L. S. (1934/1991). *Young geographers: How they explore the world and how they map the world.* New York: Bank Street College of Education.

National Geographic Joint Committee (1994). *Geography for life: The national geography standards.* Washington, DC: Author.

Natoli, S. (Ed.) (1989). Strengthening geography in the social studies. Bulletin No. 81. Washington, DC: National Council for the Social Studies.

NCGE (National Council on Geographic Education). (1994). The eighteen national geography standards. http://www.ncge.org/publications/tutorial/standards. (Accessed May 30, 2004).

NCSS (National Commission on Social Studies in the Schools). (1989). *Charting a course: Social studies for the 21st century.* New York: Author.

NCSS (National Council for the Social Studies). (1998). *Curriculum standards for social studies: Expectations for excellence.* Washington, DC: Author.

North American Association for Environmental Education. (1994). *Environmental education guidelines for excellence: What school-age learners should know and be able to do.* Oregon, IL: Author

Olds, A. R. (1989). Nature as a refuge. *Children's Environments Quarterly, 6*(1), 27–32.

Piaget, J. (1965). *The child's conception of the world.* Totowa, NJ: Littlefield Adams.

Rivkin, M. S. (1995). *The great outdoors: Restoring children's right to play outside.* Washington, DC: National Association for the Education of Young Children.

Trifonoff, K. (1998). Introducing thematic maps in the primary grades. *Social Studies and the Young Learner, 11*(1), 17–22.

Wilson, R. A. (1993). *Fostering a sense of wonder during the early childhood years.* Columbus, OH: Greyden Press.

Wilson, R. A. (Ed.). (1994). Environmental education at the early childhood level. Washington, DC: *North American Association for Environmental Education.*

Woyke, P. (2004). Hopping frogs and trail walks. *Young Children, 59*(1), 82–85.

SUGGESTED READINGS

Earth Works Group. (1990). *50 Simple things you can do to save the Earth.* Kansas City, MO: Andrews and McMeel.

Gibbons, G. (1996). *Recycle! A handbook for kids.* Boston: Little, Brown.

Gold, J. (1998). *From a distance.* New York: Orchard Books.

Guthrie, W. (1998). *This land is your land.* Boston: Little, Brown.

Harlow, R., & Morgan, S. (2002). *Garbage and recycling.* Boston: Houghton Mifflin.

Hirsch, E. (1996). *The block book.* Washington, DC: NAEYC.

Hopkinson, D. (1995). *Sweet Clara and the freedom quilt.* New York: Dragonfly Books.

Joyce, W. (1987). *George shrinks.* New York: HarperTrophy.

Keller, L. (1998). *The scrambled states of America.* New York: Henry Holt.

Leedy, L. (1999). *Celebrate the 50 states!* New York: Holiday House.

Priceman, M. (1996). *How to make an apple pie and see the world.* New York: Dragonfly Books.

Rogers, L. (1997). *Geographic literacy through children's literature.* Portsmouth, NH: Teacher Ideas Press.

Schnett, S. (1995). *Somewhere in the world right now.* New York: Dragonfly Books.

Showers, P. (1993). *Where does the garbage go?* New York: HarperCollins.

Weiss, G. (1995). *What a wonderful world.* New York: Antheneum.

CHAPTER 8
History

OBJECTIVES

After reading this chapter, you should be able to:

➤ Identify and define the five types of historical thinking.

➤ Discuss the importance of young students enhancing their sense of self through the study of historical themes.

➤ Plan a history lesson, based on the use of children's literature and arts.

➤ Reflect on the importance of your own personal history as it relates to your teaching of historical concepts to young children.

➤ Evaluate literature, songs, and poetry in terms of their value in teaching historical concepts.

The supreme purpose of history is a better world.

Herbert Hoover

Encouraging children to work together makes
history much more fun.

INTRODUCTION

If you ask students—elementary, high school, and university students alike—
what they think about History, most will respond, "b-o-r-i-n-g." Many of us
remember history class as endless hours of reading the dry textbook and
"answering the questions at the back of the chapter." Good students mem-
orized the names, places, and dates just long enough to pass the inevitable
multiple-choice test, then promptly forgot that information. When dates and

times are learned in isolation, they become bits of useless information, unconnected to the greater understanding of historical concepts.

Developing a sense of history takes more than just memorizing facts. History is about people (Hakim, 1997). The richness of the stories of those people and events is often left untapped in the elementary school social studies curriculum. History is a true multidisciplinary subject. *Everything* that happened yesterday and before is history! Art, music, literature, science— all are history. It is the responsibility of the early childhood teacher to bring it to life for his or her young students.

Studies have shown that the historical knowledge young Americans possess is less than most of us would prefer (Cheney, 1986). Content history is practically absent from the K–3 curriculum in most schools (Ravitch, 1987). Including standards for history in the early grades is important for many reasons. Foremost among these is that "knowledge of history is the precondition of political intelligence. Without history, a society shares no common memory of where it has been, of what its core values are, or of what decisions of the past account for the present circumstances. Without history, one cannot undertake any sensible inquiry into the political, social, or moral issues in society and without historical knowledge and the inquiry it supports, one cannot move to the informed, discriminating citizenship essential to effective participation in the democratic processes of governance and the fulfillment for all our citizens of the nation's democratic ideals" (National Center for History in the Schools, 1996, p. 1).

Through the balanced study of the people and cultures of the world, young children can develop an understanding and appreciation of the similarities among the world's people. This can, in turn, encourage mutual respect among an ever-changing and more diverse population.

BIOGRAPHY

Ralph Waldo Emerson said, "There is properly no history, only biography." History is a *story*. With young children, the story begins with themselves. Then the story extends to their families. As teachers of young children, we know that they love to tell us stories about themselves and their families. This should be the focus of our lessons in history with young children—start where they are!

The study of history has been defined by the National Council for the Social Studies (1994) as "a time-oriented study that refers to what we do know about the past." It deals with the concepts of change and the continuity of human life and includes knowledge gained from critical systematic investigation of the past.

Encouraging mutual respect in the classroom promotes
understanding of one's differences.

Learning about history contributes to the education of the
public citizen, but is also very important for the individual student.
"Historical memory is the key to self-identity, to seeing one's place in
the stream of time, and one's connectedness with all of humankind"
(National Center for History in the Schools, 1996, p. 1). History is
exciting for young children! Even the youngest children can begin to
build historical understandings. As teachers of young children, it is
important that we supply an environment conducive to our students'
natural curiosity and imagination.

One of the most effective ways to bring history alive for young
children is to center the study on the *people* of history. Through the
study of people in history, students can be introduced to the use of historical artifacts, field trips, and historical fiction. Historical study should
be used to help students formulate effective questions, locate events in
time and space, and explain historical causes and consequences, and to
use primary sources to accurately portray life in the past.

Recitation of names, dates, and places is not the heart of historical study. Real historical understanding requires students to truly
engage in historical thinking. This does not happen using only rote
memory and worksheets. Early childhood teachers must provide
opportunities to develop the five types of historical thinking.

CONNECTION TO CHILDREN'S LITERATURE

The Memory Coat by Elvira Woodruff

Young children will make an immediate connection to this story of a family immigrating to the United States from Russia. The hardships of the voyage and the fear of being turned away because of an injury offer opportunities to talk about the sacrifices of immigrants who left their own countries for the promise of America.

Though the book *I Was Dreaming to Come to America: Memories from the Ellis Island Oral History Project* by Veronica Lawlor is probably too difficult for young students, this collection of stories from the Ellis Island Oral History Project offers an excellent source of background information for the teacher. Fifteen vignettes chronicle the journey as remembered by the immigrants, all of whom were children at the time. This book would be a great one to use as an inspiration for a story-telling session with your young students.

THE FIVE TYPES OF HISTORICAL THINKING

1. Chronological Thinking
2. Historical Comprehension
3. Historical Analysis and Interpretation
4. Historical Research Capabilities
5. Historical Issues—Analysis and Decision-Making

Even though these five types of historical thinking are described separately, it is important to remember that they are interactive and mutually supportive. For example, a child cannot develop skills in historical analysis and interpretation without also working to develop an understanding of chronological thinking. To develop effectively, each of the skills requires historical content.

National Center for History in the Schools, p. 4.

For young children, daily activities using the calendar provides an effective way to build concepts about time.

Standard 1: Chronological Thinking

Chronological thinking is at the center of understanding history. Without a clear concept of historical time, students will not be able to make sense of the events that are being explored. Working with concepts of specific time words such as morning, afternoon, daytime, and nighttime is an important beginning for young children, and relational words such as early, tomorrow, and before are important concepts to develop with young children. Specific duration words such as minute, hour, day, week, and so forth are also important to teach to children. Holidays and special days are another way to explore chronological thinking. Birthday, holiday, vacation, and weekend are concepts that can help students develop chronological thinking.

What children know about time is directly related to their own lives. These concepts can be taught effectively only by making the lessons relevant to a child's own life experience.

The traditional calendar time during the morning meeting is an effective routine to help children explore chronological thinking. Having students use the appropriate vocabulary as they discuss their daily activities helps to develop this important standard, which undergirds the rest of the historical instruction in your early childhood classroom.

Standard 2: Historical Comprehension

Students must develop the ability to understand the literal meaning of historical passages. They must learn to identify the central questions of the passage and to draw on the data presented to understand a passage. Frequent use of historical fiction in whole-group read-aloud sessions offers an excellent opportunity to model historical comprehension. During interactive read-alouds of historical fiction, model metacognitive strategies for the students. For instance, during the reading of a particular page you may stop and ask the students how the dress of the character gives clues about the time the story was taking place. When the teacher models the thinking process for students, they are able to see, first-hand, the way that this kind of thinking is developed.

Standard 3: Historical Analysis and Interpretation

In all areas of instruction, one of the most important skills is that of analytical thinking. This is particularly important when helping students to develop historical knowledge and understanding. Inherent in the study of history are the exciting and engaging stories that bring real-life dilemmas and experiences to life. Through the use of these stories, teachers of young children can help foster analytical thinking and problem-solving skills.

History is replete with charts, artifacts, and other kinds of records that lend themselves to analysis and interpretation. Through interaction with these authentic materials, students can learn to distinguish between fact and fiction, compare and contrast different versions of the same stories, and make hypotheses about different paths history could have taken if different choices had been made.

Standard 4: Historical Research Capabilities

History offers wonderful opportunities for student research. Field trips, observation of historical artifacts, interviews with older family members, and photographs offer endless possibilities for authentic and meaningful research.

The job of the early childhood teacher is to provide students with the opportunity to visit the school library, to use the Internet responsibly, to understand what makes a reliable source of information, and to allow time for students to explore the varied materials.

Standard 5: Historical Issue-Analysis and Decision-Making

Developing the abilities of students to identify problems confronting people in history is an important part of an effective social studies curriculum. Early childhood teachers must offer ongoing opportunities for students to do this and to analyze the decisions made concerning the problems identified.

Students can gain insight into history and the perspective of historical characters by developing alternate solutions to the problems

GROUP ACTIVITY

WHO AM I?

The following activity can be used to focus students of any age on the importance of people in history. The activity can be tweaked to focus on historical characters specific to a particular time in history (e.g., the Civil War) or a particular group of people (e.g., U.S. presidents). This activity gives students an opportunity to walk around the classroom, meet and greet fellow class members, and enjoy interaction with other students. This activity also provides practice in developing questioning strategies, as students have to formulate yes/no questions in order to discover the identity of the name on their backs. Fun.

To prepare the cards, make a list of the historical figures (these could also be created for geographic features, anthropological terminology, etc.). Print the names, one at a time, on index cards, punch a hole in the corner of the card, and attach the card to a large safety pin. As students enter the classroom, greet

them, ask them to turn around, and pin the cards to their backs. Students then go to their seats for the introduction of the lesson for the day (anticipation rising!) and an introduction to the lesson.

This fun, active focus never fails to encourage interaction and to activate prior knowledge about the historical figures. Try this in your university classroom, and then try it with young students. Here's how:

1. The name of a historic figure has been pinned to your back.
2. To discover the identity of your "person," you will ask other students in the class a single yes/no question.
3. When you determine the name on your back, write three facts about him or her.
4. You may get help from your classmates in determining the three facts about your person.

presented. In reality, this is probably the most important function of history—to guide students in developing their analyses of events and to think of ways that they might use what has already happened in history to solve present-day problems.

Excellent, well-researched children's literature titles can help present historical events to young children in a way that they can understand. These stories offer a springboard for discussion and analysis (McGowan & Guzzetti, 1991).

KEY CONCEPTS OF HISTORY IN THE EARLY CHILDHOOD CLASSROOM

There are four key concepts to explore when teaching history to young children:

1. Time
2. Space/Place
3. People
4. Events

Time

Teaching the concept of time to young children is quite difficult. They believe that their 25-year-old mothers are ancient and it takes forever for Christmas to get here! Thus, they have a great deal of difficulty dealing with the concept of long ago. Early childhood teachers can help students develop a sense of "passing of time" by giving them the responsibility of being the timekeeper in cooperative learning activities, by the calendar activities that are completed during the Class Meeting each morning, and by involving students in cooking activities (Van Scoy & Fairchild, 1993).

Chronological thinking, which helps children differentiate between what has happened in the past, what is happening now, and what will happen in the future, should be in place, to a degree, by the age of 8. Again, this kind of thinking can be encouraged through the use of appropriate vocabulary and activities completed during Calendar Time, and throughout the school day. Something as simple as making a point to talk about "after lunch" or "before recess" is one way to incorporate the teaching of chronological thinking in the early childhood classroom. While it seems so simple to the adult, many young children do not come to school with this concept in place.

Through regular interaction and modeling, this concept, central to the teaching of history, can be developed.

Look for songs and poetry that involve sequencing. One such chant, the well-known "Peanut Butter and Jelly," is perfect for reinforcing sequencing skills. Reciting this fun and silly chant, incorporating movement, and illustrations of the different steps in the process can help children to understand chronological thinking. *The Very Hungry Caterpillar* by Eric Carle is another great source of inspiration for teaching chronological thinking. There are many children's literature selections with storylines perfect for teaching about time (McClure, 1998; McGowan & Guzzetti, 1991). Use of these on a regular basis can help develop this important historical concept.

Change over time is another important historical concept related to a child's understanding of time (Davis, 2003). History involves the notion of change—change in people, in events, in towns and cities, and in countries. History also involves internal change—such as a change of opinion or a change of plans.

Cooking experiences are excellent sources for teaching children about change over time. Put the bread in the oven as a blob of dough, and in a short amount of time, that bread has changed into a crisp, fragrant loaf that students can enjoy together. Help children understand this change by pointing out the "ingredients" of the event, the causes of change (the oven temperature), and what happened as a result of the cause. Explore what might have happened if the cause had been different. What if the bread dough had been placed in the refrigerator rather than the oven? What if the yeast had been left out of the recipe? Change over time—a wonderful, multisensory example.

Young children understand the world in terms of their own experience. Understanding time is no different. They learn about the concept of time through their own personal experiences: "Once I was a baby, now I'm big." "My birthday is in October." "Summer vacation begins in two weeks."

Children thrive on routine. Developing a consistent classroom routine is an effective way to teach children about time. Even the youngest student will know (and will tell the substitute teacher) if snack time is in the wrong sequence of the morning, or if the "real teacher" reads a story at a particular time of day. The development of a routine is an important part of an effective early childhood classroom, which helps make students feel more secure, and which also serves as a tool for teaching children about time.

When working with young children, introduce them to the words that invoke time images. We use general words such as "time, age, generation" when we talk about time. Specific words, such as "morning, afternoon, day, and night" and relational words such as "tomorrow, long ago, and before" are also concepts that will lead to early development of historical understanding. Specific duration words, such as "minute, second, and day" are also important concepts to reinforce with young children. Take every opportunity to use these words and to relate them to the personal experience of the child. The way that they learn these important concepts is through personal experience and relating to meaningful life events.

Space/Place

The second key concept in history is that of space and place. For children to make a connection to the event they are studying, they must understand the setting of that event. If they are not already familiar with the setting, how can the early childhood teacher help them make a link from their own experience? Building on the map-making skills that were discussed in an earlier chapter, the teacher can help children develop a sense of space/place through block play, taking a walk and identifying different places in their environment, and providing photographs of familiar places. Through the use of children's literature, early childhood teachers can help students to identify settings, helping them to develop a sense of space and place.

People

The third key concept in history is the people. People are the actors of an historical event. The people and their stories are what bring history alive. As teachers introduce history to young children, it is important to talk about the characters involved. What makes them interesting? Do their characteristics remind the students of people in their own lives? What makes us like them or not like them? How did these personal characteristics contribute to the historical event being studied?

Children's literature offers beautifully illustrated biographies of people from all walks of life—from historical heroes to "regular" children from different places and times. Incorporate this important resource in your teaching of history. These books offer different perspectives on events in history, and often, young children are able to relate to the characters in the literature.

Events

The fourth key concept in history is events. This is often the focus of history education—what happened? Within any historical event, in order to make it meaningful for young students, teachers must find a link to their own experience. What did the event mean to them? How significant is the event to the child's life? Helping children make those connections will make the historical event meaningful.

SUPPORT FOR HISTORICAL THEMES IN EARLY CHILDHOOD EDUCATION

Some teachers believe that historical themes are developmentally inappropriate for young children. Good history instruction can be exciting, active, and engaging to young children. As with almost every topic or discipline, young children are able to grasp complex concepts if they are introduced in an active, hands-on way, on the child's level.

History education is consistent with a child's natural curiosity. Young students come to school ripe for learning. The adventures that are an integral part of history engage that curiosity and focus young students on the fascinating stories of exploration, immigration, and heroism. Through appropriate, active exploration of historical events and concepts, early childhood teachers can help students to maintain that natural curiosity about the world.

Historical themes in early childhood teaching promote an understanding of one's own culture and that of others. Through exploration of the people and events that formed their lives, students can make a connection to their own culture and open their minds and hearts to the culture of others. Through the study of history, students learn an appreciation for culture through the stories, celebrations, and traditions that they study.

Far from being inappropriate, the active exploration of the people and events of history offers a rich opportunity for students to learn who they are by studying who others are. Incorporating children's literature, which transports us back in time, allows even the youngest of students to experience a slice of life from the past and to begin to make connections to the way things were.

History and the Arts

Including the arts in concept development is a powerful way to bring to life the important events of history. Through music, dance, cooking, and visual arts, we can understand the cultural aspects of a historical event. Bring these kinds of experiences to your young students as a way to make connections between the past and the present.

Through the ages, people have expressed themselves through the arts. Exposing children to the cultural aspects of a particular era in history helps them to connect to the spirit of the people who lived in those times. Whatever your historic topic, bring in the music, dance, theater, and visual arts of the time. Children will remember much more about your teaching through these avenues than they ever would through other means.

Music: Did your mother sing to you? Try to remember the words to the songs that she sang. How did it make you feel when she sang? How does it make you feel now, when you remember?

Dance: Involve your students in dances that represent the historical eras you are studying. Square dancing, line dancing, learning to hula—all are memorable activities that can bring the study of history to life.

Theater: Involve students in historical events by developing (or leading them to develop) Reader's Theater scripts based on historical events. In one fourth-grade classroom, the students took the story of Harriet Tubman, *Go Free or Die,* which they had used in Guided

CONNECTING TO ADMINISTRATION

Recently, one very effective third-grade teacher allowed individual students to choose and research historical figures, then report out to the class, dressed in costume. Students chose such diverse people as Betsy Ross, Babe Ruth, and Florence Nightingale to represent. The performances took place every Friday morning, and the principal made it a regular event to attend every week. This gave the principal an opportunity to see, first hand, the ongoing history instruction in the classroom.

Make it a point to invite your principal to participate in classroom activities as often as possible. This gives him or her a chance to see the learning that is taking place in the classroom, while giving students confidence, having the head of the school there to watch their performances.

Dramatic play helps bring history alive.

Reading groups, and made it into a Reader's Theater script. Students had had experience in changing genres during a guided lesson earlier in the year. In small groups, they took sections of the book, using the dialog already present to create the script. The students enjoyed performing the skit, with generic dress-up clothes as costumes. While this lesson took place in January, the students continued to enjoy the script throughout the spring semester since the teacher put copies of that script and others in the Drama Center. Many of the students worked voluntarily in that center, increasing their fluency in reading, after completing other assigned work. A small group of students even video-taped their performance and "took it on the road" to other classrooms.

USING HISTORICAL FICTION WITH YOUNG CHILDREN

Primary social studies curricula have traditionally stayed away from a formal study of history because of the young child's difficulty in developing time concepts (Piaget). Teaching history through narra-tive, however, provides "a temporal scaffolding for historical under-standing that is accessible event to quite young children" (Downey and Levstik, 1988, p. 338).

Historical fiction is an important tool in opening the past for young children. It illuminates time periods for young children, helping to integrate the curriculum and bringing to life the cultural aspects of an era (Freedman, 1994). The use of historical fiction in the early childhood classroom, in conjunction with the adopted textbook, online resources, maps, and other print materials, enriches the curriculum.

The use of historical fiction brings the *people* back to history instruction. Good historical fiction presents individuals as they are, "neither all good nor all bad" (Lindquist, 2000, p. 2). Use of picture books to introduce a unit of study is an excellent way to arouse the curiosity of young children, as well as to build a knowledge base con-cerning the historical events to be studied. Good historical fiction builds visual clues about the ways that people lived during a partic-ular time period, enriching the understanding of the era for young children. Historical fiction also helps children to build a sense of multiple perspectives. Through the use of multiple pieces of litera-ture concerning a specific event or person, the students can begin to experience the different ways that people view the same event or per-son. This is also a good first lesson for young students about the interpretive nature of history.

In historical fiction, the characters are usually fictional, though they frequently interact in some way with historically famous people. Storylines can involve events in history or can simply be set, accurately, in the historical era. "Historical fiction is judged by the same criteria as any other piece of fiction: strength of character development and plot,

Students illustrate a study of artists throughout history.

writing style, definition of setting, handling of theme" (Jacobs & Tunnell, 2004, p.118). In addition, there are several criteria to consider, specific to the genre of historical fiction. First, historical accuracy is important. The story can be fictionalized to a degree, but the facts must not conflict with historical records. The characters and settings should be presented realistically. Stereotypes and myths should be avoided. When choosing historical fiction for use in the classroom, the teacher must research the background of the author, making sure that he or she is qualified to present an accurate story.

Historical fiction involves a good story that can be enjoyed as a read-aloud or by a child independently. Historical fiction can help young children to develop a sense of time. It can also help bring to life the historical facts and events presented in the social studies curriculum. An abundance of historical fiction is available to the classroom teacher. Sharing a variety of literature is very effective in bringing history to life for young learners.

USING BIOGRAPHY WITH YOUNG CHILDREN

The genre of biography focuses on the lives of human beings, generally those who are famous. When using biography in the history curriculum, it is important to look for accuracy (Fertig, 2003). The facts must be accurate, and it is important for biographers to acknowledge their sources and credentials for writing about the subject. Although it is impossible for biographers to be totally objective, they must avoid making personal judgments in the text (Jacobs & Tunnell, 2004, p. 135). Presentation of a balanced view of the biographical subject is important in order to allow students to see the humanity of the people in history.

Biographies need to be measured against the standards of other books used in the social studies curriculum. They need to be engaging for students, while bringing the era of the subject to life in an authentic way. Bringing stories of the people in history to the students is an excellent way to illustrate the important aspects of historical study.

SUMMARY

The study of history is integral to an understanding of the world in which children live. History can be a vibrant part of the social studies curriculum, offering children an insight into the world of the past and giving them an opportunity to build a bridge of understanding between their current lives and people who lived in the past.

History is not an endless series of names and dates. By exploring the lives of people—both famous and not widely known—throughout history, young children can begin to understand the important characters and events that helped shaped their own present-day lives.

▶ THEMATIC STRANDS AND FOCUS QUESTIONS

Culture

1. How can students come to understand a historical era through the popular customs represented by that era?

2. How can young children connect to a historical era through the arts of those times?

Time, Continuity, and Change

1. How can students develop a sense of historical time?

2. What activities can be presented to students to develop an understanding of change over time?

People, Places, and Environments

1. How can young children develop an understanding of the physical and human characteristics of the historical events that are studied?

2. How can students develop a sense of *place*?

Individual Development and Identity

1. How can the early childhood teacher help students to understand themselves in relation to historical events?

2. How do special events in a child's life relate to events in history?

Global Connections

1. How do young children view the events of history as they affect them?

2. What resources can the early childhood teacher use to help make young children aware of the effects of global issues?

KEY TERMS

events
people
space/place
time

REFERENCES

Cheney, L. (1986). *American memory: A report on the humanities in the nation's public schools.* Washington, DC: National Endowment for the Humanities.

Davis, J. (2003). Preschool children's mental constructs of time and space. *Social Studies and the Young Learner, 15*(4), 18–19.

Downey, M., & Levstik, L. (1988). Teaching and learning history: The research base. *Social Education,* September, 336–342.

Fertig, G. (2003). Using biographies to explore social justice in U.S. history. Social *Studies and the Young Learner, 16*(1), 9–10.

Freedman, R. (1994). Bring 'em back alive. Writing history and biography for young people. *School Library Journal, 40*(3), 138–141.

Hakim, J. (1997). History at the center of the curriculum. *Teaching K–8,* November/December, 52–53.

Jacobs, J., & Tunnell, M. (2004). *Children's literature, briefly.* Upper Saddle River, NJ: Pearson.

Lindquist, T. (2000). Why and how I teach with historical fiction. http://www.teacher. scholastic.com/lessonrepro/lessonplans/instructor/social1.htm (Accessed October 27, 2004).

McClure, A. A. (1998). Choosing quality n onfiction literature: Examining aspects of writing style. In R. A. Bamford & J. V. Kristo (Eds.). *Making facts come alive: Choosing quality nonfiction literature K–8* (pp. 39–54). Norwood, MA: Christopher-Gordon.

McGowan, T., & Guzzetti, B. (1991). Promoting social studies understanding through literature-based instruction. *The Social Studies, 82*(1), 16–21.

National Center for History in the Schools. UCLA. (1996). National standards for history grades K–4: Expanding children's world in time and space. http://w3.iac.net/~pfilio/stand.txt. (Accessed May 31, 2004).

National Council for History Education. (1996). Reinvigorating history in the U. S. schools. http://www.nche.net (Accessed April 17, 2005).

National Council for the Social Studies. (1994). *National Standards: History for grades K–4.* Los Angeles: Author.

Ravitch, T. (1987). Tot sociology, or what happened to history in the grade schools? *The American Scholar, 56,* 343–354.

Van Scoy, I., & Fairchild, S. (1993). It's about time! Helping preschool and primary children understand time concepts. *Young Children, 48*(2), 21–24.

Vygotsky, L. (1996). *Thought and language.* Cambridge, MA: MIT Press.

▶ SUGGESTED READINGS

Cobblestone: The history magazine for young people. (published monthly, except June, July and August by Cobblestone Publishing. 7 School Street, Petersborough, NY.

Czartoski, S., & Hickey, G. (1999). All about me: A personal heritage project. *Social Studies and the Young Learner, 11*(4).

Davis, J. (2003). Identifying with ancestors: Tracking the history of America. *Social Studies and the Young Learner, 16*(2),13–16.

Hopkinson, D. (1993). *Sweet Clara and the freedom quilt.* New York: Alfred A. Knopf..

Inzerella, M. (2002). Using biographical poems in a fifth grade class. *Social Studies and the Young Learner, 14*(3), 4–5.

National Center for History in Schools. (1994). *National standards: History for grades K-4.* Los Angeles, CA: Author.

Schwartz, S. (2000). My family's story: Discovering history at home. *Social Studies and the Young Learner, 12*(3), 6–9.

Wheeler, R. (1996). *Teaching the ten themes of social studies.* Grand Rapids, MI: McGraw-Hill Children's Publishing.

Zarnowski, M. (1995). Learning history with informational books: A social studies educator's perspective. *The New Advocate, 8,* 184–196.

Zarnowski, M. (1998). It's more than dates and places: How non-fiction contributes to understanding social studies. In R. A. Bamford & J. V. Kristo (Eds.). *Making facts come alive: Choosing quality nonfiction literature K–8* (pp. 93–108). Norwood, MA: Christopher-Gordon.

CHAPTER 9
Economics, Anthropology, and Archaeology

OBJECTIVES

After reading this chapter, you should be able to:

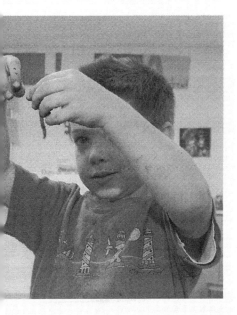

➤ Identify ways that young children develop economic concepts.

➤ Develop activities to help young children make good economic decisions.

➤ Create a classroom environment conducive to introducing young children to the concepts of producer and consumer.

➤ Explore the use of artifacts in an early child-hood classroom

➤ Describe the use of folktales to help young children learn about world cultures.

Never doubt that a small group of thoughtful, committed citizens can change the world. Indeed, it is the only thinking that ever has.

Margaret Mead, anthropologist

Providing environments for hands-on exploration helps children feel involved.

INTRODUCTION

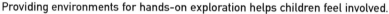

Economics and Anthropology and Archaeology. . . in preschool and primary school? Absolutely! But how does an elementary teacher incorporate the complex subjects into the classroom for young children? How can these important concepts and reasoning strategies become accessible and understandable to young children? The exciting nature of archaeology and anthropology and the relevancy of economics make these topics particularly appropriate for young children.

ECONOMICS

Young children are bombarded with economics information on a daily basis. They make consumer choices regularly, deciding on whether to save or spend money, watching and interpreting commercials on television, and seeing the effects of unemployment and inflation in their own families. As important as the economic information gained from direct instruction in economics are the analytical skills developed through the appropriate implementation of economics education.

Have students do their own cost analysis to develop economic education.

As with all concept development with young children, hands-on, developmentally appropriate, and interesting presentation make all the difference. As with all subjects and lessons, young children can learn anything, if the material is presented in an interesting and appropriate way, by teachers who want to teach the subject, who are knowledgeable about the topic, and who are willing and able to spend time and resources necessary to accomplish the goal. Since our students must have knowledge and skills about economics in order to earn a living and make decisions about how to spend that money, learning about economics is essential to the goal of educating an informed citizenry (Chapin & Messick, 1999). A recent study by Sosin, Dick, & Reiser (1997) found that students can and do learn economic concepts *when they are taught.*

In teaching, the term **authentic** is used to describe teaching that provides opportunities for students to use prior knowledge, recent learning, and critical-thinking and problem-solving skills to complete tasks that are relevant to their lives. Young children, understandably, have naïve understandings of how the economic world works. It is the job of the teacher to help replace these misconceptions with ideas based on inquiry. The teacher must, then, give ample opportunity for exploring these concepts of the real world. Practice in thinking about and working through economics concepts is vital to growth in understanding. It is imperative that teachers make economic learning meaningful and memorable. M. L. Kourilsky (1983) suggested some specific guidelines for employing experience-based economics instruction:

- Introduce new economic ideas through real-life experiences.
- Provide active economic experiences.
- Allow students to experience the consequences of their economic decisions.
- Use direct instruction to focus attention on economic ideas to be gleaned from their own real-world experiences.
- Reinforce experience-based economic learning with various experiences (role-play, literature, pictures, games, cooperative learning activities).

Key Concepts

Keeping in mind the ultimate goal of social studies education, as well as public education in general, to develop an informed citizenry, what could be more important than teaching young children about economics (Saunders & Gilliard, 1996)? Learning about taxation, goods and services, money, inflation, unemployment, and international trade are basic to informing students about the way the economic world works. The National Council on Economic Education (NCEE) has developed a publication, **Voluntary National Content Standards in Economics** (1997), that outlines "enduring themes," concepts, and principles basic to the teaching of economics. Within this publication are outlines for development of complex thinking and problem-solving skills, inherent to the discipline of economics. The National Council on Economic Education (1997) targets life-long knowledge and skills in order to help children become:

- Productive members of the work force
- Responsible citizens
- Knowledgeable consumers
- Prudent savers and investors
- Effective participants in a global economy
- Competent decision makers

  (National Council on Economic Education, 1997, p. 3)

The five key economic concepts—scarcity, production, distribution, exchange, and consumption—can be explored effectively by young children. The appropriate early childhood classroom offers many opportunities to help young children build their knowledge of economics (Suiter, 1998). Through active exploration, children can begin to develop an understanding of these complex concepts.

- Scarcity: Understanding that there are limited amounts of some resources
- Production: Understanding jobs that people have; exploring where different goods are produced
- Distribution: Understanding how products reach the market
- Exchange: Understanding how trade works
- Consumption: Understanding the difference between wants and needs and making appropriate use of resources

Scarcity

All children understand the concept of "wants." Developing an understanding of the difference in wants and needs is a more difficult task. This concept is, however, key to understanding economic principles. Understanding economics is essential as children make choices about personal resources.

Many classroom activities can be used to introduce the concept of scarcity. For example, participating in a recycling project can help bring the issue of scarcity to the attention of young students.

Production

The function of production is to meet the needs or the wants of consumers. Children can begin to understand the concept of production by understanding the work that their parents do. Workers are producers of either goods or services.

Distribution

Many children believe that goods just appear on the store shelves. An integral part of economic education is developing an understanding of how those goods are produced and distributed. Young students can investigate how products reach the marketplace in several ways. One suggestion is to have students research the origin of materials used in the classroom, then trace the path that the goods take before reaching the classroom for consumption.

Exchange

Young students come to school with some basics about the concept of exchange. Almost all of them have had experiences exchanging money received as gifts or allowance for a toy or piece of candy. In this way, children begin to develop an understanding of trade. From this base, the effective teacher can help children make connections to understanding how trade among countries makes goods available.

Consumption

Children are consumers! They have all had experiences in making purchases. Helping children to understand that money is required to pay for services and that work is required to obtain money is a key to developing a healthy understanding of consumption.

There are many ways to prepare the classroom environment to encourage economic understanding. Transforming the Home Living Center into a store makes it possible for students to practice making choices. Helping children to discriminate while watching television is another way to help them understand how to make wise choices. The effective teacher can help children understand that television commercials are designed to affect consumer behavior.

The use of learning centers supports and reinforces student learning of economic concepts. Centers offer students an opportunity to practice the skills that have been introduced in economics education. When paired with appropriate instruction and illustrative children's literature, the use of learning centers can help young students to develop the complex concepts presented in economics education.

Exploration of Careers in Economics Education

Careers provide a purpose and a direction for a person's life (Dewey, 1944). Exploration of careers in the early childhood classroom is important, appropriate, and can take many forms. Exploration of careers can begin by having students choose classroom jobs. Through development of responsibility for classroom tasks, young students begin to understand the basics of career development. Students can be introduced to a variety of career options through a study of community helpers. Teachers can also point out different career

LEARNING CENTERS WITH ECONOMICS THEMES

Home Living

Transform the home living center into a pizza parlor. Through participation in the restaurant, students can practice ordering supplies (distribution), cooking (production), delivering (distribution and exchange), purchasing and eating the pizza (consumption), and collecting money (exchange). Pizza restaurants in the area will frequently give teachers pizza boxes, which helps make the experience more real for students. Have students develop the menu, setting prices. They can take orders on a pad provided by the teacher, and work with play money. Aprons, rolling pins, pizza pans and boxes, a cash register, and telephone can help bring the activity to life.

Theater Center

Encourage children to incorporate economic principles in their dramatic play. Provide scripts and props that have settings with economic themes. Such settings as the grocery store or bank encourage students to consider scenarios having to do with economics.

Block Center

Provide a variety of models of transportation in the block center. Even the youngest student can begin to develop an understanding of the transportation of goods by playing with trucks and trains in the block center.

options as presented in the literature shared through social studies instruction.

At this early age, the important elements of career education are:

1. Introducing students to the importance of work
2. Offering a broad survey of careers important to their own lives
3. Creating an awareness of women and minorities in all careers

USING CHILDREN'S LITERATURE IN ECONOMICS EDUCATION

As with all other disciplines in the early childhood classroom, the curriculum can be greatly enhanced through the use of children's literature. Children's books help to deepen the concept development for all involved. Many classroom teachers, not experts in economics, can examine basic economic concepts themselves, through the use of

CONNECTING WITH ADMINISTRATION

Invite your principal to visit your classroom while students are engaged in the learning center developed for economics education. Point out the active ways in which students are developing mastery over the complex concepts introduced in the economics standards.

With the principal's understanding of the way that you are introducing higher-level thinking skills with your young students, lobby for a field trip to the bank or grocery store, or maybe the bakery in town. Invite your principal to accompany your class.

GROUP ACTIVITY — USING LITERATURE TO TEACH ECONOMICS CONCEPTS

With a small group (three or four) develop a book list of children's literature to address each of the Economics Education Voluntary

standards. Bring the books to class to share with the rest of the group. Add these selections to your Children's Literature Data Base.

children's literature. By using children's literature to explore economics concepts, we are basically "killing two birds with one stone" and extending time available for social studies instruction by including these topics in our reading instruction.

As teachers, we all want our students to expand their content knowledge and to become competent, independent users of literacy. Content learning and literacy learning occur concurrently. "As children engage in reading and writing to gain information on social studies themes, they simultaneously develop their ability to read and write (Johnson & Janish, 1998, p. 9). Many children's books have an underlying theme of economics education. While the formal terminology of economics usually will not be found in children's literature,

READ-ALOUD SUGGESTIONS FOR ECONOMICS

The Go-Around Dollar by Barbara Adams.
Round and Round the Money Goes: What Money Is and How We Use It by Melvin Berger.
Eyewitness: Money by Joe Cribb.
City Green by D. Ryan-DiSalvo.
Uncle Willie and the Soup Kitchen by D. Ryan-DiSalvo.
Once upon a Company: A True Story by W. Hallperin.
The Great Pet Sale by M. Inkpen.
Follow the Money by Loreen Leedy.
The Story of Money by Betsy Maestro.
Mommies at Work by E. Merriam.

To Market, to Market by A. Miranda.
Families by A. Morris.
Lemonade for Sale by Stuart Murphy.
Money, Money, Money: The Meaning of the Art and Symbols on United States Paper Currency by Nancy Parker.
If You Made a Million by David Schwartz.
Sheep in a Jeep by N. Shaw.
Alexander, Who Used to Be Rich Last Sunday by Judith Viorst.
Making Cents: Every Kid's Guide to Money: How to Make It, What to Do with It by Elizabeth Wilkerson.

the concepts will be beautifully illustrated, and the teacher can supply the correct terminology.

Children's literature is a powerful tool in helping children develop complex concepts and thinking skills. In their publication, *Teaching Economics Using Children's Literature* (1997), Day, Folts, Heyse, Marksbary, and Sturgeon (1997) sum up the importance of using children's literature in economics education by saying, "as economic concepts are taught within the context of literature, students realize that economics is a very real part of life around them."

ANTHROPOLOGY IN EARLY CHILDHOOD EDUCATION

Anthropology is defined as the scientific study of the origin; the behavior; and the physical, social, and cultural development of humans. Learning about other cultures is an exciting adventure for young children (Black, 1998; Mamola & Bloodgood, 2002). Children enjoy exploring the different traditions of people around the world through the use of folktales. Through a study of traditional tales from different

At an early age, children begin to develop economic concepts.

cultures, students can glean important elements of those cultures and compare them to what they know about their own culture (Fuhler, Ferris, & Hatch, 1998). Children particularly enjoy reading and comparing some of the hundreds of versions of the Cinderella story.

CONNECTION TO CHILDREN'S LITERATURE

Throw Your Tooth on the Roof: Tooth Traditions From Around the World, by S. Beeler

This fun book is particularly appropriate for first-graders, who are obsessed with their disappearing teeth! It explores traditions around the world having to do with what happens to teeth once they are out! Since six-year-olds are very interested in their ongoing loss of teeth, some first-grade teachers even keep "lost tooth" graphs in the classroom. This fun activity builds on the natural interests of the children at this stage of development. Their inherent curiosity about this particular subject makes this a perfect time for students to explore the traditions of children around the world.

Young students have also enjoyed studying other cultures through the literature describing different foods and traditions. Some favorites include *Everybody Cooks Rice* by Norah Dooley (she has also written other books in this same vein) and *Bread Is for Eating* by David Gershator. These books open the discussion and understanding that most cultures share commonalities. This also, of course, provides an excellent opportunity for appropriate cooking activities.

Anthropology offers an interesting and exciting insight into the traditions inherent in diverse cultures. Again, children's literature brings these traditions into the early childhood classroom, making the traditions and customs come alive for young children. Some suggestions for read-alouds having to do with anthropology are shown in the text box.

ARCHAEOLOGY

Archaeology is defined as the science or study of prehistoric antiquities such as the remains of buildings or monuments, bones, or other relics. A favorite dinosaur book for young children is Aliki's *Digging Up Dinosaurs.* While prehistoric history is not readily understandable to young children, they all know about dinosaurs and enjoy the study. It is easy to capture student interest by using these huge creatures as a hook.

READ-ALOUD SUGGESTIONS FOR ANTHROPOLOGY

Wee Sing around the World by P. Beall and S. Nipp.

Throw Your Tooth on the Roof: Tooth Traditions from around the World by S. Beeler.

A life Like Mine by H. Belafonte.

Paper through the Ages by S. Cosner.

Pancakes for Breakfast by T. dePaola.

Cranberry Thanksgiving by W. Devlin.

Everybody Cooks Rice by N. Dooley.

Everybody Bakes Bread by N. Dooley.

How People Live by D. Freeman.

The Gift of the Sacred Dog by P. Goble.

Children Just Like Me: Celebrations! by A. Kindersley.

Welcoming Babies by M. Knight.

People around the World by A. Mason.

Mommies at Work by E. Merriam.

Houses and Homes by A. Morris.

Families by A. Morris.

Sun through the Window: Poems for Children by M. Rilon.

When the Earth Wakes by A. Rucki.

If You Made a Million by David Schwartz.

Chicken Soup with Rice by M. Sendak.

Me on the Map by J. Sweeney.

A GLOBAL PERSPECTIVE
DESIGN A LESSON TO EXPLORE OTHER CULTURES

With a partner, develop a lesson plan based on objectives from the discipline of anthropology. Find the standards in your district/state standards. Use children's literature as a basis for your instruction.

Include some kind of active participation—cooking, art, dance, etc.

Share with the class, keeping notes for use in your own classroom later on.

Of course, archaeology is much more than the study of dinosaurs. This is just an exciting topic that readily engages young children in discovering archaeological concepts. Gauge the interest of students in the classroom to determine how much more of this kind of information

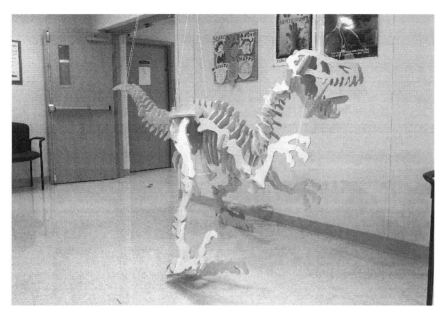

Children love dinosaurs.

READ-ALOUD SUGGESTIONS FOR ARCHAEOLOGY

My visit to the dinosaurs by Aliki.

Digging up dinosaurs by Aliki.

Dinosaur bones by Aliki.

Fossils tell of long ago by Aliki.

The magic school bus in the time of the dinosaurs by J. Cole.

Bodies from the bog by J. Deem.

Eyewitness: Fossil by D. Taylor.

National geographic prehistoric mammals. by A. L. Turner.

they are capable of handling. The purpose of archaeological study in early childhood classrooms is not necessarily to teach facts and details about the topic, but to whet students' appetites for learning and to stimulate interest in learning more about the world around them.

Children's literature offers many interesting titles related to the study of prehistoric times. Books listed in the box above are excellent hooks for engaging young children in the world of archaeology (Morris, 1998).

SUMMARY

Preschoolers and primary-school-aged students are capable of understanding complex concepts in all disciplines of the social studies. The fascinating worlds of anthropology and archaeology offer tempting morsels of information, ready to whet the appetite of the eager learner. Use of children's literature opens these complex disciplines to the understanding of young children. As with all other subjects, these must be taught in a developmentally appropriate way, assessing a child's prior knowledge and redirecting misconceptions.

Economics education is also an important part of an effective social studies program. Through the media, young children are constantly surrounded with information concerning economics. It is important that they learn to make wise decisions about their money, through study of the way the economic world works. When taught in appropriate ways, young children can understand and embrace the complex concepts presented in the study of economics. Through experience-based learning, young children are able to begin to develop sound economic decision-making strategies.

▶ THEMATIC STRANDS AND FOCUS QUESTIONS

Culture

1. How can young children engage in archaeological study to learn about other cultures?

2. How can the early childhood teacher use fairy tales to highlight cultural similarities and differences?

People, Places, and Environments

1. How can hands-on activities help young children connect to the societies from long ago?

2. How can the early childhood teacher structure lessons to help young children understand the importance of economics to the people around the world?

Production, Distribution, and Consumption

1. Which materials and activities can be used by early childhood teachers to introduce and reinforce the concept of "wants and needs" to young children?

2. How can children's literature be employed to introduce the concepts of distribution and consumption to young children?

Science, Technology, and Society

1. How can young children explore the relationships among science, technology, and society to gather and process information?

2. How can the early childhood teacher help young children explore the relationship between technology and culture?

Global Connections

1. Which materials and activities can the early childhood teacher employ to help young children understand the interdependence we have with people around the world?

2. How can early childhood teachers use economic concepts to introduce and reinforce global connections?

▶ KEY TERMS

anthropology
archaeology
authentic
Voluntary National Standards in Economics

▶ REFERENCES

Black, M. (1998). Using archaeology to explore cultures of North America through time. *Social Studies and the Young Learner., 11*(1), 12–13.

Chapin, J., & Messick, R. (1999). *Elementary social studies: A practical guide* (pp. 177–178). New York: Longman.

Day, H., Foltz, M., Heyse, K., Marksbary, C., & Sturgeon, M. (1997). *Teaching economics using children's literature*. Indianapolis, IN: Indianapolis Indiana Department of Education.

Dewey, J. (1944). *Democracy and education*. New York: Free Press.

Fuhler, C, Farris, P., & Hatch, L. (1998). Learning about world cultures through folktales. *Social Studies and the Young Learner, 11*(1), 23–24.

Johnson, M., & Janisch, C. (1998). Connecting literacy with social studies content. *Social Studies and the Young Learner, 10*(4), 6–9.

Kourilsky, M. (1983). *Mini-society experiencing real world economics in the elementary school classroom*. Reading, MA: Addison-Wesley.

Mamola, C., & Bloodgood, J. (2002). The enticements of archaeology: An interdisciplinary experience. *Social Studies and the Young Learner, 15*(2), 9–14.

Morris, R. (1998). Using artifacts as a springboard to literacy. *Social Studies and the Young Learner, 10*(4), 14–16.

National Council for the Social Studies. (1998). *Social studies for early childhood and elementary school children: Preparing for the 21st century.* Washington DC: Author.

NCEE (National Council on Economic Education). (1997). *Voluntary national content standards in economics.* New York: NCEE.

Saunders, P., & Gilliard, J. (1996). *A framework for teaching basic economic concepts.* New York: National Council on Economic Education.

Sosin, K., Dick, J., & Reiser, M. (1997). Determinants of achievement of economics concepts by elementary school students. *Journal of Economic Education, 28*(2), 100–121.

Suiter, M. C. (1998). Authentic Teaching and Assessment in Economics Education. *Social Studies and the Young Learner, 11*(2), 22–25.

▶ SUGGESTED READINGS

Beeler, S. (2001). *Throw your tooth on the roof: Tooth traditions from around the world.* Boston: Houghton Mifflin.

Bohan, C. (2000). A fair to remember: elementary economics. *Social Studies and the Young Learner, 16*(1), 6–8.

Kehler, A. (1998). Capturing the "economic imagination": A treasury of children's books to meet content standards. *Social Studies and the Young Learner, 11*(2), 26–29.

Meszaros, B., & Engstrom, L. (1998, Nov/Dec). Voluntary National Content Standards in Economics: 20 enduring concepts and benchmarks for beleaguered teachers. *Social Studies and the Young Learner, 11*(2), 8–10.

CHAPTER 10

Bringing It to Life
Drama, Art, Music, Movement, Field Trips, Cooking, and Storytelling

OBJECTIVES

After reading this chapter, you should be able to:

➤ Develop a list of movement activities designed to correspond with social studies concepts.

➤ Design and describe an effective dramatic play center for young students that will complement the social studies curriculum.

➤ Plan a field trip proposal to address social studies standards, complete with objectives for student learning, budget, permission slips, and notes home to parents.

➤ Design a social studies lesson based on a cooking experience, using children's literature as a base.

➤ Conduct a storytelling session addressing a social studies standard.

Live a balanced life—learn some and think some, and draw and paint, and sing and dance, and play and work every day some.

Robert Fulghum, 1989

Incorporating play encourages participation.

INTRODUCTION

Although social studies instruction has, in many cases, been relegated to a few minutes of reading the textbook and answering the questions at the back of the chapter, the subject matter available through the social studies can make for the most exciting instruction in the elementary curriculum. The vast array of real-life topics offers to the imagination of the creative teacher a vast smorgasbord from which to choose.

Teachers of young children are free of the necessity of being a master artist in any one discipline, and can explore and increase their own creative interests while working with young students. Five-year-olds don't care if the teacher can sing on key or if the dance steps are exactly right. This frees the teacher to explore a variety of experiences in the arts.

Through the ages, cultures have expressed themselves through the arts (Lutz & Kuhlman, 2000), offering the teacher meaningful examples of music, visual and performing arts, dance, and culinary arts that can be used as illustrations of particular skills in the social studies. The choices of beautifully illustrated children's literature, based on social studies topics, offer yet another way to connect the standards for which we are accountable to the interests of the students and to the arts.

In the classic, *Walden,* Henry David Thoreau stated, "There is an incessant influx of novelty into the world, and yet we tolerate incredible dullness."

For teachers of the most creative and enthusiastic population in our schools, there should never be a dull moment! Every standard can be brought to life through the efforts of a creative teacher, who sings, dances, dramatizes, and cooks his or her way through the curriculum.

Throughout this chapter, we explore ways that the early childhood teacher can engage students in social studies exploration through the arts, cooking, **field trips,** and realia. Topics from the social studies offer a variety of possibilities for exploration by young children.

DRAMA AND SOCIAL STUDIES

"Early childhood educators agree that children learn best through active engagement with objects and people in their environment" (Cooper & Dever, 2001, p. 59). By integrating curriculum, the interest and imaginations of young learners are engaged, and involving students in sociodramatic play is an effective way to communicate social studies concepts. Combining play with content supports children's understandings and conceptual development.

The early childhood teacher can encourage sociodramatic play by preparing the environment properly. Creating centers where children can develop their own props and write their own scripts provides a meaningful context for children to practice complex skills and explore complex concepts. Learning is a sociocultural event (Vygotsky, 1962), and dramatic play encourages social interaction as well as a context in which children can develop social studies knowledge and concepts.

Incorporating the dramatic play center into the daily lives of young children is an effective way to extend understanding of social studies concepts (Church, 1992; Crawford, 2004; Fayden, 1997). Through the use of a few simple materials, the early childhood teacher can allow students the opportunity to explore and extend information that was presented in social studies instruction. A dramatic play center does not need to be elaborate to be effective. Providing a few props, space for children to move and interact, and time for them to explore will allow students to use their imaginations to create the meaning necessary for successful dramatic play. Some simple props include:

Mirrors

Dolls

Cash registers, mail boxes, grocery store supplies

Costumes: hats, ties, coats, dresses, accessories, shawls

Sociodramatic play is an effective way to learn social studies.

Puppets

Transportation toys

Butcher paper/paint/crayons for scenery development

Dishes, plastic food (representing many cultures)

Creating a Play-Rich Environment

Creating a play-rich environment for school-aged children is as important as creating such an environment for very young children (King, 1987; Levin, 2004). High-quality play provides experiences for students that promote underlying skills necessary for improving memory, developing oral language, literacy skills—and the list goes on! This kind of play for older children involves planning and commitment. It also involves *time*. On the average, it takes from 30 minutes to an hour for a young child to develop and act out a good play scenario (Leong & Bodrova, 2003). Scheduling time for play in the elementary school classroom is an important part of an effective social studies curriculum. Students, given time and opportunity to play, develop problem-solving, social, and oral language skills.

The introduction of new social studies concepts, along with new historical characters and settings, offers a plethora of ideas for elementary school-aged students to incorporate in their play. The addition of student-made **Reader's Theater** scripts allows students to bring to life the words that they have written.

Blurred Lines Between "Work" and "Play"

The ideal classroom for young children incorporates "work" and "play" in such a way that the lines between them are blurred (Perlmutter & Burrell, 1995). Young children thrive on the excitement of learning. The early childhood teacher's responsibility is to help maintain and encourage the love of learning that young children exhibit before starting school.

Primary school-aged children still need lots of time to play (Smilansky & Shefatya, 1990). The social studies curriculum allows multiple opportunities to encourage creative and dramatic play. This active involvement allows students to construct an understanding of the complex concepts developed in the social studies curriculum, while providing important opportunities for children to practice social skills needed to thrive in a democracy. For example, in the home center, children can explore the roles of family members, look into economics as they make the home center into a grocery store, or act out historical accounts studied in their literature books.

In a 1987 study, N.R. King found that children called what the teacher tells them to do "work" and what they choose to do "play." This insight encourages teachers to allow choice in the classroom to meet the needs of individual students *and* the district's curriculum. An informal survey of adults found that they either *loved* or *hated* social studies as children, and that their feelings about this education were based on the delivery methods of the teacher. Active, relevant instruction in the social studies makes all the difference in the way students perceive this important aspect of their overall education. When teachers allow and encourage a choice of interesting and relevant educational experiences in the social studies, they stand a greater chance of engaging students and bringing them into the fascinating world of social studies.

STORYTELLING AND SOCIAL STUDIES

Folklorists define storytelling as "the art or craft of narration of stories in verse and/or prose, as performed or led by one person before a live audience; the stories narrated may be spoken, chanted, or sung, with or without musical, pictorial, and/or other accompaniment and may be learned from oral, printed, or mechanically recorded sources, one of its purposes may be that of entertainment" (Pellowski, 1991, p. 15). Storytelling is one of the true joys of working with young children. They love to be read to, but they come alive when you *tell* the story. There is just something magical about the art of storytelling.

Again, you do not need to be a professional storyteller to be effective in the social studies classroom. Young children just appreciate the effort! There are many reasons to participate in storytelling with your young students, some of which include: (1) introducing children to the patterns of oral language, (2) contributing to social and cognitive development, (3) developing listening skills, (4) entertaining, (5) introduction of classic tales from different cultures, (6) connecting to specific curricular objectives, and (7) helping the child appreciate his own and others' cultural heritage.

Storytelling is the oldest form of passing culture from generation to generation, and continues to be an effective way to pass down information and cultural understanding to children. When you are working with young students to develop an understanding of the complex concepts presented in the social studies, storytelling is a natural extension of the instructional "bag of tricks." Try a simple story first. Practice, practice, practice, then jump into it! You will be a little frightened at first, as we always are with a new experience. But, you will ultimately find developing your storytelling skills to be a joyful part of your teaching.

Tips for Storytelling

1. Find a story that you love.

2. Read, reread, and reread again.

3. Outline the characters in the story.

4. What is the style of the story? Is it funny, scary, matter-of-fact?

5. Outline the story on index cards, with only a few words on each card to cue you to the next portion of the story.

6. Practice telling your story. First practice in the mirror several times, then move on to family members or friends.

7. Tell the story to your students. Critique your performance, then make notes on things you would like to change.

8. Practice again.

9. Tell the story again to your students. They love to hear stories over and over again.

10. After you perform a few times, the story will belong to you.

GROUP ACTIVITY

TELL A TALE

1. Using your district/state social studies standards and year-long plan from Chapter 4, choose a theme for your storytelling.

2. Using the Internet, anthologies of children's stories, songs, or your own memories from childhood, choose a story that will illustrate an important point from your chosen theme.

3. Following the "Tips for Storytelling" given earlier in this chapter, practice your story.

4. Develop props or costumes, if you choose to use them.

5. In small groups of four or five classmates, perform your storytelling.

6. Make a time to conduct a storytelling session for a group of children.

7. Discuss: How did you feel about the storytelling? What went well? What could you improve on? How was this experience different from reading a story aloud?

8. Tell the story again, to your original group of classmates. Have an open discussion about the performance.

VISUAL ARTS AND SOCIAL STUDIES

In his book *The Art Lesson*, Tomie dePaola gives an autobiographic account of his experiences in elementary school. Throughout his early life, this gifted artist was encouraged by his family in his art. His parents taped his artwork on the refrigerator, took examples of his artwork to their workplaces to show off his abilities, and enthusiastically reinforced his natural talents. They made him feel like the artistic genius that he was. He then went to school, where he was required to copy the teacher's template and was not allowed to "do" art the way that he interpreted it. He became frustrated and closed down, refusing to participate in the activities that had brought him so much pleasure at home. Fortunately for him and for the thousands of children who have enjoyed his artwork, dePaola finally had the good fortune to meet with a knowledgeable and caring teacher, who encouraged him and allowed him to follow his own artistic path.

dePaola's experience is not, unfortunately, uncommon in our public schools. Young children come to school as passionate learners. At home, they were tauted as artistic geniuses, their masterpieces displayed on the refrigerator door gallery for all to see! All too often, their enthusiasm and excitement about learning is squelched by the teacher, who is intent on covering the curriculum. Encouraging the young child to express him- or herself through the **visual arts** is a natural way to maintain this passion (Bredekamp, 1993; Epstein, 2003; Jensen, 2001; Lasky & Mukerji-Bergeson, 2001). The gifted teacher can introduce techniques and materials to extend the child's artistic ability while maintaining an appreciation for the child's individual style and talent.

When young children use art materials, much incidental learning occur. Feelings of self-worth, cooperation, and taking turns are lessons that come from sharing ideas and materials. Art experiences offer a wealth of possibilities for young children to assimilate knowledge about their world, while providing a natural means for integrating learning from other curriculum areas.

When teachers value the artwork of their young students, those students develop an awareness and appreciation for painting, drawing, and sculpting. It is important to provide children with access to a variety of materials and to encourage them to use those materials in their own way, emphasizing process over product. Artwork can be used as a springboard from which the students can explore different cultures, different art techniques, and various social issues. In terms of social development, teachers can use art experiences to help children learn to respond to others' work in nonjudgmental ways and to accept the responses of others.

Valuing children's art encourages awareness
and enforces endless possibilities.

Reggio Emilio

The topic of visual arts in early childhood education cannot be examined without at least a mention of the Reggio Emilio Community, in beautiful northern Italy. The Reggio Approach began in Reggio Emilia, Italy at the end of World War II. Loris Malaguzzi, a psychologist, became the educational leader for a group of 19 schools for young children. Influenced by the work of Dewey and Piaget, Malaguzzi and the teachers set forth to develop new ways of teaching that would support the democratic society accomplished with the fall of the Fascist dictatorship (Malaguzzi, 1993).

Reggio teachers emphasize visual and expressive arts as tools to be developed for learning by young children (Bredekamp, 1993; Edwards, 1993). Malaguzzi believed that visual training was very important and should be developed from a very early age. In Reggio schools, in addition to the focus on visual arts, music is always playing in the background, while the children work on projects and play.

Reggio teachers do not use checklists or standardized tests. Instead, portfolios are used as the basis of student assessment. The teacher's role is more that of an observer and a facilitator/co-learner. The teacher acts as co-learner by providing opportunities for projects and creating an environment that is conducive for learning.

By incorporating some of the strategies employed in Reggio schools, the classroom teacher can encourage creativity in young children. Providing opportunities for children to engage in creative and imaginative activities that relate to classroom instruction allows students to explore these concepts in an appropriate and exciting way.

READ-ALOUD SUGGESTIONS FOR ART

Camille and the Sunflowers: A Story about Vincent Van Gogh by L. Anholt.

Degas and the Little Dancer: A Story about Edgar Degas by L. Anholt

Picasso and the Girl with a Ponytail: A Story about Pablo Picasso by L. Anholt.

Leonardo and the Flying Boy: A Story about Leonardo Da Vinci by L. Anholt.

Visiting the Art Museum by L. Brown.

Artist in Overalls: The Life of Grant Wood by J. Duggleby.

Katie and the Sunflower by J. Mayhew.

Henri Matisse: Drawing with Scissors by J. O'Connor.

Suzette and the Puppy: A Story about Mary Cassatt by J. Sweeney

My Name Is Georgia: A Portrait by Jeanette Winter by J. Winter.

Diego. by J. Winter.

Children's literature selections offer interesting and appropriate ways to introduce the work of artists to young children. Some of those titles are shown in the box.

MUSIC AND SOCIAL STUDIES

From birth, babies are biologically primed to respond to the human voice with pleasure. Babies take pleasure in the familiar songs sung by their mothers, and they gradually begin to imitate and sing along. Music is part of our biological heritage and is hard-wired into our genes as a survival strategy (Jensen, 2001). Cave paintings more than 70,000 years old depict the use of music. It is a part of the human experience. In fact, Howard Gardner (Multiple Intelligences Theory; see Chapter 3) suggests that the musical intelligence is the first to emerge (Gardner, 1993).

Children are first exposed to music in the womb, hearing the sound and rhythm of the mother's heartbeat. They love to sing! Singing gives playful opportunities to practice oral language, dramatic expression, and creative movement. In a recent article in *Young Children*, children's singing guru Hap Palmer said, "I started combining music and movement and writing songs that invite children to get out of their seats and experience the world through active engagement (Palmer, 2001, p. 13). A preponderance of evidence from the research suggests that music should be a significant part of every child's education.

Music is a significant factor in increasing learning and information retention in all core areas for students. "As children grow and develop, their musical involvement widens through opportunities for moving, listening, creating, and singing" (Hill-Clarke & Robinson, 2004, p. 92). The inclusion of music can be an important and successful educational strategy. Music can create and activate prior knowledge, creating a "hook" on which students can attach new information. The use of music in the classroom is consistent with theories of multisensory learning. These theories confirm what educators have known all along—that there are many avenues to learning, and music is one of the most powerful. By weaving it naturally into a child's day, learning through music can be inseparable from learning in other areas (Bayless & Ramsey, 1991).

When planning musical experiences for young children, the teacher must take into account a child's individual development and growth. Singing, movement, and language development are closely related for the young child. Inclusion of these important experiences

Music can help students remember and learn.

is effective in extending the social studies curriculum to meet the developmental needs of all students in the class.

Music has generally been considered a pleasant addition to an early childhood curriculum, but oftentimes it has not been considered terribly important. Teachers of young children battle time constraints on a daily basis. There is simply not enough time in the day to teach all that needs to be taught. Combining subjects, or multitasking, is one way to deal with this problem (Barclay & Walwer, 1992). Whenever possible, combine singing activities with the reading lesson, and combine both with social studies instruction. Using an integrated, center-based approach to teaching, teachers are able to present the information that children need, while addressing skill development in an appropriate way.

Music is so powerful in our lives because of the way it helps us remember events (Riggenberg, 2003). When we hear an old song on the radio, we are all transported back to a particular event or time. Students are able to recall facts presented in songs long after they have forgotten the factual information presented in the textbook.

There are many ways that we can incorporate music into classroom experiences (Fogarty, 1991). While music is an integral part of most preschool and kindergarten classrooms, these experiences often diminish as children move up the grade levels. An increased focus on academics often makes it more of a challenge to incorporate musical experiences in the upper primary and intermediate grades. Musical experiences at the upper grade levels can, however, offer excellent curricular reinforcement and extension.

Making connections between singing, children's literature, and social studies curriculum is natural (Barclay & Walwer, 1992). Books such as James W. Johnson's African-American anthem, "Lift Every Voice and Sing," offer opportunities to incorporate singing and literature into the study of the African-American experience. Jeanette Winter's "Follow the Drinking Gourd" offers similar opportunities, as do a multitude of children's literature selections. Folk songs, traditional American music, and songs written with social studies instruction in mind are all available to engage the musical intelligences of young students and to bring to life the stories told in social studies instruction. Research supports the use of music as a mnemonic device for learning skills and concepts in the content area.

There are many easy and interesting ways to incorporate music into the social studies curriculum. Putting factual information to music or chants or raps is an effective way to help students memorize discrete facts. While memorization of specific dates, places, and events is not the basis of an effective early childhood social studies program, developmentally appropriate introduction of these can form a basis for more complex concept development.

Singing with students also serves to increase group identification and cohesion. Beginning the class meeting with a song each

READING THE ROOM

1. Chart songs that students enjoy singing on a regular basis.
2. Post the charts around the room.
3. Provide a variety of pointers for students to use as they "read the room."

4. When students finish assigned work, instead of doing more paperwork, they can move around the room, practicing reading (singing) and increasing fluency.

morning helps children to become familiar with each other and to become comfortable singing in class. Through songs, children build **language fluency** that permeates every area of the curriculum.

Cornett (2001) recommends integrating music into the curriculum because music:

- "is a learning vehicle,
- unites affective, cognitive, and psychomotor domains,
- solves problems,
- increases creativity, sensitivity, and self discipline,
- gives aesthetic enjoyment" (pp. 337–340).

Musical Instruments

Using and creating musical instruments is another way to incorporate social studies concepts and skills. Students can research the kinds of musical instruments used in different periods of history being studied, look at materials used in making musical instruments and the parts of the world from which those materials come, work cooperatively to build their own instruments, and use instruments in performances based on social studies instruction. Musical instruments are motivational for children, who love to experiment with different sounds and to perform. Tying these interests into the social studies curriculum can extend student understanding of cultures being studied while motivating students to use research skills and to collaborate with classmates.

Far from being "fluff" in the curriculum, musical experiences can form a basis for student learning in the content area. The effective early childhood teacher will incorporate musical experiences into social studies instruction, bringing to life the important concepts being presented to students.

CREATIVE MOVEMENT AND SOCIAL STUDIES

Young children love to move! Using their bodies is the primary way in which young children learn about and explore the world. Between the ages of four and six, muscular coordination improves, and with it, a child's interest in experimenting with space and movement in rhythmic activities (Christianson, 1938, pp. 31–32). An effective curriculum offers children many opportunities for movement through direct experience. Children should have chances to move in a variety of ways—through block play, art, dramatic play, and dance. They can run, skip, dance, climb, throw and catch a ball, ride a tricycle or scooter, and dance. Brain-compatible learning indicates that teachers should weave math, movement, geography, music, drama, art, science, and physical education into an integrated curriculum.

Japan, Hungary, and Netherlands, three countries near the top in rankings of math and science scores, all have intensive music and art classes built into their elementary programs (Jensen, 2001, p. 87). Current research establishes significant links between movement and learning. Educators must be purposeful about integrating movement activities into lessons on a daily basis.

Teaching simple dances to accompany specific social studies units is a fun and effective way to incorporate movement in your classroom. Through the use of dance activities, the teacher can incorporate social studies, language arts, and physical education. Interpersonal skills are also learned and practiced as students listen to dance instructions, pay attention to the rhythm of the music, and work cooperatively with other students in the classroom (H'Doubler, 1936).

Movement activities can be integrated into almost every social studies unit (Green, 2002). Students can work with rhythm sticks, jump ropes, and square dancing to add creative and expressive movement to poetry and songs (Nilges & Gallavan, 1998). While the students are sometimes self-conscious at first, they soon come to enjoy the freedom they are given to move and explore space with their bodies.

In times of tight budgets and a focus on basic skills, many short-sighted school officials have made the decision to cut physical education courses. With rising childhood obesity rates and increased stress on children, this is a mistake. Recent research indicates that there are strong links between the cerebellum and memory, spatial

CONNECTION TO CHILDREN'S LITERATURE

Legend of the Bluebonnet: An Old Tale of Texas

In this classic retelling, Tomie dePaola's illustrations bring to life the experiences of She-Who-Is-Alone, who lived with the Comanche tribe. In this beautifully illustrated tale, the people were suffering because of an ongoing drought. The tribe's dancers continued their efforts in vain, and finally the shaman told the people that the Great Spirit wanted offerings of their most prized possessions. She-Who-Is-Alone offered her beloved doll as a sacrifice, scattering the ashes to the four corners of the Earth. The next morning, the hillside was covered with blue flowers—a sign of forgiveness. The people offered their thanks as the rains came.

Students can act out the story, using their body movements to illustrate the different aspects of the story. Invite students to offer suggestions for ways that they might move to depict rain or fire. They can stretch their arms and pretend to scatter the ashes of the doll to the four corners of the classroom.

It is also effective for students to move in response to music (Pica, 2004). In the Peter, Paul, and Mary classic, "Garden Song," there is an opportunity for students to move as the singers describe the growth of the plants in the garden. Young children love to move and these kinds of activities allow them to hone their listening skills by responding to the words of a book, poem, or song.

perception, language, attention, emotion, nonverbal cues, and even decision-making. Incorporating movement activities into the social studies curriculum is one important way to help children discover ways that their bodies work, while reinforcing skills and dispositions necessary to a successful social studies curriculum.

Why Physical Movement Is Important

Approximately 65 percent of students in the United States do not participate in physical education on a daily basis (Brink, 1995; CDC, 1996). Researchers James Pollatschek and Frank Hagen (1996) report, "Children engaged in daily physical education show superior motor fitness, academic performance and attitude toward school as

Outdoor activity is important to overall development.

compared to their counterparts who do not participate in daily physical education" (p. 2). Particularly in light of the trend toward doing away with physical education because of budget cuts and a "back to basics" mentality in the nation's schools, the classroom teacher must offer relevant and appropriate movement activities for children throughout the curriculum.

FIELD TRIPS AND SOCIAL STUDIES

John Dewey (1941) believed that learning was active and that schooling was unnecessarily long and restrictive. He believed that history could be learned best by experiencing how people lived and that geography could be best learned by knowing about the plants and animals that grew in different areas. Field trips enable teachers to expand students' knowledge beyond the walls of the classroom, much in the spirit of John Dewey's theory of learning and education.

Field trips allow students to acquire knowledge through hands-on experience with the rich resources in their community. Field trips increase a student's knowledge of a subject and provide opportunities to develop a student's socialization and citizenship skills. In these days of budget cuts and a return to basics instruction, teachers must plan effectively and choose appropriately the field trips that will be offered to students. It is important that we plan well and develop effective units that complement our classroom instruction and extend and deepen the learning for our children.

Careful attention must be paid in planning all aspects of a field trip. Again, because of budget cuts and curricular constraints, most public schools limit field trips to one or two per year. It is important to maximize the impact of these trips through careful selection, planning, implementation, and follow-up. We will discuss curricular issues, as well as safety, funding, parent involvement and concerns, and administrative support.

Selecting an Appropriate Trip

Many elements need to be considered when planning a field trip for your young students. The first is always safety. As you make decisions about your choice of field trips, keep safety foremost in your mind. A trip to the active rock quarry at the edge of town may be just the thing to augment your study of the Earth, but can you ensure the safety of 22 five-year-olds in that setting? Maybe. It depends on the particular rock quarry, as well as the people who own it and work there and their willingness to stop work while your students observe. We will talk more about safety as we discuss procedures for the field trip.

Curricular Considerations for Field Trips

Field trips should be tentatively identified during the summer prior to the school year, when the initial year-long plan is created. When looking at the year's themes, the teacher can consider all of the possibilities for an effective and appropriate field trip. (Many teachers get to April and remember that there is money budgeted for field trips, then make hasty plans for a trip). Given plenty of time to research and plan, you will be able to choose fun and unique field trips, which extend and reinforce the social studies curriculum.

Begin by reviewing the standards for your grade level. When creating the year-long plan, look for opportunities to extend those standards. You might begin with an Internet search of museums, theaters, libraries, factories, and so forth. In the larger cities, the museums have traveling exhibits, which may mesh beautifully with the thematic units chosen for the year. The Internet provides a valuable resource for selection of appropriate field trips, offering the classroom teacher information about specific opportunities available in the area.

Field trips offer meaningful connections to the social studies curriculum.

TIPS FOR SELECTING A SUCCESSFUL FIELD TRIP

1. Create the year-long plan, based on social studies themes and objectives.
2. Identify the objectives to be addressed with the field trip and develop a rationale for this choice.
3. Research possibilities in the area.
4. Write a proposal for the field trip, developing a tentative budget. Identify objectives and detail how this field trip will reinforce the social studies program.
5. Make a preliminary visit to the field trip site.
6. Seek administrative approval of the proposal.
7. Make arrangements with the appropriate office at the field trip site. Book a date and time.

After selecting the perfect location for the field trip, you will need to do the actual preparation for the trip. One of the most volatile aspects of planning a field trip for young children seems to be dealing effectively with the parents. There are two opposite but equally tricky problems when getting parent chaperones.

PLANNING GUIDE FOR THE TRIP

Two weeks before the trip:

1. Write a letter to the parents, outlining the details of the field trip. Make particular note of the educational objectives that will be met through this field trip.
2. Attach the district-approved field trip permission slips. Make a class list and check off students' names as they turn in the slips. Set a deadline of several days before the field trip date.
3. Contact the cafeteria so that they can prepare sack lunches for those children who are on free/reduced lunch plans. If those children not on this plan would like to order a sack lunch for the trip, those names should be turned in as well.
4. Contact the people in charge of transportation for the field trip. It is usually a good idea (though not absolutely necessary) to provide lunch for the drivers. Their jobs are difficult and often uncomfortable and boring. Anything you can do to make their jobs more pleasant will make your field trip more successful.
5. Identify your chaperones.
6. Divide students into small groups, with a chaperone attached. Decide if you will have parents work with their own child, or with a different group of children. There are pros and cons to each plan.

Two days before the trip:

7. Call parents two or three days before the trip if a child has not yet turned in his or her permission slip. Children cannot go on the trip without permission, and it is very distressing to them if they have to miss the trip.
8. Copy the permission slips (which should contain emergency contact information) and place on a clipboard, which you will take on the trip.
9. On the clipboard, place a class list, with four or five columns following each name. Throughout the day, take roll several times. This method will give you a systematic way to check on the students throughout the course of the field trip.
10. Have a class meeting with the students, going over procedures and expectations for learning and behavior.
11. Prepare nametags for the students and the chaperones. It is helpful to color code the groups for easy identification. Encourage students to wear their school t-shirts or a particular color t-shirt so they can be easily identified as they move through the field trip site.

(continued)

The problem that many teachers have with pre-kindergarten and kindergarten children's parents is an overabundance of desire for participation. Often there are too many parents wanting to chaperone, and cutting it down to a manageable number of escorts can be a political nightmare! Decide, before you ever mention the field trip to parents, how you will deal with this situation. How many

(continued)

12. Develop a field notebook for each parent chaperone. Prepare one page, reminding parents of the rules and expectations for student behavior, the schedule for the day (lunch, departure time, etc.), followed by some background information on the field trip location and some questions and activities that the parents might lead during their exploration of the field location.

On the day of the trip:

13. Dress comfortably! Be sure to wear comfortable shoes.
14. Hold a brief class meeting to remind students of your expectations for their learning and behavior.
15. Pass out nametags and introduce chaperones to their assigned students.
16. Take inventory of food, equipment, and so forth.
17. Take a last-minute restroom break with the students.
18. Take a cell phone and class list/permission slips in a tote bag.
19. Take along an emergency kit.

After the trip:

20. Allow students to share observations and reactions to the field trip.

21. Have one or two specific assignments as follow-ups to the field trip. Don't overdo this. You want the students to be able to enjoy the memory of the trip.
22. Create a scrapbook or bulletin board about the trip.
23. Have students create and send thank-you notes to the field trip hosts, chaperones, bus drivers, cafeteria workers, and so forth. They might include a photograph or drawing of their trip.
24. Send a follow-up report to the parents and administration about the trip. Again, be sure to highlight curricular objectives that were met through the trip. Presenting the field trip as a newspaper article, on your class Web page, or as a slide show at a PTA meeting are all good ways to publicize the academic aspects of your field trip.

Evaluating the field trip:

25. Did the students meet your objectives/expectations?
26. What were the positive aspects of the trip? How could it have been better?
27. Was there adequate supervision?
28. What was student feedback?

chaperones will you need? How will you divide the children into small groups? How will you select the parents who will participate? What will you do about those who are not needed for this field trip? Another difficulty, with the very young children, is the fear that parents have in allowing children to attend the field trip if the parent is not along as well. In addition, a policy concerning the attendance of younger brothers and sisters is one that needs to be in place early on.

On the opposite end of the spectrum is the difficulty of getting enough parents to help with field trips, because they work, have younger children at home, or have transportation issues. In this case, recruiting instructional aides or other school personnel to accompany you would be necessary.

While it seems simple on the surface, planning for a field trip is actually quite complex. Making a field trip meaningful and educationally relevant, while making sure every child is safe and feels secure during the trip is a difficult task. Through careful planning and appropriate supervision, field trips can offer excellent extensions to the regular social studies curriculum.

When field trips are planned and carried out in a thoughtful manner, they provide valuable ways to expand student interest and knowledge of a particular topic. They provide opportunities to experience things that cannot be duplicated in a classroom setting. Field trips also provide excellent opportunities to hone social skills among students and to make positive connections with parents and other community members.

GROUP ACTIVITY — PLANNING A FIELD TRIP

1. Pair up with a class member interested in teaching the same grade level you are interested in teaching.
2. Using the social studies standards for your state and district and the year-long plan outline that you developed in Chapter 4, choose a standard that you would like to address through the experience of a field trip.
3. Using the Internet or print sources, choose a field trip destination in your area that would lend itself to teaching those standards.
4. Using the Trip Planning Guide presented earlier in this chapter, plan the field trip from beginning to end.
5. Prepare a role-play in which you "sell" this field trip idea to your principal. Pretend that your principal is not a fan of field trips and will need a great deal of persuading. You will have had to prepare a budget, a lesson plan (complete with homework and extension activities), a plan for choosing chaperones, and so forth. Be ready to present this to your classmates.
6. Prepare a brochure, guiding parent chaperones in making the field trip successful.

Cranberry Thanksgiving by Harry Devlin

The "Cranberry" books (Halloween, Thanksgiving, Christmas, Valentine's Day) are wonderful jumping-off points for cooking activities with children. *Cranberry Thanksgiving* (1990), the first in this series, chronicles the days leading up to Thanksgiving in a New England cranberry bog. Maggie, the heroine of the story, and her grandmother invite a guest to Thanksgiving dinner, featuring Grandmother's own secret recipe for cranberry bread. A mystery ensues and ends up in a heartwarming exchange. The "secret recipe" is printed in the back of the book, and offers a wonderful,

ready-made connection between cooking and literature.

While it is not appropriate to base the social studies curriculum entirely on holiday themes, this series of books offers a nice connection throughout the year. Students remember Cranberry Halloween as you introduce Cranberry Thanksgiving, and so on. As a small portion of what you do in your cooking classroom, this is an effective way to help students to understand the passage of time.

COOKING AND SOCIAL STUDIES

Cooking activities in the classroom lend themselves to a whole realm of learning opportunities for children. Cooking experiences integrate easily into the social studies arena, revolving around themes and units of study. Cooking is an enjoyable activity for children and teachers alike. Literature-related cooking experiences involve children in all of the language-arts skills. In cooking activities, they read, write, use oral language, develop new vocabulary, listen, think critically, and problem-solve. Combining cooking activities with children's literature is an excellent way to focus student attention on a current topic of study. Social skills are encouraged, since cooking must be preceded by developing a set of rules for safety, and then requires cooperation as children cook and clean up. Students can be exposed to authentic recipes and techniques that relate to the social studies units being explored.

Since cooking is a basic life skill, it helps to foster a child's sense of independence. Cooking experiences are excellent introductions to the concept of change over time, and change as we alter the environment. Cooking also encourages a child's ability to reason and problem-solve. Involving all of the senses in cooking and eating experiences helps to make lasting impressions and connections for students as they study the foods of different times and parts of the world.

Social skills are encouraged during cooking activities through the development of safety rules and the inherent requirements of cooperation and planning. The act of eating itself is community building. Researching and participating in culinary experiences from other cultures gives students an insight into those cultures and peoples. The possibilities are endless.

Benefits of Cooking

Cooking helps develop skills in many areas—oral language, written language, reading, mathematics, fine motor development, and social

A GLOBAL PERSPECTIVE

CONNECTING TO DIVERSE CULTURES

It is the job of teachers of young children to help children develop a positive self-image and pride in who they are. A first step in helping to foster these feelings of pride is to help children reflect on the diversity around them. Exploring the arts is a meaningful and appropriate way to help children notice the beauty of the differences around them.

Begin with an exploration of the different cultures represented in your own classroom. Invite parents, grandparents, and other family members to share their special expertise in cooking, dance, drama or visual arts. Ask them to dress in traditional costume, if appropriate, and share with the students the different traditions and cultural aspects of their or

their ancestors' homelands. It is important to talk with the students concerning the commonalities among cultures as well as the differences. One common theme across cultures is the love of a parent for his or her child. These kinds of common denominators should be explored, as well as the differences.

Take pictures! Have students write about the visits from classmates' families, have them practice the native dances with the family members, and have them create art in the style of the culture represented. Enjoy the diversity of experience represented in your classroom, and use this diversity to help your students recognize their own self-worth and uniqueness.

skills. Pairing cooking with children's literature and social studies instruction is a natural fit. During cooking activities, children integrate their math, social studies, science, language arts, nutrition, and basic economics skills. They explore foods from other cultures and make connections between those foods and the geographic regions from which they come. Students are encouraged to research other recipes, to make plans for successful cooking experiences, and are given purposeful and challenging reasons to read, write, and learn.

SKILLS DEVELOPED THROUGH COOKING EXPERIENCES

A variety of skills are introduced and developed through the classroom use of cooking experiences. Since children enjoy cooking activities so much, they frequently forget that they are learning! When participating in cooking activities as the teacher, keep in mind the multitude of skills that are being addressed. Some are listed below.

Social Skills Development

Sharing

Trying new experiences

Taking turns

Taking responsibility for clean-up

Table manners

Mealtime conversation

Sensorimotor Development

Fine motor development (chopping, stirring, mixing)

Large muscle development (kneading)

Taste differentiation

Smell differentiation

Texture differentiation

Language Development

Reading recipes

Planning sequence of recipe

Vocabulary development

Following written/verbal directions

Writing

Asking questions

Mathematics

Fractions

Classifying

Ordering

Measuring

Spatial conceptual development

Time

Temperature

Social Studies

Change over time—concept development

Cultural understanding

Geographic differences in food

Ethnic differences/regional differences

Some Cautions When Cooking With Children

When planning for cooking experiences with young children, several things need to be taken into consideration. It is important to talk with parents during the Back-to-School night concerning plans for cooking in the classroom. This gives the parents an opportunity to discuss any food allergies their children may have, or other concerns that they may have about food experiences in the classroom. It is also a good idea to check the students' permanent records for food allergies and to send a note home the day before the cooking activity, just to make sure that the child will have no difficulty with the ingredients of the recipe. Of particular concern are children with allergies to peanuts. This can be a deadly allergy and should be taken very seriously. Always check with parents before cooking with children!

Childhood obesity has tripled since 1980 (Center for Disease Control and Prevention, 1996). Overweight children have a 70 percent likelihood of becoming overweight adults, and overweight adults are at higher risk for developing heart disease, diabetes, high blood pressure, and some kinds of cancer. At school, it is important that students learn about nutrition and have an opportunity to practice what they have learned through cooking and gardening activities. When planning cooking lessons based on social studies topics, keep in mind that you are modeling good food choices.

The school environment is a powerful influence on students' attitudes concerning food. Schools are currently struggling to improve academic achievement, and are cutting back on physical education and recess time in the school day. They are requiring more homework for students, cutting into the amount of time they have to play outdoors after school. In addition, unsafe neighborhoods and parks make it less likely that parents will allow children out to play alone. Increased television viewing and playing video games take children's attention away from the physical activity in which children have been engaged in the past.

Some state governments are stepping into the discussion, by requiring school cafeterias to present more nutritious meals for students, and by requiring schools to remove candy and soft drink machines. In addition, in some states, teachers are not allowed to give candy and sweet snacks to students during the school day. Be sure to check the requirements of your own state before planning cooking experiences with your students.

Inviting guest chefs in to cook with the students is a wonderful way to connect to the parents of your students, other school personnel, and the greater community. It is important to hold a brief training session for interested volunteers, so that they know your behavior and academic expectations for the students. You might model a literature/cooking lesson for the volunteers, giving them ideas about ways they might extend the experience. At the very least, prepare a brief handout or booklet to help guide volunteers in their lessons. Tapping into the diversity of the community is a great way to help students extend their knowledge of ethnic foods and cultures.

HINTS FOR COOKING IN CLASS

Cooking with young children is an exciting way to make the social studies come alive in the classroom. There are, however, several important things to keep in mind when planning cooking experiences with young children.

1. Check for food allergies.
2. Lobby for a cooking room in your school. Some primary schools have such rooms, but areas can be designated in all schools. Second-hand stoves and refrigerators may be obtained from parents or community members. Faculty and parents can stock the kitchen with measuring spoons and measuring cups, bowls, mixers, and so forth. This makes it much easier to incorporate cooking activities in your classroom.
3. If the preceding is not possible, a toaster oven and ice chest in your classroom will work.
4. Send a note home the day before the cooking activity. You might ask for volunteers to bring in ingredients. This is a judgment call. If you are working in a school with children from less advantaged backgrounds, do not put this added strain on the family budget. You might work with your principal to build funds into the budget for cooking experiences. You can also look for grants to help you with this expense.
5. Reproduce the recipe for the students. Students can use the recipe for many skills in language arts and math.
6. Reproduce the recipe on a large chart. This can be used for large-group instruction and shared reading.
7. Offer one or two extension activities for the cooking experiences. Occasionally, just allow students to enjoy the cooking, with no requirements for follow-up.
8. Allow students to write and draw about their cooking experiences. It's always nice to create a class big book with these cooking experiences. Then students can revisit the experiences throughout the year.
9. Share your experiences and recipes with parents each week. Newsletters are great ways to connect home and school activities. Encourage students to take their copy of the recipe home to re-create with their families.
10. Have fun! If you plan well and have behavior expectations in place for students, cooking is a piece of cake!

Safety in the School Kitchen

Safety is, of course, the most important consideration when cooking with young children. By establishing rules before the activity ever begins, and by following some simple procedures, cooking in the classroom can be a safe and meaningful activity. Some safety considerations are:

1. Use electrical appliances and sharp utensils only under adult supervision. (Use plastic knives with young children.)
3. Cut away from your body.
4. Use thick potholders when handling hot pots and pans.
5. Unplug all electrical appliances when not in use.
6. Wipe up spills immediately.
7. Wash hands with warm water and soap before handling foods.
8. Wash, dry, and put up utensils after cooking.

Keeping parents informed about the cooking experiences in the classroom is important for several reasons. First of all, a letter to the parents prior to the cooking activity gives an additional opportunity for you to make sure there are no allergies or other health concerns relating to the dish to be prepared. In addition, communicating with

LETTER TO PARENTS

Dear parents,

The second graders in Room 9 will be reading *How to Make an Apple Pie and See the World* by Marjorie Priceman. Through this book, our students will explore economic wants, how people use resources, and different geographic regions of the world. They will also explore measuring, change over time, and cooperation.

The ingredients in the recipe (which the students will bring home on Friday) are eggs, flour, cinnamon, butter, salt, sugar, and apples. Please let me know if your child has any allergies that would be affected by this recipe.

Be watching for the recipe when your child brings it home on Friday. You may want to have him/her help you prepare the recipe at home.

Sincerely,

the parents concerning the cooking experience gives you an excellent opportunity to model effective, active learning for the parents. Many times, parents will follow up on a school cooking activity by re-creating the experience in their own kitchens. This allows young children to spend meaningful time with parents, acting as an "expert" with a recipe that they have already cooked in the classroom. A sample letter to parents is provided, introducing the cooking lesson to be taught and tying it to a piece of literature.

Making Picture Recipes

Cooking with young children offers many benefits. One important benefit is that of supporting literacy development. Recipes provide an authentic reason for children to practice their reading skills. When cooking in the classroom, it is often effective to make picture recipes, for even the youngest students. These chart-sized recipe cards help very young children to make the connection between the written word and the cooking task at hand.

For older students, picture recipes allow and encourage practice of new reading skills, continuing to make the connection between the written word, sequence of directions, and new vocabulary. The pictures drawn to represent each ingredient in the recipe help cue developing readers about new vocabulary words.

You might choose for students to use the picture recipe as a guide for writing their own recipe cards in a writing center. These cards can be taken home and shared with the family, encouraging family involvement in the social studies curriculum.

How to Make a Picture Recipe

1. Use chart paper to create a poster-sized recipe.
2. Write down the word for each ingredient, with a picture of a label on each card.
3. Number the steps to the recipe and draw as much of the process as possible.

Supplies for Classroom Cooking

Many teachers avoid cooking in the classroom because of the expense and preparation-intensity of these activities. These difficulties can be reduced by working with grade-level partners, developing a common supply closet for cooking equipment. In some schools, parents are willing and able to help provide materials and some principals allow funds for cooking experiences. As you begin to plan for cooking in the classroom, the following supplies, kept in a common area, reduce the preparation time for each cooking activity:

1. Measuring cups and spoons
2. Mixing bowls
3. Large mixing spoons
4. Rotary mixer
5. Plastic spoons, knives, and forks
6. Paper plates
7. Small cutting board
8. Pitcher
9. Napkins and paper towels
10. Aprons
11. Pot holders
12. Antibacterial soap

CONNECTING TO DIVERSE POPULATIONS

Incorporating the Arts

Learning about other cultures and ethnicities is one way to combat prejudice. As children learn about new cultures and add that new information into their existing schema, they can appreciate the uniqueness and similarities of others and not rely on racial and ethnic generalizations (Davidson & Davidson, 1994).

The arts provide opportunities for students to learn about themselves, as well as the world around them. Through experiences in visual arts, music, and movement, young children can become more aware of the contributions of people of all races and ethnicities through the ages. The arts provide a means for young children to express their own emotions and to learn about the feelings of others. When the arts are integrated into the social studies curriculum, information about other cultures can be better understood and embraced.

SUMMARY

The Association for the Advancement of Arts Education states, "The arts are worth studying simply because of what they are. Their impact cannot be denied. Throughout history, all the arts have served to connect our imagination with the deepest questions of human existence: Who am I? What must I do? Where am I going? Studying responses to those questions through time and across cultures—as well as acquiring the tools and knowledge to create one's own responses—is essential not only to understanding life but to living it fully" (Association for the Advancement of Arts Education).

Incorporating arts into the social studies curriculum is a natural for young learners. Throughout the ages, people have expressed their culture through the arts. It is only fitting that we incorporate these into the study of social studies in the early childhood years.

The good news about working with young children in the arts is that we don't have to be masters. If we have two left feet or if we can't carry a tune, our students don't care. The joy of expressing ourselves and allowing the students to express themselves through the arts is far more important than technique or singing on key. Enjoy your teaching! "... learn some and think some, and draw and paint, and sing and dance, and play and work every day some." It's the only way.

THEMATIC STRANDS AND FOCUS QUESTIONS

Culture

1. How does the sociodramatic play of young children reflect their culture? How can the early childhood teacher use sociodramatic play to expand the cultural horizons of the young child?

2. How can the art of storytelling inform young students about other cultures?

Time, Continuity, and Change

1. How can the study of the arts help young children understand the concept of change over time?

2. How can cooking activities help young children to develop a sense of time with young children?

People, Places, and Environment

1. What are the physical and human characteristics of the places/events represented in historical stories?

2. How are the people in history represented through their art?

Individual Development and Identity

1. How do events in history affect the individual development and identity of the child? How can the early childhood teacher help the child discover this connection?

2. How can the biographies of artists from the past help young children develop a sense of self? Which strategies can the early childhood teacher employ to encourage this discovery?

Global Connections

1. How can integration of the arts help young children to see the interconnectedness of people around the world? What can the early childhood teacher do to encourage this understanding?

2. How can early childhood teachers use international music and dance to address social studies standards?

▶ KEY TERMS

field trips
language fluency
mnemonic device
performing arts
Reader's Theater
storytelling
visual arts

▶ REFERENCES

Association for the Advancement of Arts Education. (1994). *National Standards for Arts Education. What every young American should know and be able to do in the arts* [Electronic version]. Rowley, MA: Author. [Online]

Bayless, K., & Ramsey, M. (1991). *Music: A way of life for the young child* (4th ed.). New York: Merrill.

Barclay, K., & Walwer, L. (1992). Linking lyrics and literacy through song picture books. *Young Children, 47*(4), 76–85.

Bredekamp, S. (1993). Reflections on Reggio Emilia. *Young Children, 49*(1), 13–17.

Brink, S. (1995). Smart moves. *US News and World Report* May (online database).

CDC (Centers for Disease Control and Prevention). (1996). Guidelines for school health programs to promote lifelong healthy eating. *Morbidity and Mortality Weekly Report, 45*(RR-9). www.cdc.gov/mmwr/preview/mmwrhtm/00042446. htm (Accessed May 31, 2002).

Christianson, H. (1938). *Bodily movements of young children in relation to rhythm in music.* New York: Columbia University Press.

Church, E. (1992). *Learning through play: Music and movement.* New York: Scholastic.

Cooper, J., & Dever, M. (2001). Sociodramatic play as a vehicle for curriculum integration in first grade. *Young Children, 56*(3), 58–62.

Cornett, C. (2001). *Creating meaning through literature and the arts.* Upper Saddle River, NJ: Merrill-Prentice Hall.

Crawford, L. (2004). *Lively learning: Using the arts to teach the K–8 curriculum.* Greenfield, MA: Northeast Foundation for Children.

Davidson, F., & Davidson, M. (1994). *Changing childhood prejudice: The caring work of schools.* Westport, CT: Bergin & Garvin.

Dewey, J. (1941). *Education today.* London: George Allyn & Unwin.

Edwards, C. (1993). *The hundred languages of children: The Reggio Emilia approach to early childhood education.* Norwood, NJ: Ablex.

Epstein, A. (2001). Thinking about art: Encouraging art appreciation in early childhood settings. *Young Children, 56*(3), 38–43.

Epstein, A. (2003). Supporting young artists: The development of visual arts in young children. Ypsilanti, MI: High Scope Press.

Fayden, T. (1997). Children's choice: Planting the seeds for creating a thematic sociodramatic center. *Young Children, 52*(3), 15–20.

Fogarty, R. (1991). Ten ways to integrate curriculum. *Educational Leadership,49*(2), 61–65.

Fulghum, R. (1989). *All I ever really need to know I learned in kindergarten.* New York: Ballantine.

Gardner, H. (1993). *Frames of mind: The theory of multiple intelligences*(2nd ed.). New York: Basic Books.

Green, C. (2002). Moving to literature. *Texas Child Care, 26*(1), 12–21.

H'Doubler, M. (1936). *The dance and its place in education.* New York: Harcourt, Brace.

Hill-Clarke, K., & Robinson, N. (2004). It's as easy as A-B-C and do-re-mi: Music, rhythm, and rhyme enhance children's literacy skills. *Young Children, 59*(5), 91–95.

Jensen, E. (2001). *Arts with the brain in mind.* Alexandria, VA: Association for Supervision and Curriculum Development.

King, N. R. (1987). Elementary school play: Theory and research. In J. Block & N. R. King (Eds.). *School play source book*(pp. 143–165). New York: Garland.

Lasky, L., & Mukerji-Bergeson, R. (2001). *Art: Basic for young children.* Washington, DC: NAEYC.

Leong, D., & Bodrova, E. (2003). *Educational Leadership 60*(7), 50–53.

Levin, D. (2004). Rethinking Children's Play: Changing times, changing needs, changing responses. http://www.pta.org (Accessed March 17, 2004).

Lutz, T., & Kuhlman, W. (2000). Learning about culture through dance in kindergarten classrooms. *Early Childhood Education Journal, 28*(1), 35–40.

Malaguzzi, L. (1993). For an education based on relationships. *Young Children, 49*(1), 9–12.

Nilges, L., & Gallavan, N.(1998). How can I make social studies move? *Social Studies and the Young Learner, 10*(4), 5–8.

Palmer, H. (2001). The music, movement, and learning connection. *Young Children, 56*(5), 13–17.

Pellowski, A. (1991). *World of storytelling.* New York: H. W. Wilson.

Perlmutter, J., & Burrell, L. (1995). Learning through "play" as well as "work" in the primary grades. *Young Children,* July, pp. 14–21.

Piaget, J. (1954). *The construction of reality in the child.* New York: Ballantine Books.

Pica, R. (2004). *Experiences in movement: Birth to age 8* (3rd ed.). Clifton Park, NY: Thomson Delmar Learning.

Pollatschek, J., & Hagen, F. (1996) *Smarter, healthier, happier."* International Health, Racquet, and Sportclub Association Booklet, Boston, MA.

Priceman, M. (1994) *How to make an apple pie and see the world.* New York: Alfred A. Knopf.

Riggenberg, S. (2003). Music as a teaching tool: Creating story songs. *Young Chidren, 58*(5), 76–79.

Smilansky, S., & Shefatya, L. (1990). *Facilitating play: A medium for promoting cognitive socioemotional and academic development in young children.* Gaithersburg, MD: Psychological and Educational Publications.

Thoreau, H. D. (1854/2001). *Walden: Or life in the woods.* New York: Dover.

Vygotsky, L. (1962). *Thought and language.* Cambridge, MA: MIT Press.

SUGGESTED READINGS

Beierle, M., & Lynes, T. (1992). *Book cooks.* Cypress, CA: Creative Teaching Press.

Derman-Sparks, L., & the ABC Task Force. (1989). *Anti-bias curriculum: Tools for empowering young children.* Washington, DC: NAEYC.

National Association of Music Education Staff. (2000). *Music makes the difference: Music, brain development, & learning.* Washington, DC: Music Educators National Association.

CHAPTER 11
Assessment

OBJECTIVES

After reading this chapter, you should be able to:

➤ Develop and apply a rubric to the work of young children.

➤ Perform a role-play of an effective parent conference.

➤ Describe ways that accountability can be established in a developmentally appropriate way for young children.

➤ Describe the three aspects of assessment.

➤ Develop an observational checklist for use with young children in social studies instruction.

As long as there are tests, there will be prayer in public schools.

Anonymous

305

Simply observing children is one of the most valuable assessment srategies available to the early childhood teacher.

INTRODUCTION

Children are "smart" many different ways. Just as it is inappropriate to teach all children in the same fashion, it is inappropriate to assess them in the same way. Standardized testing is a fact of life that is here to stay. Even though many early childhood educators have serious philosophical, moral, and ethical concerns about the inappropriate nature of high-stakes testing, the fact of the matter is that we will continue to be judged by the standardized test scores of our students and students will continue to be judged academically by their standardized test scores (Herman, 1997; Kamii, 1991; Karp, 2002).

Classroom teachers are responsible for helping young children do well on those tests, while doing what is *really* important—learning! Fortunately, for excellent teachers, this is not only possible, but also an exciting challenge!

In response to the growing demand for accountability in the classroom, teachers must use a variety of assessment measures to gauge learner performance and understanding. "Assessment is the process of observing, gathering evidence of a child's knowledge, behaviors and dispositions; documenting the work children do and how they do it; and making inferences from that evidence" (Moore, 2002, p. 12). There are many ways to assess student learning in an appropriate way. Several options are explored throughout this chapter.

AUTHENTIC ASSESSMENT IN THE EARLY CHILDHOOD CLASSROOM

Authentic assessment includes written products, experiments, performances, portfolios, observation, checklists, and group projects, to name a few (National Center for Fair and Open Testing, 1991). An authentic assessment approach, a form of naturalistic assessment, occurs when a child is observed while performing tasks in real-life situations as these would naturally occur during the routines of the day (Losardo & Notari-Syverson, 2001).

Authentic assessment originated in the arts and apprenticeship systems, when those evaluating the ability of a young musician or apprentice observed and gave feedback on the performance of the young person. The idea of authentic assessment extends this principle of evaluation to all areas of the early childhood curriculum. In the social studies, products and performances provide data on how well concepts are being learned, and are valuable tools in the early childhood classroom.

FUNCTIONS OF ASSESSMENT

While assessment is traditionally viewed as a way to "get a grade in the grade book" or as an end-of-the-year standardized view of the student's growth, assessment should be an ongoing, important part of the instructional cycle. Students' progress toward achieving their goals should be assessed at every stage of the lesson. Assessment should inform the instruction designed by the early childhood teacher, and is an ongoing, fluid process.

Initial assessment identifies the current knowledge of the students as of the beginning of the instructional unit. Through this assessment, the teacher will develop a plan to address the strengths and needs of each student as he or she relates to the unit to be taught. In an ongoing fashion, the teacher will evaluate student growth as the unit progresses. The informal assessment along the way will serve to guide the teacher in monitoring and adjusting as the lesson unfolds. The final assessment will help to evaluate unit effectiveness, along with the individual growth of each child.

COMPONENTS OF ASSESSMENT IN THE EARLY CHILDHOOD SETTING

1. Documentation
2. Evaluation
3. Communication

Documentation

Document, document, document. There is nothing more powerful, in a meeting with parents, administration, or in an ARD (Admission, Review, Dismissal—for special education services) than the teacher who has well organized documentation of a student's work over time. Many teachers keep a large three-ring binder of informal assessments. Divide the binder into sections for each student, and file the informal reading running records, observational records, rubrics, and so forth. This is an efficient way of having documentation at your fingertips.

Evaluation

Evaluation is simply determining if a standard has been met, and to what degree the student has met that standard. The teacher can use

CONNECTING TO ADMINISTRATION

INVOLVING THE PRINCIPAL IN ASSESSMENT

Talk to your principal about developing an appropriate way to share evaluations of students with their parents. In many states, it is not a requirement to give number or letter grades to young children on the report card. Many times, however, in an effort to make evaluation tools equal across the grade levels, principals choose to have early childhood teachers present report cards for young children. Not only is this inappropriate, but it also gives very little meaningful information to the parents.

Talk with your principal and early childhood team members about ways that you can appropriately report progress of young children to the parents. This might involve parent conferences, parent visitations, more frequent informal interaction with parents, etc. Devise a plan.

a variety of tools to evaluate a student's progress toward a standard. There are many suggestions following in this chapter. It is important that evaluation be "authentic." Again, authentic means that the way we evaluate students is meaningful and relates to their real-life experiences. Such assessments as observations, interviews, journals, drawings, and work samples are examples of authentic assessment. Examples of assessments that are not authentic are the use of standardized testing, multiple-choice tests (in most cases), and answering the questions at the end of the book.

Communication

The third component of assessment in the early childhood setting is communication with parents. Until parents are informed of the child's progress, true assessment has not taken place. It is important to develop an open relationship with the parents of your students from the very beginning of the school year. Don't wait until a problem occurs, and don't wait until the end of the six-weeks planning period to make contact with the parent. Make phone calls to report a positive change in the student. Send home notes on a regular basis, and make a habit of sending weekly folders with student work. Have documentation readily available and complete. Parents appreciate and respect the teacher who is ready with specific examples of the child's work.

OPTIONS IN ASSESSMENT

In addition to written tests and standardized tests, it is appropriate to use a variety of other kinds of assessments. With time always in short supply, many effective early childhood educators use assessments that also offer an ongoing opportunity for learning. By honing "kid-watching" skills, early childhood teachers are able to extend student assessment to many of the classroom activities that are planned for instruction

Visual Presentations

Visual presentations allow students to demonstrate complex learning in an interesting and meaningful way. Visual presentations can be completed by individual students, but are also an effective product from a cooperative group. Some examples of these follow in the next subsections.

GROUP ACTIVITY
A PARENT CONFERENCE

With a partner, develop a profile of a child who is having difficulty in school. Outline the specific problems the child might be having, the different assessments that you may assemble for a parent meeting, and a script for a role-play of the conference that you will have with that parent.

With your partner, present the role-play to the class. First, outline the problems that the child is having, what you have done to help remediate the problem, and the documentation that you will have on hand to share with the parent.

The class will discuss and critique each performance.

Graphs/Charts

Students as young as pre-K and kindergarten are able to represent the learning that has occurred through the use of charts and graphs. Students can represent their graphs on chart paper, or can use the computer to develop graphs. Creating a chart or graph indicates higher-order thinking, as students must take information that they have learned, synthesize, and then represent that learning in a different way.

Illustrations

Teachers can learn a great deal by simply looking at a child's drawing. For those students who are not as able as others to represent their learning in written form, assessment through illustration can be a powerful tool. Attention to detail can tell a teacher a great many things about what a child has learned in a given lesson. The Art Center is a great addition to a classroom at any level. Allowing children to illustrate their understandings of complex concepts in the social studies through illustrations is an effective way to assess their learning.

Murals

Murals are a wonderful way for students to work cooperatively to display what they have learned in a social studies study. Murals lend themselves to displays of change over time, allowing children to work on several different scenes from a single unit of study. Murals can be used as an assessment tool, as well as a tool for effective instruction of social studies concepts.

Videotapes

Most schools have video cameras available for use by students. With some basic training, most children in grades 2–4 are able to safely operate a video camera. The camera itself offers an incentive to students to prepare, practice, and perform original skits, songs, poems, and so forth. This assessment activity encourages higher-order thinking. Students must take what they have learned, synthesize that information, add to it with additional research, apply skill for scene development, costume design, etc. in order to make videotaped presentations.

Students worked in cooperative groups to develop this mural as a part of their study on the arts.

Multimedia Presentations

PowerPoint is a great way for students to present information they have learned in social studies instruction in a meaningful and visually powerful way. Students as young as kindergarten age have the ability to add photographs, charts/graphs, and information from the Internet, which provides meaningful extensions for student presentations.

Quilts

Making quilts with young children is a creative way to represent learning in the social studies. Although this form of assessment can be time intensive, the finished quilts serve as a reminder of learning that has taken place in the social studies classroom, and also are a source of pride for young children. There are many ways to create quilts with young children. One easy and attractive way to create a class quilt is to have students illustrate, with crayons, a representative event in a unit that has been presented, on a square of muslin. Quilts can also be done on manila paper, putting squares together with tape

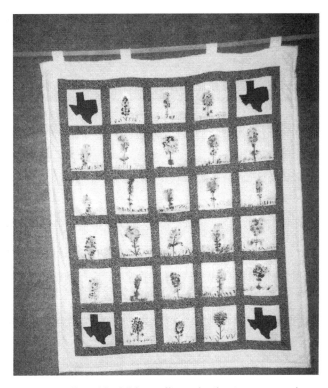

Creating quilts with children offers a lasting treasure and can
illustrate their understanding of a topic being studied.

or yarn. This is a wonderful way to see what students really gleaned
from the unit of study.

Making quilts with children also provides an opportunity to
employ parent and community volunteers. Involving volunteers in
working with the children to create a quilt, and ultimately, to put it
together, provides a meaningful volunteer activity.

Models

Models are a fun and effective way to assess learning in many disciplines of the social studies. Representations of ships, communities, or
period dress are just a few of the endless ways modeling can be used
to assess understanding in a particular social studies area. Again, this
offers students the opportunity to extend what has already been learned
through additional research. Modeling also offers an opportunity for

A GLOBAL PERSPECTIVE — CONNECTING TO PARENTS FROM A DIFFERENT CULTURE

Working with children from different cultures offers many challenges in terms of appropriate assessment (Robles de Melendez & Osertag, 1997). One of those challenges involves communicating with a parent who does not speak English.

With a partner, discuss how you might have a meaningful parent conference with a parent who does not speak English. What special accommodations will you need to make for this parent? What preparations do you need to make before meeting with this parent? Share with the class and make a chart for suggestions from the entire class.

students to use higher-order thinking skills by applying the knowledge previously learned in a social studies unit to a new activity.

Museum Exhibit

One way to assess understanding of a topic, to extend learning, and to whet the appetite for continued learning on a topic is to have students develop an exhibit of materials based on a specific topic. Students might bring in artifacts, photographs, models, and videotapes on the assigned topic. This allows the children to showcase their understanding of the topic at hand and to encourage the interest of the other students concerning this topic.

Story Maps

The use of story maps is a creative way to assess students' understanding of a particular story or concept. As an assessment tool, this strategy is low pressure for the students and gives a great amount of information to the assessor. By examining a student's completion of a story map, the teacher can note the level of detailed understanding that a student has about a particular concept. The teacher can also determine what kinds of misunderstandings a child has, by examining the process of making the story map, as well as the final product.

A Kindergarten Museum of Art.

To create a story map, students could, for example, illustrate the different locations where the story takes place. They could use a concept presented in a history lesson, illustrating a timeline of the historical events. Students can complete story maps independently or in small groups of students.

Oral Presentations

Oral presentations allow students to demonstrate their understandings of social studies concepts in front of an audience. Oral presentations can be group presentations or individual presentations. This is an effective way to showcase the understanding of students on a particular topic. Oral presentations also provide an opportunity to deepen the understanding of a topic for the audience members. Some examples of oral presentations are given in the following subsections.

Skits, Plays, and Interviews

The use of historical events as a basis for student-written skits and plays are powerful assessment tools. In plays and skits written by students, teachers can assess student's understanding of the setting and customs of an era, as well as the reality of the characters in the play. Again, this assessment strategy offers rich opportunities to assess what the students know about the topic, as well as an opportunity to extend the knowledge and understanding of audience members during performances. Use of a video camera can further extend the activity for the students and create a lasting artifact for assessment.

Oral Reports

Teaching students to use effective research tools is one of the most important things we can do as social studies teachers. The amount of information available to students is astounding, and it is important to help students understand how to access that information, then pare it down to a manageable amount. Oral reports are an effective way to assess that ability. Students are given a limited amount of time to present the *most important* facts of their research. Additional benefits of this kind of assessment include encouragement and practice for students to feel more comfortable in public speaking and the enrichment of the audience members as information is presented.

Simulations

Reenactments of actual events allow students an opportunity to showcase their understanding of events in history. Students may simulate battles, explorations, campaigns, presidential speeches, and so forth, allowing them to showcase their understanding of the event. While commercial simulations are available and are valuable teaching tools, allowing students to develop their own simulations, based on information gained from a unit of study, is a very effective means of assessment.

Songs, Poetry, and Choral Readings

Students enjoy the use of original songs, poetry, and choral reading passages. Students, usually in small groups, work to develop a song, poem, or choral reading passage, using the information they have gained from a unit of study. Giving students an interesting and non-traditional assignment, such as using their knowledge of an historical event to write a song, is both motivational to the student and beneficial to the assessor. In a short time, the classroom teacher is able to listen to the original work of the students and determine to what extent the information presented has been learned and understood on a higher level.

Written Assessments

Performance-based writing is a fairly typical form of assessment. This kind of assessment encourages students to use knowledge and understandings from unit study to create a written product.

Research Reports

Research reports are a mainstay of social studies instruction. Children as young as kindergarten age can begin to develop research skills, presenting them in written form. Research reports are valuable for assessment, as a teacher can identify understanding of a specific topic, by taking note of the pieces of the report that the students have synthesized from their research. "Teachers in the primary grades can support children in their quest for knowledge by establishing an environment that is conducive to inquiry, and by helping children develop basic research skills (Barclay & Traser, 1999, p. 215).

Giving students a clear understanding of your expectations for their research projects is a first step to success. Checklists can be developed with the students before they begin the project, helping them to understand the steps to take to complete their research. These should, of course, be designed with the developmental needs and abilities of each child in mind. One example is shown in Table 11-1.

Songs and Poetry

We previously discussed the strength of the presentation of songs and poetry developed in response to study in a particular unit. The act of conceptualizing, writing, and editing songs and poetry offers a powerful synthesizing experience for students. The natural outgrowth of the writing of songs and poetry would be performance.

Biographies

Biography is a powerful force in bringing the social studies to life for children. The *people* in history, the *people* in archaeology, and the *people* in geography are what make these disciplines of study relevant to the lives of young children. When students write biographies of a historical figure, of an inventor, of a geographer, when they study geographic

TABLE 11-1

Example of Checklist for Early Childhood Classroom Research Projects

WHAT CHILDREN CAN DO	ASSESSMENT DATE	COMMENTS
1. Identify topic for research.		
2. Identify materials needed for research project.		
3. Work independently on research project.		
4. Work cooperatively in small group.		
5. Meet timeline dates.		
6. Create materials necessary for presentation.		
7. Present material in appropriate fashion.		
9. Work cooperatively with others.		

information, they must truly know about the entire surrounding elements of the person. When writing a biography, a student would have to understand the setting and purpose of the subject's life and times. Writing a biography creates a meaningful opportunity for young students to showcase the synthesis of their understanding concerning a specific person represented in the social studies.

Newspapers

A creative way for students to display their learning is through the development of a classroom newspaper. This format allows children to write about the information they have learned in their social studies instruction, either from their own perspective, or from the assumed perspective of a historical character. This format has the added benefit of encouraging cooperation among students in the classroom. The classroom newspaper offers an effective vehicle for communication with parents and administration concerning curricular issues presented in the classroom. When student work together to create a classroom newspaper, they have an authentic reason to write and show great pride in the final product.

Journals

Journaling is one of the most powerful tools we can use for assessment and continuous learning with our young students. The possibilities

The most important assessment is that of the teacher interacting one-on-one with the student.

are endless—beginning with children as young as pre-K and kindergarten, dictation and illustration can be done with a focus on the social studies topics currently being addressed in the classroom. This process allows the teacher to observe misconceptions and true understandings of the concepts addressed. With older elementary students, journaling provides an opportunity and a vehicle for students to use to document their understandings and feelings about specific learnings and readings in the social studies. An added benefit is the convenience and organization of a single document to use in tracing the progress of student understanding throughout the course of the school year.

Creative Writing

Using the factual information presented in social studies instruction, students can expand their knowledge and understandings through writing of fictional material. Creative stories, journals, letters, television and movie scripts, radio shows, and so forth can be written based on the historic information students have learned. Development of fictional characters living in historically correct settings can be a motivational way for students to display their knowledge of information presented.

HOW CAN I GRADE THESE KINDS OF ASSESSMENTS?

Many teachers, both experienced and novices, would love to incorporate these kinds of assessments, but hesitate to do so because of district mandates for a minimum number of grades to be taken during each grading period. There are many ways to get the requisite "grades for the book" *and* to do the appropriate kinds of assessments which will give needed information about the students' understanding of the concepts being presented.

Rubrics

A **rubric** is simply a guideline for what will be expected by the teacher on a particular assignment. A rubric can be as simple as a "yes" or "no" response to a statement. Rubrics can be very specific and detailed or very basic. The most important element of a rubric is the students' understanding of the scoring criteria prior to beginning the assignment. When students understand the appropriate use of scoring rubrics, they are able to self-assess their work along the way.

Guidelines for Developing a Rubric

1. Determine which concepts or skills you are assessing.
2. Rewrite the concepts or skills into statements, which reflect performance components (e.g., Student used correct punctuation in 100% of the essay).

3. Determine the number of points to be used in your rubric. A three- or four-point scale is most appropriate for young children.

4. Starting with the desired level of performance on the task, develop a description for each score.

5. Analyze the student's work and compare it to the rubric.

GROUP ACTIVITY

DEVELOPING A RUBRIC

In small groups of three or four, develop a rubric to assess a social studies lesson that you have prepared for an earlier chapter. Discuss the merits of using this kind of assessment with young children. What are the benefits? What are the drawbacks? How could this kind of assessment be used in a parent conference?

Peer Assessment

Rubrics can be used by student peers as well as the person completing the assignment. This assessment strategy allows classmates to give input on the work of the assessed student. The child completing the assignment is given the benefit of several points of view of their work and the assessors are given an opportunity and a motive for paying close attention to the work of their classmates. While a teacher would need to be careful in incorporating these forms of assessments into a final grade for the assessed student, it is an important piece to the assessment puzzle.

Kidwatching

Baseball great, Yogi Berra said, "You can observe a lot by watching." While it seems a little silly on the surface, that statement actually has a great dealt of merit. Of the multitude of assessment strategies available to teachers, **kidwatching** is the one of the most valuable. The classroom teacher, with training, experience, and specific knowledge of curriculum and individual students, is the most important tool in assessing true student learning. Watching students as they play and as they work is a very useful medium for gathering information on student learning. This is true because, as children play and complete authentic assignments, they are free to display their real-world abilities. The information gained from such observations can inform instruction and give valuable information about the program and individual students.

Checklists

There are countless ways to do appropriate observations. One of the most common forms of formalizing "kidwatching" is through the use of **checklists.** It is important for the teacher to develop a checklist to identify the specific behaviors to be observed. The teacher must develop a strategy for cycling students through the observation process. Many teachers use a clipboard, complete with index cards labeled with each child's name. This makes "walk-arounds" constant assessment opportunities. When the index card is filled, simply file it behind the name of the student in an index card file.

Checklists are convenient ways for teachers to systematically evaluate the children's progress. Checklists can be formal, published documents provided by the school district or specific publishers. Teacher-made checklists are more targeted and give more beneficial information to the teacher's evaluation of her individual students.

Anecdotal Records

Anecdotal records are another way to formalize your kidwatching. A very beneficial way to report to parents or other professionals concerning the progress of your individual students is to take anecdotal records as he or she works and plays. Nothing is more powerful than to be able to cite specific instances, words, and actions of a particular child when reporting on his or her progress. This can be done in a variety of ways, but many teachers find that keeping a pad of sticky notes and labeling with the name of the child and the date of the record works well. When the Post-it® note is full, just stick that note on the child's page in your assessment notebook, to organize and type up when you have time.

Informal Questioning

Informal questioning is a very effective way to obtain information about the learning of your students. This can and should be done on an ongoing basis, whenever the opportunity presents itself. Making

Maintaining documentation of student progress helps to make
parent-teacher conferences more meaningful to the student.

sure to provide time for each student is an important part of the
informal questioning process. One way to do this is to set up a schedule, during the daily SSR (Sustained Silent Reading) time. The teacher
can take the opportunity presented by all students being engaged in
their reading for 15 uninterrupted minutes to systematically choose a
student or two to "interview." Proponents of SSR would insist that the
teacher spend this time reading as a model to the students, but some
teachers find this time better spent working individually with students.
This is a time that can be used to talk with the students about the
books they are reading, which frequently will be related in some way
to the current social studies theme. This can be enhanced by having a
variety of books on the current topics available to students for their
independent reading. Seizing on the time provided by having the class
engaged in an independent activity to interview individual children
can give the classroom teacher an otherwise unavailable opportunity
to gain insight into the thought processes of each student. By keeping
a list of student interviews, the classroom teacher can be sure to have
individual time with each child over the course of a two-week period.
It is helpful to keep anecdotal records of these interviews, as this gives
additional information to the teacher in terms of assessment, and also
provides a starting place for subsequent interview opportunities.

EXAMPLE OF CHECKLIST FOR INDIVIDUAL STUDENT INTERVIEWS

Teachers can gain a great deal of insight into the understanding and thought processes of their young children by conducting individual student interviews. These interviews are a very effective way of customizing instruction to meet the very individual needs and interests of each child in the classroom.

To use individual student interview checklists effectively, the early childhood teacher will develop a schedule of students to be interviewed on a particular day. These can be kept in the teacher's lesson plan book, allowing her to be sure that students have been interviewed in a timely fashion.

To begin the interview process, have in mind the level of the student being interviewed and the instructional focus for their current lesson. Spend a few minutes (5–10) with each child, using his or her responses as a springboard for the ensuing interview. Make quick notes about their responses and their current independent reading selections (Table 11–2). This will help you guide them to subsequent book choices.

TABLE 11-2
Sample Checklist for Individual Student Interviews

CHILD'S NAME	DATE OF INTERVIEW	TOPIC OF DISCUSSION	CURRENT INDEPENDENT READING
Alex	10/12	Making a map. How Clara designed a legend for her map.	*Sweet Clara and the Freedom Quilt*
Kalisha	10/12	Comparison of non-fiction and fantasy stories about the same topic.	*Aunt Harriet and the Underground Railroad in the Sky*
Marcus	10/13	Compare/contrast *Under the Quilt of Night* with *Sweet Clara and the Freedom Quilt*	*Under the Quilt of Night*
Javier	10/13	Talked about the importance of song to the slaves.	*Follow the Drinking Gourd*

STANDARDIZED TESTS

By definition, standardized tests permit the comparison of a single child's performance against those of other children of the same age. Standardized tests provide the teacher with a summative evaluation, which can be effectively used to assess the effectiveness of a total program or curriculum (Business Roundtable, 2001). Goals and objectives established by

CONNECTION TO CHILDREN'S LITERATURE

Testing Miss Malarkey by Judy Finchler

Obtain a copy of *Testing Miss Malarkey* by Judy Finchler. This fun book illustrates the teacher, Miss Malarkey, talking to the students in her class about THE test. There are no grades on the report cards, there is no extra homework, and no matter what, students will be promoted to the next grade. But, Miss Malarkey is biting her nails and is very nervous. Why?

This book helps to put the pressure of standardized testing into perspective.

Discuss: How can we minimize the negative effects of standardized testing on our students, while giving them every opportunity and incentive to do well?

someone other than the classroom teacher are assessed by standardized testing, so these kinds of tests do not offer a great deal of usable information for the individual classroom teacher and student.

The problem with standardized testing with young children is twofold: first, the great deal of time testing takes away from classroom instruction, and second, the politically charged nature of standardized testing. While the use of standardized testing will be a part of the education landscape for a long time to come, it is important for teachers of young children to take the appropriate attitude about these tests and to use them for the purposes for which they are designed—as program evaluation; *not* as a measure of a particular student, or as a single measure to from which to make decisions on a child's placement or continuation in a program.

A CALL FOR APPROPRIATE ASSESSMENT

The National Association for the Education of Young Children (NAEYC) has developed guidelines for **appropriate assessment** for young children, which reflect key points about how teachers can assess what children have learned. Some of those guidelines are summarized below.

CHECKLIST FOR LOOKING AT ASSESSMENT

- Is it based on knowledge of child development?
- Does it rely on regular/periodic observations over time?
- Does it address all domains of learning: social, emotional, physical, cognitive?
- Will the information gained help you do a better job?
- Does it rely on multiple sources of information?

- Does it reflect individual, cultural, linguistic diversity?
- Is it free of bias?
- Does it allow for learning differences?
- Is the classroom teacher the primary assessor?
- Is there accommodation for communication with parents?

In the development of appropriate assessment strategies, the individual child is the most important component of the assessment.

READ-ALOUD SUGGESTIONS FOR ASSESSMENT

Finchler, J. (2003). *Testing Miss Malarkey.* London: Walker & Company.

Prelutsky, J. (1998). *Hooray for Diffendoofer day!* New York: Knopf Books for Young Readers.

1. Assessment is congruent with and relevant to the goals, objectives, and content of the program.

2. Assessment results in benefits to the child, such as needed adjustments in the curriculum or more individualized instructions and improvements in the program.

3. Children's development and learning in all domains, as well as their dispositions and feelings are routinely assessed and are supported by the assessment.

4. Assessment relies primarily on procedures that reflect the ongoing life of the classroom and avoids approaches that place children in artificial situations.

5. Assessment recognizes individual diversity and allows for differences in styles and rates of learning.

6. Assessment utilizes an array of tools such as those described earlier in this chapter.

7. The classroom teacher is the primary assessor, although assessment is a collaborative process that ultimately involves the teacher, the students, the parents, the greater school community, and the community in general.

8. Assessment involves what a child can do now, as well as what he or she can do with assistance (in the zone of proximal development) as that shows the direction of growth.

9. Assessment information is systematically collected, recorded, and analyzed.

10. Assessment information is regularly shared with parents—not with traditional report cards relying on letters and numbers, but with meaningful, descriptive information.

CONNECTING TO DIVERSE POPULATIONS

Effective Assessment in a Diverse Classroom

The United States is an increasingly diverse society. As early childhood teachers address the social studies curriculum with young children, it is necessary to acknowledge and understand the differences that the children bring to the classroom. It is imperative that each student has equal access to the curriculum in order to meet his or her full potential.

Teachers must be prepared to facilitate the learning of each student, whatever ethnicity, cultural background, or learning style that child brings to school. Teachers must examine all educational practices, teaching methods and strategies, materials, and assessment strategies to ensure an equal opportunity for all students to succeed.

SUMMARY

Assessment is a vital part of effective teaching. As curriculum is planned and implemented, it is imperative that teachers know *what* students need to learn from the instruction, and *how* to know when those objectives have been met. Effective teaching is based on what we expect children to be doing *tomorrow*. Early childhood teachers must look at what children know *today,* plan effective instruction, and *assess* student learning in terms of what they will be learning *tomorrow.*

▶ THEMATIC STRANDS AND FOCUS QUESTIONS

Individual Development and Identity

1. What influences the way individual children learn and grow?
2. Which assessment strategies support the individuality represented by each child in the class?

Individuals, Groups, Institutions

1. What are the influences (groups/institutions) that guide assessment in public schools?
2. What is the role of the teacher, the principal, the student, and the parent in assessment?

KEY TERMS

anecdotal record
appropriate assessment
authentic assessment
checklist
kidwatching
rubric

REFERENCES

Barclay, K., & Traser, L. (1999). Supporting young researchers as they write to learn. *Childhood Education, 75*(4), 215–223.

Business Roundtable. (2001). *Assessing and addressing the "testing backlash."* Washington, DC: Author.

Herman, J. (1997). Assessing new assessments: How do they measure up? *Theory Into Practice, 36*(4), 196–204.

Kamii, C. (Ed.) (1991). *Achievement testing in the early grades.* Washington, DC: National Association for the Education of Young Children.

Karp. S. (2002). Let them eat tests. Rethinking Schools: An Urban Education Resource, 16(4). http://www.rethinkingschools.org/archive/164/Eat164, shtml. (Accessed November 10, 2002).

Losardo, A., & Notari-Syverson (2001). *Alternative approaches to assessing young children.* Baltimore, MD: Paul H. Brookes.

Moore, K. (2002). Choosing assessment tools for individual learning. *Early Childhood Today, 16*(4), 12–14.

National Association for the Education of Young Children. (1997). *Teaching and working with culturally and linguistically different children.* Washington, DC: Author.

National Center for Fair and Open Testing (1991). Authentic Assessment of Educational Achievement. http://www.uncg.edu/edu/ericcass/achieve/docs/ aut_ass.htm. (Accessed October 8, 2004).

Robles de Melendez, W., & Osertag, V. (1997). *Teaching young children in multicultural classrooms: Issues, concepts, and strategies.* Clifton Park, NY: Thomson Delmar Learning.

SUGGESTED READINGS

Bredekamp, S., & Rosegrant, T. (Ed.). (1995). *Reaching potentials: Transforming early childhood curriculum and assessment* (Vol. 2, p. 17). Washington, DC: NAEYC.

McTighe, J. (1999). What happens between assessments?" *Educational Leadership, 54*(4), 4–12.

APPENDIX I
Simple Ideas for Content-Related Learning Centers

LISTENING CENTER

Using listening posts or individual cassette players with earphones (less than $10.00 at discount stores), have students listen to and read along with a teacher-made tape.

Choose a read-aloud that addresses the social studies unit being taught. This can further extend the availability of content-related information presented to students. The use of listening centers also provides an opportunity to introduce students to biographies. By listening to a recording of the text, students are able to engage in books at a higher readability level, increasing the amount and depth of information to which they are exposed. School libraries offer a wide variety of biographies from which to choose.

Tip for recording: Read s-l-o-w-l-y. You will think that you are dragging along, but students are able to follow along much more readily when you read slowly. If there is a fluent reader in your class, you might let these upper-grade students make tapes for your class, or maybe for a primary classroom.

MAKING BIG WORDS

In her book *Making Big Words,* Patricia Cunningham offers a strategy for students to use in manipulating the letters from big words to make many smaller words. This activity is an excellent extension to a social studies lesson, giving students an opportunity to work with the vocabulary in a different way.

After going through a "Making Big Words" lesson, place the materials in a center with a pocket chart and let the students practice making big words on their own. After some experience with this technique, vocabulary words based on the social studies themes are appropriate for this center. Some "big words" for use in the social studies center might include Constitution, Declaration, Independence, or

Washington. Use the words that have been introduced in the read-aloud selections or in the textbook introduction of the units of study.

To create this center, prepare several sets of each "big word" on tagboard. Cut the word into individual letters, placing each cut-up word in a plastic sandwich bag. Students are directed to make as many two-letter words as they can form and put the letters in the bag, then as many three-letter words, four-letter words, and so forth. After they manipulate the tagboard letters into words, students write the words on a tablet or in their unit notebooks. The grand finale of this exercise occurs when the student finally makes the targeted "big word."

Example: Constitution

Two-letter words:
On
To
No
It
So

Three-letter words:
Not
Ton
Tin
Sit
Too

Four-letter word:
Cost

Five-letter word:
Stint

Six-letter words:
Notion
Cotton

Seven-letter word:
Tuition

Twelve-letter word:
Constitution

OVERHEAD PROJECTOR

Prepare an excerpt from an online or hard-copy encyclopedia, based on the social studies theme being studied. Print that passage on an overhead transparency and place in the Overhead Projector Center. Students can use markers to highlight the important words in each sentence, using some of those words to create a one-sentence summary of the selection. This is an excellent way to help students practice synthesizing passages from the content area. Students can write their summaries on index cards, punch a hole in the upper left-hand corner, and place them on a metal ring, kept in the Projector Center. Students can review the work of the previous "synthesizers."

READING CENTER

Give a free reading time for the students. The research is clear that "good readers read." Include books that you have read during large group time, which relate to the social studies unit being taught. Have some big pillows, a beanbag chair or two, and a good selection of easy reading level books for your students to read. A lamp in this corner is a nice touch, as well. This free reading time will allow for reinforcement of skills and concepts previously taught in the social studies lesson, and will allow students to explore previously read material.

GAME CENTER

Games such as *Candy Land*® and *Chutes and Ladders*® are effective for reinforcing directional concepts with young learners. More advanced games such as *Where in the World is Carmen Sandiego*® or *Risk*® are good for older, more sophisticated learners. This can be a place where students develop their own games, as well. Providing poster board, markers, scissors, dice, and materials for making spinners creates an inviting place for students to hone their social studies skills.

DICTIONARY/THESAURUS CENTER

Put several copies of the classroom dictionaries and thesauri on a small table. Develop a chart, giving students instructions for the assignment to be completed. For instance, if students are practicing the use of Guide Words in their Language Arts course of study, make a list of words from the social studies theme for them to look up. A tip: Minimize the amount of actual "copying" from the dictionary. Copying from the dictionary teaches very little. Have students write the page number or the two guide words, instead of copying selections from the dictionary.

COMPUTER

The classroom computers are a great, easy-to-prepare center. It is often effective to pair students to work on the computer. Depending on the sophistication of the students and the equipment, many things can be done to extend the social studies lessons presented. There are a variety of excellent computer programs available, which address the social studies standards. In addition, if there is an Internet connection in the classroom, this is an excellent center to use for research.

WRITING CENTER

Go out in your garage and pull out that old typewriter. Set it up with some plain white paper and let the students loose writing their own stories. They love working on the machinery. There's also something special about the kinesthetic aspect of pounding on the keys of an old typewriter that is very satisfying. This is a good way to practice spelling and vocabulary words, as it brings in that kinesthetic modality. The novelty of a typewriter intrigues children and may encourage them to write more. Start with a research topic related to the social studies unit being explored, or encourage students to do their own research on historical figures, using the typewriter to complete the report.

Of course, this center can be incorporated into the computer center, or students can be provided with a variety of paper, pens, and markers, if a typewriter is not available.

ADDING MACHINE

Do the same thing with an old adding machine. Provide some catalogs and/or newspaper advertisements and have students develop a budget for a dinner party or a trip to the mountains. This is a motivating way to interest students in economic principles.

MOUNTAIN SOCIAL STUDIES

Mountain Math is an excellent program that can be purchased for use in the elementary classroom. This adaptation works well to reinforce skills in social studies. Each week, you will have 10–15 different problems on a bulletin board. Such questions as, "Which states would you pass through on a trip from Florida to Texas?" will require students to hone their map skills. Students will use a spiral notebook to keep their work in for the entire year. Have students complete 4–5 problems each day during center time. Provide an answer key so that the center can be self-correcting.

STORY STARTERS

Cover a coffee can with bright contact paper. Inside of the can, place many pieces of paper, each with a story starter written on it. Have students do a "quick write" (no huge editing process needed here) and share their stories with other members of their center group. Change the story starters as the social studies units change, to reflect the unit topics.

PHOTO STORY STARTERS

A great use for those *National Geographic* photos! Cut out a large number of photos from *National Geographic* and have them available in a large brown envelope. Have students choose a picture from the envelope and write a descriptive paragraph about the photo. Special instructions can change, according to the topic being studied at the time. For instance, during a study of map skills, the instructions might include finding the location of the photograph on a map and including latitude and longitude within the paragraph.

BLOCKS

Blocks, Legos®, etc. are great for children of any age. When working with a partner or two, this is a great time for continued oral language development, fine motor development, and creative thinking. Special instructions for this center can include creating a map with the blocks, then transferring the map to a piece of graph paper. Instructions could include building a set for a puppet theater, then writing a script to use in that center. Your imagination (and that of the students) is the only restriction here. Focus of the center can change as the social studies units change throughout the school year.

READER'S THEATER

Reader's Theater is defined as a minimal theater in support of reading and literature. Few props are required, and most scripts are adaptations of literature. The Reader's Theater center can help students increase oral language skills, reading fluency, and interpersonal interactions while exploring topics and themes presented in the social studies coursework. The Reader's Theater Center is also an excellent motivation for having students read and write their own plays, based on stories read during the social studies thematic instruction. Great sites for obtaining scripts for Readers' Theater are also available on the Internet. Provide a hat rack with different simple props (hats, aprons, old shirts, etc.) or a trunk of old clothing for students to use as they work through the process.

Some Web sites for Reader's Theater include:
http://www.aaronshep.com
http://www.fictionteachers.com

BOOK MAKING

To encourage students to edit their work and publish, it is beneficial to have materials and instructions available for them to bind their own books. Instructions can involve including characters, settings, or events that are being studied in the social studies units. Have some cardboard (cereal boxes work great), different colors of tape, interesting contact papers, and so forth. This center can be used in conjunction with the computer or writing center, or can be free-standing. The book making center also works well with parent volunteers or older students.

RESEARCH CENTER

At the beginning of each new unit of study, have the large group brainstorm things that they would like to know more about. Post the brainstormed chart in the Research Center, along with the encyclopedias, research books for the social studies unit, and the computer, and allow students to choose the area they would like to extend through research. At the end of the unit of study, bind the research studies for the unit and place in the Research Center for student use.

JOURNALS

Journaling is an effective way to engage children in thinking about the social studies themes and lessons being addressed. Students can keep the journals at their own desks or there can be a specific center where these are kept. Vary the journaling activity by giving starters (questions, sentence starters, etc.) sometimes, and allowing the students to choose their own topics for writing. The journals offer excellent documentation of the students' work and of their understanding of the complex concepts presented in the social studies instruction.

RECYCLED MATERIALS CENTER

Toilet paper rolls, scraps of foil, scraps of fabric, stickers, stamps, and so forth can be used by students to create *stuff*. Students can then use the *stuff* as an object to write about. To address the Science, Technology, and Society Theme, students can develop a product description, giving uses for the item they have created. This center offers an excellent opportunity for the teacher to reinforce the reduce–reuse–recycle theme of environmental education.

PUZZLES

Jigsaw puzzles from the discount store or a garage sale are excellent materials for use in the early childhood classroom. These are great activities for problem-solving, developing oral language, cooperative learning, and so forth. Use of puzzles illustrating a specific part of the world being studied, or different modes of transportation, and so forth are ways to extend the social studies curriculum.

WORD SEARCH/CROSSWORD PUZZLES

Young children love word searches and crossword puzzles. Computer programs available on the Internet that can help teachers develop puzzles for any unit being studied. Simply decide on the terms to be reinforced and plug them into the program. Students enjoy this activity, and this provides an excellent opportunity to reinforce vocabulary study.

FILMSTRIPS

Most older schools have several unused filmstrip projectors in the library or media center. Since schools don't use filmstrips much any more, the projectors are available more readily. Check the library for filmstrips that your students can use in small groups. Set up a center for filmstrip viewing. While some filmstrips have taped narratives, many have the words written right on the filmstrip. This is a fun way for students to practice reading, while reinforcing skills and concepts presented in the social studies unit.

PHONE BOOKS, TV GUIDES, CATALOGS

Collect out-of-date materials and put in a center. To begin with, give the students an assignment, looking up information in these resources. After some practice in large group settings, they will be able to make up problems for each other. This center provides an excellent way to work on alphabetization, reading a schedule, filling out forms, real-life application, and even applying economic principles.

PARTNER READING

During center time, have students pair up and read to each other. There's just something about their being able to choose a friend to read with that motivates everyone. Choose books that are easily read by the students in the class and that extend the information being taught in the social studies unit.

OBSERVATION CENTER

Provide a bean sprouting, or a tadpole growing, or a mouse running around in its cage. Have students make daily entries in their journals, making note of whatever they are observing. The idea here is to have ongoing observations. Students will then be able to go back and see the progression over time. This is an excellent way to help students develop that all important sense of time.

SONG CENTER

Introduce new songs to students on a regular basis. Type out the words to the song and make a copy for each student. Keep in a folder in a corner of the room. Students can go to the Song Center and sing their songs, reinforcing their reading skills as they follow along in their song-books. Using songs from periods being studied in social studies is a good thematic tie-in. One example is "Follow the Drinking Gourd," as upper-level students study the issue of slavery.

PUPPET CENTER

Along the same lines as Reader's Theater, students can get together to make puppets and put on a puppet show. Many books and Web sites give written directions for making specific kinds of puppets. This activity gives students an opportunity to follow written directions, sequence, work together cooperatively, speak in front of a group, display audience manners, and so forth, meeting many national standards. Students can put on a show from a book or the Internet, or make one themselves.

★TIP: In any of these performance-based centers, getting to give a performance to the younger students in the school, at recess, to parents, and so forth is a real motivation for children to do good work.

TIPS FOR CENTER WORK

- Go over procedures for center work *daily*.
- Introduce only one or two centers each couple of days, in the beginning.
- Make centers an exciting part of the curriculum.
- Maintain strict codes of conduct in the centers
- There *will* be noise. Teach students about the "12 inch voice"—the voice that can be heard only from a foot away.
- Make students responsible for cleaning the centers before moving on to the next activity.

- Decide how you will hold students accountable for their center work.

- Do you want each student to visit EACH center each week?

- Are there some centers that are more important to you than others?

- Are some centers mandatory, while others can be a choice?

- Which Standard(s) are you addressing in each center? How will you document this?

- You don't have to have room for a separate table for each center. Some centers lend themselves nicely to a plastic tub, which the student can take to his or her own desk to work. Just be sure to let the students know your expectations in terms of clean-up, making sure all of the pieces are together, and so forth.

- You don't have to have all of these centers available on the same day (week, or month, for that matter). You may be more comfortable with a more controlled environment, in which you assign students to a specific center. After they learn the ropes, you can extend it.

- Just about anything you do in the classroom can be made into a center activity, with a little creative thought.

- The most positive effect of center work is that you'll have time to work with small, guided groups while the rest of the class is busy and engaged in meaningful work. These centers make excellent extension and reinforcement centers for social studies skills. This is just one more way to make sure students are receiving social studies instruction all day, every day.

Find more ideas on Content-Related Learning Centers on Social Studies, All Day, Every Day's Online Companion™ at http://www.earlychilded.delmar.com

APPENDIX II
Professional Organizations/Contacts

NATIONAL COUNCIL FOR THE SOCIAL STUDIES (NCSS)

National Council for the Social Studies (NCSS) is the largest association in the nation dedicated to social studies education. The association supports social studies educators and advocates for social studies education. NCSS published *Expectations of Excellence: Curriculum Standards for Social Studies,* which provides an articulated K–12 social studies program. This document serves as a framework for the integration of other national standards in social studies, with the stated purpose of guiding social studies decision makers in K–12 schools to help children achieve academic and civic competence.

Available on the NCSS Web site are position statements concerning appropriate and effective social studies instruction and links to Social Studies Curriculum Standards. This Web site also offers a link to the National Council for the Social Studies' *Notable Trade Books for Young People.*

Membership in National Council for the Social Studies is open to any person or institution interested in the social studies.

Contact Information:

National Council for the Social Studies
PO Box 79078,
Baltimore, Maryland 21279-0078,
1-800 296-7840
http://www.ncss.org

THE NATIONAL ASSOCIATION FOR THE EDUCATION OF YOUNG CHILDREN (NAEYC)

The National Association for the Education of Young Children (NAEYC) is the nation's premier organization for early childhood professionals. NAEYC's mission is to serve and act on behalf of the needs, rights, and well-being of all young children with primary focus on the provision of educational and developmental services and resources (NAEYC Bylaws, Article I., Section 1.1).

NAEYC provides professional development opportunities and resources for those who work for and with young children. The organization strives to build public understanding and support by setting and publicizing standards that promote excellence in early childhood education and early childhood professional preparation. NAEYC also advocates for public policies and funding to support a comprehensive system of high-quality early childhood education for all young children and families.

Membership in the National Association for the Education of Young Children is open to teachers, administrators, parents, policy-makers, and others committed to bringing high-quality early education and care to all young children.

Contact Information:

National Association for the Education of Young Children
1509 16th Street, NW
Washington, DC 20036
(202) 232-8777
(800) 424-2460
http://www.naeyc.org

THE ASSOCIATION FOR CHILDHOOD EDUCATION INTERNATIONAL

The mission of the Association for Childhood Education International (ACEI) is to "promote and support in the global community the optimal education and development of children, from birth through early adolescence, and to influence the professional growth of educators and the efforts of others who are committed to the needs of children in a changing society."

The ACEI Web site offers links to the organization's position statements on such topics as War and Peace Education, the importance of Play, A Child's Right to Creative Expression, and Standardized Testing, to name a few.

The Association for Childhood Education International welcomes the membership of classroom teachers, administrators, university professors, and others interested in the welfare of children around the world.

Contact Information:

Association for Childhood Education International
17904 Georgia Ave, Suite 215
Olney, Maryland 20832
(301) 570-2111
(800) 423-3563
Fax: (301) 570-2212
http://www.acei.org

U.S. DEPARTMENT OF EDUCATION—EDUCATION PUBLICATIONS CENTER

In 1980, Congress established the U.S. Department of Education (ED). Under this law, ED's mission includes encouraging increased involvement of the public in federal education programs, promoting improvements in the quality and usefulness of education through federally supported research, evaluation, and sharing of information.

Any publication produced or funded by the U.S. Department of Education since its creation in 1980 that appears in ERIC, the world's largest bibliographic database of education literature, can be accessed by the public. The database currently lists 34,117 publications and includes documents produced or funded by the U.S. Department of Education and entered into the ERIC database through July 2004. The **Education Publications Center (ED Pubs)** is the Department's one-stop center for access to ED information products, including publications, videos, brochures, posters, and other mailings.

Contact Information:

Education Publications Center
1-877-ED-PUBS (877) 7827
http://www.edpubs.org

NATIONAL GEOGRAPHIC SOCIETY

The National Geographic Society has pursued its mission to increase and diffuse geographic knowledge, making a special effort to *motivate and enable each new generation to become geographically literate*. The National Geographic Society offers lesson plans, professional development, online learning communities, and many other resources to educators.

Contact Information:

National Council for Geographic Education
206A Martin Hall
Jacksonville State University
Jacksonville, AL 36265-1602
Phone: +1 256 782 5293
Fax: +1 256 782 5336
http://www.nationalgeographic.com

THE NATIONAL COUNCIL FOR HISTORY EDUCATION

The National Council for History Education (NCHE) is a nonprofit corporation dedicated to promoting the importance of history in schools and in society. The NCHE welcomes membership of teachers, school administrators, historians, museum and historical society personnel, authors, publishers, parents, and others interested in history and history education.

The NCHE Web site offers links to websites concerning historical events, locations, and organizations, as well as contact information for others interested in history education.

Contact Information:

National Council for History Education
26915 Westwood Rd., B-2
Westlake, OH 44145
Ph: 440-835-1776
FAX: 440-835-1295
http://www.history.org/nche/

CENTER FOR CIVIC EDUCATION

The mission of the Center for Civic Education is to "promote an enlightened and responsible citizenry committed to democratic principles and actively engaged in the practice of democracy in the United States and other countries." The National Standards for Civics and Government were developed through a partnership with the Center for Civic Education and the U.S. Department of Education.

The Web site for the Center for Civic Education offers links to Teacher Resources and the National Standards for Civics and Government.

Contact Information:

Center for Civic Education
5145 Douglas Fir Road
Calabasas, CA 91302-1440
Tel: 818-591-9321
Fax: 818-591-9330
http://www.civiced.org

AMERICAN ANTHROPOLOGICAL ASSOCIATION

The Anthropology Education Committee, a committee of the American Anthropological Association (ASA) promotes high-quality, effective, and equitable teaching of anthropology as a means of increasing public understanding of anthropology. Of specific interest to the early childhood professional is the Committee's commitment to identify, develop, and promote high- quality curriculum and methodology for the teaching of anthropology in K–12.

Contact Information:

American Anthropological Association
2200 Wilson Blvd, Suite 600,
Arlington, VA 22201
703/528-1902
fax 703/528-3546
http://www.aaanet.org

NATIONAL COUNCIL ON ECONOMIC EDUCATION

The National Council on Economic Education (NCEE) is a nationwide network that leads in promoting economic literacy with students and their teachers. Their mission involves helping students learn to think and choose responsibly as "consumers, savers, investors, citizens, members of the workforce, and effective participants in a global economy."

The NCEE Web site offers lesson plans, a link to the National Standards, and other curriculum materials for teachers.

Contact Information:

National Council on Economic Education
1140 Avenue of the Americas
New York, NY 10036
Phone: 212.730.7007 or 1.800.338.1192
Fax: 212.730.1793
http://www.ncee.net

THE SOCIETY FOR AMERICAN ARCHAEOLOGY

The Society for American Archaeology (SAA) is an international organization whose mission is to promote the research, interpretation, and protection of the archaeological heritage of the Americas. SAA offers sample lesson plans for grades 3–12 on their Web site.

Contact Information:

Education Manager
Society for American Archaeology
900 Second Street NE, #12
Washington, DC 20002-3557
(202) 789-8200
http://www.saa.org

INTERNATIONAL READING ASSOCIATION STORYTELLING—SPECIAL INTEREST GROUP

The International Reading Association (IRA) has developed a special interest group for those interested in storytelling. The mission of this special interest group is to promote storytelling as an instructional tool. Storytelling is a particularly effective way to enrich the social studies curriculum.

Contact Information:

International Reading Association
Headquarters Office
800 Barksdale Rd.
PO Box 8139
Newark, DE 19714-8139

USA
Tel. 1-800-336-READ (1-800-336-7323), U.S. and Canada
+302-731-1600, elsewhere
Fax +302-731-1057
http://www.reading.org

Glossary

A

anecdotal record — informal note taking; documentation of behaviors of children while they work.

anthropology — the scientific study of the origin; the behavior; and the physical, social, and cultural development of humans.

anti-bias curriculum — curriculum that addresses race and ethnicity, along with consideration of gender, language, religious diversity, sexual orientation, physical and mental abilities, and socioeconomic class.

anticipatory set — the "hook" that grabs the attention of the student and focuses that attention on the learning that is about to be introduced.

application — the ability to use learned material in new situations.

appropriate assessment — assessment that reflects key points about how teachers can assess what children have learned.

archaeology — the science or study of antiquities; prehistoric antiquities such as the remains of buildings or monuments, bones, or other relics.

Association for Childhood Education International (ACEI) — international association whose stated mission is to "promote and support in the global community the optimal education and development of children, from birth through early adolescence, and to influence the professional growth of educators and the efforts of others who are committed to the needs of children in a changing society."

Association of Teacher Educators (ATE) — an individual membership organization devoted solely to the improvement of teacher education.

authentic — teaching that provides opportunities for students to use prior knowledge, recent learning, and critical-thinking and problem-solving skills to complete tasks that are relevant to their lives.

authentic assessment — assessment of a child's ability, completed in a natural setting, while the child is performing tasks in real-life settings (e.g., portfolios, checklists, group projects).

B

Bloom's Taxonomy — hierarchy of educational objectives.

bodily/kinesthetic — intelligence related to physical movement and an understanding of the physical body.

C

cartographer — mapmaker.

character — the inherent complex of attributes that determine a person's moral and ethical actions and reactions.

check for understanding — in this phase of teaching, the teacher makes sure that every child has a firm understanding of the learning that has taken place so far. This may be done by questioning strategies, by whole-group responses (such as "thumbs up" to indicate a "yes" answer), or by the use of individual chalkboards or dry erase boards.

checklist — forms used by teachers to identify the specific behaviors to be observed.

class meeting — regularly scheduled group meeting with students designed to encourage development of problem-solving strategies.

classroom environment — the setup of the classroom in its entirety; the physical setup, the level of respect extended to class members, and the materials chosen for the class.

closure — brings the lesson to an academic end. This is a time for the teacher to reinforce important points that have been discussed, and to emphasize the learning that has taken place.

Code of Ethical Conduct — NAEYC's guidelines for responsible behavior that set forth a common basis for resolving the principal ethical dilemmas for early childhood educators.

compass rose — identification of the directions on the map. Points out cardinal directions.

comprehension — the ability to gain meaning from material.

constructivism — the idea that learners construct knowledge for themselves, both individually and socially, as they learn.

constructivist learning — a philosophy of learning that refers to the idea that learners construct knowledge for themselves.

cooperative learning — specific strategies designed to teach and encourage children to work toward a common educational goal.

culture universals — the totality of socially transmitted behavior, arts, beliefs, and institutions.

curriculum — all of the concepts and information that children are expected to learn. An organized framework that delineates the content children are to learn.

D

democracy — form of government in which citizens choose the nation's leaders by voting for them. In this text, democracy is used to describe more than a political system—it is described as a way of life; a way of being with other people.

democratic principles — the fundamental beliefs and constitutional principles of American society that unite all Americans.

developmentally appropriate practices — any activity involving young children (birth to age 8) that is based on knowledge of the stages of child development, each child's

individual development, and each child's cultural background.

discovery method — allowing students to explore mathematical concepts on their own, in a thoughtfully designed environment. This kind of learning can be facilitated by guided learning strategies, which focus on active, hands-on opportunities. Discovery learning is based on the notion that experience has the most important role in obtaining new knowledge.

dispositions — beliefs that guide behavior.

distributed practice — a part of independent practice. It involves having students practice a skill or the application of a concept several times in the early days of learning that skill. Then later, revisit the skill occasionally throughout the remainder of the school year.

E

environmental education — education in, about, and for the environment.

evaluation — determining if a standard has been met, and to what degree the student has met that standard.

events — a significant occurrence or happening.

expository text — text written by authors to inform, explain, describe, present information, or persuade.

F

facts — can be looked up in the encyclopedia, or seen for ourselves.

field trip — a group excursion for the purpose of first-had experience; historic site, museum, zoo, library, and so forth.

formal lesson cycle — specific formula for developing an effective, direct instruction lesson.

free appropriate public education (FAPE) — in 1975, the U.S. Department of Education passed P.L. 949-142, which was the first law to ensure that each child with a disability was to be given a free appropriate public education.

full inclusionists — believe that children with special needs must be placed full-time in the general education classroom.

G

generalizations — broad statements that relate to and provide a focus for a theme.

genre — a category of language that is used to classify its form and content.

geography — the study of people, places, and the environments and the relationships among them (National Geographic Society).

graphic organizer(s) — visual organizer such as a map, web, chart, or diagram, used to organize general information and ideas.

guided practice — practice, under the direct guidance of the teacher.

H

heterogeneous groups — classes made up of students of different abilities, genders, and cultures.

high-stakes testing — use of achievement test results that carry serious consequences for students or for educators, such as an inability to progress to the next grade level in the case of a student, or reassignment or termination of employment for the educator.

human–environment interaction — ways that people impact the physical world and the physical world impacts people.

I

inclusion — educating children with special needs together with their same-age peers.

independent practice — practice of a learned skill or concept individually.

Individuals with Disabilities Education Act (IDEA) — enacted June 4, 1997. An extension of provisions made in 1975 by PL 94–142. This act strengthened the academic expectations and accountability for children with disabilities.

informational texts — text written with the primary purpose of conveying information

about the world, typically from someone more knowledgeable on the subject.

input — in the input phase of a formal lesson plan, the teacher provides the information that the students need for the lesson. This can be in the form of a lecture, film, read-aloud, etc. At this point, the teacher is actually "putting in" information that will be used at a later time.

inquiry teaching — the process of asking and answering key questions. In an inquiry lesson, the students develop questions, collect and organize data related to the questions, analyze the data, and draw conclusions from the data to answer those questions

intelligence — "way of knowing."

interdisciplinary learning — integrated learning, organized around themes and projects rather than along traditional subject-matter boundaries.

interactive read-aloud — a read-aloud strategy that encourages childen to interrupt, question, and participate as the teacher reads aloud to the group.

interpersonal — intelligence involving the ability to cooperate, communicate, and collaborate with others.

intrapersonal — intelligence having to do with knowing ourselves.

K

kidwatching — observing students as they play and work as a medium for gathering information on student learning.

knowledge — remembering learned material

KWL chart — a graphic organizer, incorporating what children **K**now, **W**ant to know, and **L**earned in a unit of study.

L

language fluency — ability to speak and write easily.

learning centers — areas set up in the classroom, which are designed to encourage independent understanding of the concepts presented.

legend—explanation of the symbols on the map.

logical/mathematical—intelligence associated with deductive reasoning, inductive thought, and scientific thinking.

M

methodology—a system of principles and procedures of inquiry followed in a particular discipline.

mnemonic device—a device, such as a formula or rhyme, used as an aid in remembering.

modeling—showing the students examples of what is expected from them.

multicultural education—the infusion of varying cultural viewpoints, ideas, and perspectives into the curriculum and learning environment.

Multiple Intelligence Theory—psychologist Howard Gardner's view that intelligence is made up of many kinds of abilities. He proposes that every individual possesses several different and independent capacities for solving problems and creating products and ideas.

musical/rhythmic—intelligence related to music and rhythm. One of the earliest intelligences to be developed.

N

National Association for the Education of Young Children (NAEYC)—national association that "exists for the purpose of leading and consolidating the efforts of individuals and groups working to achieve healthy development and constructive education for all young children."

National Council for the Social Studies (NCSS)—national organization whose stated mission is to "provide leadership, service, and support for all social studies educators."

naturalist—intelligence involving the understanding of the natural world.

No Child Left Behind (NCLB)—legislation signed by President George W. Bush in January, 2002, that involves: (1) stronger accountability for results, (2) more freedom for states and communities, (3) encouragement of proven teaching methods, and (4) more choices for parents.

O

objectives—the specific purposes or teaching techniques that interpret the goals of planning, schedules, and routines. These objectives are designed to meet the physical, intellectual, social, emotional, and creative development of young children.

opinion—an expression of how people feel about something. It does not have to be based on truth or even logic.

orienteering—use of specific tools for navigation (maps, compass, etc.).

P

people—humans, considered as a group.

performing arts—arts performed before an audience: dance, drama, music.

perspective—looking at objects from various positions.

P.L. 94–142—in 1975, the U.S. Department of Education passed P.L. 94–142, which was the first law to ensure that each child with a disability was to be given a free appropriate public education.

play—exercise or activity for amusement or recreation; to act or imitate the part of a person or character; fun or jest, as opposed to seriousness.

project—an in-depth study of a particular topic that one or more children undertake.

R

Reader's Theater—an efficient and effective way to present literature in dramatic form, with no memorizing, no props, no costumes, no sets (Aaron Shepard).

realia—objects used to relate classroom teaching to real life.

re-teach—when a student does not understand a particular concept, it is important to teach the concept again in a different way (not just louder and slower!) before allowing the child to practice and move on to the next concept.

rubric — a guideline for what will be expected by the teacher on a particular assignment.

S

scaffolding — use of social interaction as support for learning

scale — representation of the size of real objects in proportion to other objects on the map.

schedule — the basic daily timeline of a classroom.

schema — a way of organizing information.

sociomoral atmosphere — refers to the entire environment in the classroom — the relationships among the children, between the teacher and the children, between the parents and teachers, and so forth.

space/place — the location where human activities and natural phenomena take place.

sponge activity — an activity designed to produce learning during the times taken up by "administrivia." The term was originally coined by Madeline Hunter.

standards — a framework for program design, which serves as a guide for curriculum decisions by providing performance expectations. Standards are provided by many state education agencies as well as organizations, such as the National Council for Social Studies.

storytelling — the art or craft of narration of stories in verse and/or prose, as performed or led by one person before a live audience.

synthesis — the ability to put parts together to form a new whole.

T

technology — refers primarily to computer technology, but this can be extended to include related technologies, such as telecommunications and multimedia, which are becoming integrated with computer technology (NAEYC position statement).

thematic learning — explores the human dimensions of any important topic.

theme — an overriding thrust for the entire school year.

time — a concept, central to the study of history, that defines the measurement of the duration and sequence of events in an experience.

topic — subject to be studied.

U

unit — a selection of the curriculum based on the unifying theme around which activities are planned.

V

verbal/linguistic — intelligence linked to written and spoken language.

visual arts — arts appealing primarily to the visual sense: painting, photography, sculpture.

visual/spatial — intelligence involving the ability to visualize an object and to create mental images and pictures of objects.

Voluntary National Content Standards in Economics — publication by the National Council on Economic Education, which outlines "enduring themes," concepts, and principles basic to the teaching of economics.

W

wait time — practice of waiting approximately 3 seconds after asking a question, before asking another question or answering the question yourself.

Z

zone of proximal development (ZPD) — the distance between a child's actual developmental level as determined by independent problem solving and the level of potential as determined through problem solving under adult guidance or in collaboration with more capable peers. First described by Lev Vygotsky.

Index

Made in the USA
Monee, IL
10 October 2024

67519091R00208